DATE DUE

JAN. 1 0 1983			
DEC. 1 1983			
OC 3 1 '85			
MY 1 7 '89			
MY 17 '00			
		Printed	

W9-AYO-255

648.5
C1   Cleaning.

WITHDRAWN

EAU CLAIRE DISTRICT LIBRARY

90349

CLEANING

Other Publications:

PLANET EARTH
COLLECTOR'S LIBRARY OF THE CIVIL WAR
LIBRARY OF HEALTH
CLASSICS OF THE OLD WEST
THE EPIC OF FLIGHT
THE GOOD COOK
THE SEAFARERS
THE ENCYCLOPEDIA OF COLLECTIBLES
THE GREAT CITIES
WORLD WAR II
THE WORLD'S WILD PLACES
THE TIME-LIFE LIBRARY OF BOATING
HUMAN BEHAVIOR
THE ART OF SEWING
THE OLD WEST
THE EMERGENCE OF MAN
THE AMERICAN WILDERNESS
THE TIME-LIFE ENCYCLOPEDIA OF GARDENING
LIFE LIBRARY OF PHOTOGRAPHY
THIS FABULOUS CENTURY
FOODS OF THE WORLD
TIME-LIFE LIBRARY OF AMERICA
TIME-LIFE LIBRARY OF ART
GREAT AGES OF MAN
LIFE SCIENCE LIBRARY
THE LIFE HISTORY OF THE UNITED STATES
TIME READING PROGRAM
LIFE NATURE LIBRARY
LIFE WORLD LIBRARY
FAMILY LIBRARY:
    HOW THINGS WORK IN YOUR HOME
    THE TIME-LIFE BOOK OF THE FAMILY CAR
    THE TIME-LIFE FAMILY LEGAL GUIDE
    THE TIME-LIFE BOOK OF FAMILY FINANCE

This volume is part of a series offering homeowners
detailed instructions on repairs, construction
and improvements they can undertake themselves.

HOME REPAIR
AND IMPROVEMENT
CLEANING
BY THE EDITORS OF
TIME-LIFE BOOKS

FAU CLAIRE DISTRICT LIBRARY

TIME-LIFE BOOKS
ALEXANDRIA, VIRGINIA

1182 . Silver Burd. #0962

Time-Life Books Inc.
is a wholly owned subsidiary of
TIME INCORPORATED

Founder	Henry R. Luce 1898-1967
Editor-in-Chief	Henry Anatole Grunwald
President	J. Richard Munro
Chairman of the Board	Ralph P. Davidson
Executive Vice President	Clifford J. Grum
Chairman, Executive Committee	James R. Shepley
Editorial Director	Ralph Graves
Group Vice President, Books	Joan D. Manley
Vice Chairman	Arthur Temple

TIME-LIFE BOOKS INC.

Editor	George Constable
Executive Editor	George Daniels
Director of Design	Louis Klein
Board of Editors	Dale M. Brown, Thomas H. Flaherty Jr., William Frankel, Thomas A. Lewis, Martin Mann, John Paul Porter, Gerry Schremp, Gerald Simons, Kit van Tulleken
Director of Administration	David L. Harrison
Director of Research	Carolyn L. Sackett
Director of Photography	Dolores Allen Littles
President	Carl G. Jaeger
Executive Vice Presidents	John Steven Maxwell, David J. Walsh
Vice Presidents	George Artandi, Stephen L. Bair, Peter G. Barnes, Nicholas Benton, John L. Canova, Beatrice T. Dobie, James L. Mercer

HOME REPAIR AND IMPROVEMENT

Editor	Kit van Tulleken
Senior Editor	Betsy Frankel
Designer	Ed Frank

Editorial Staff for Cleaning

Text Editors	Robert A. Doyle, Brooke Stoddard (principals), Lynn R. Addison, Brian McGinn, Peter Pocock, Mark M. Steele, William Worsley
Writers	Tim Appenzeller, Kevin D. Armstrong, Carol Jane Corner, Rachel Cox, Stuart Gannes, Leon Greene, Kathleen M. Kiely, Kirk Y. Saunders
Copy Coordinator	Diane Ullius
Art Assistants	George Bell, Fred Holz, Lorraine D. Rivard, Peter C. Simmons
Picture Coordinator	Betsy Donahue
Editorial Assistant	Cathy A. Sharpe
Special Contributor	William Doyle

Editorial Operations

Production Director	Feliciano Madrid
Assistant	Peter A. Inchauteguiz
Copy Processing	Gordon E. Buck
Quality Control Director	Robert L. Young
Assistant	James J. Cox
Associates	Daniel J. McSweeney, Michael G. Wight
Art Coordinator	Anne B. Landry
Copy Room Director	Susan Galloway Goldberg
Assistants	Celia Beattie, Ricki Tarlow

Correspondents: Elisabeth Kraemer (Bonn); Margot Hapgood, Dorothy Bacon (London); Susan Jonas, Lucy T. Voulgaris (New York); Maria Vincenza Aloisi, Josephine du Brusle (Paris); Ann Natanson (Rome).

THE CONSULTANTS: William H. Oster is president of Baltimore Mat Company and The Matman, two companies that manufacture, sell and lease industrial floor-protection matting. An expert in industrial housekeeping, he also advises building managers on the durability of tile, carpet and floor finishes used in high-traffic and high-maintenance areas. He is co-author of a building-maintenance newsletter.

Roswell Ard is a consulting structural engineer and a professional home inspector in northern Michigan. Trained as a mechanical and electrical engineer, he has worked as a design consultant specializing in automatic controls for industrial machinery.

Thomas Hearns is a Baltimore, Maryland, cleaning contractor. His specialty is cleaning and restoring the stonework of churches.

John and Jeff Lefever are operators of Alco Appliance, Inc., in Beltsville, Maryland. The Lefever brothers have worked for many years repairing appliances and managing appliance-repair companies.

Harris Mitchell, special consultant for Canada, has worked in the field of home repair and improvement since 1950. He is Homes editor of Today magazine, writes a syndicated newspaper column, "You Wanted to Know," and is the author of a number of books on home improvement.

Dr. George Rambo, a plant pathologist, has been the Director of Technical Operations with the National Pest Control Association since 1978. He has been a frequent consultant on pest-control matters and has also worked in the Pesticide Regulation Department for the Maryland Department of Agriculture.

Paul Wahler is part owner of Poolservice Company, located in Arlington, Virginia. He has been maintaining and repairing swimming pools since 1970.

For reader information about any Time-Life book, please write:
Reader Information
Time-Life Books
541 North Fairbanks Court
Chicago, Illinois 60611

Library of Congress Cataloguing in Publication Data
Time-Life Books.
  Cleaning.
  (Home repair and improvement; 33)
  Includes index.
  1. Cleaning. I. Time-Life Books. II. Series.
TX324.C58   648'.5   82-5717
ISBN 0-8094-3492-X   AACR2
ISBN 0-8094-3491-1 (lib. bdg.)
ISBN 0-8094-3490-3 (retail ed.)

© 1982 Time-Life Books Inc. All rights reserved.
No part of this book may be reproduced in any form or by any electronic or mechanical means, including information storage and retrieval devices or systems, without prior written permission from the publisher, except that brief passages may be quoted for reviews.
First printing. Printed in U.S.A.
Published simultaneously in Canada.
School and library distribution by Silver Burdett Company, Morristown, New Jersey.

TIME-LIFE is a trademark of Time Incorporated U.S.A.

Contents

1 **A Cleaner for Every Occasion** 7

Assembling a Battery of Cleaning Supplies 8

Reviving Protective Finishes on Wood 12

Caring For Wickerwork and Caning 15

Cleaning and Repolishing Wood Floors 16

Removing Grime from Brick, Concrete and Stone 20

Dealing With Atmospheric Assaults on Metal 28

Keeping Up the Appearance of Plastics 34

Making Cloudy Glass Perfectly Clear 38

Cleaning Porcelain Plumbing Fixtures 40

First Aid for Dingy Walls and Ceilings 42

2 **Caring For Textiles** 47

Matching Care to Fiber Content 48

A Methodical Approach to Removing Spots 50

Procedures for Stain Removal 56

Rejuvenating Soiled Rugs and Carpets 60

Shampooing Fabric-covered Furniture 68

3 **Lightening the Big Loads** 71

Retrofitting a Vacuum System into the Walls 72

Hooking Up an Exhaust Line 79

Removing Dirt from Labor-saving Appliances 80

Cleaning Filters That Purify Air 90

Keeping a Swimming Pool Clear and Clean 92

Dealing With the Aftermath of a Disaster 98

4 **Pestproofing a House** 105

A Multipronged Approach to Controlling Pests 106

Extermination: Taking Punitive Action 112

A Glossary of Common Pests 118

Picture Credits and Acknowledgments 126

Index/Glossary 127

A Cleanser for Every Occasion

Inundating crystals. A chandelier festooned with cut-glass prisms is doused with a special aerosol spray that makes it unnecessary to dismantle the delicate fixture for cleaning. With the light bulbs turned off and tightened, the glass is simply sprayed until it is dripping wet. A drop-cloth below catches the dust-filled liquid.

Cleaning is the universal home improvement. People who would not even dream of painting a door or putting up a set of bookshelves will regularly embark on cleaning projects: They wash windows, shampoo rugs, wage war on clothes moths and cockroaches, scrub mildew from bathroom walls and rust from backyard fences. In performing these tasks they call upon a staggering array of cleaning compounds and chemicals *(pages 8-9)* and an arsenal of cleaning tools, ranging from humble sponges and mops to sophisticated machines that can flush dirt from deep within carpet pile or sandblast grime from the barbecue.

The necessity for these varied cleaning supplies is a direct result of the diversity of materials encountered in the typical house. In the course of an average cleaning day, the resolute house cleaner, moving from room to room, may deal with several dozen different surfaces. In the kitchen are plastic-laminate countertops, a stainless-steel sink, porcelain-enamel appliances, vinyl flooring and wooden cabinets. The living room presents another set of challenges: carpeting, textured upholstery, furniture made of wood, glass, metal or plastic. The den may have wood-paneled walls, an acoustic-tile ceiling, and a brick fireplace with a flagstone hearth. On to the bedrooms, where the house cleaner may need to cope with patterned wallpaper, venetian blinds, glass mirrors, and bedsteads of materials as different as lacquered brass and painted wicker. Then, finally, to the bathrooms, with their ceramic-tile floors, porcelain sinks and toilets, and fiberglass tubs.

While general-purpose detergents and household cleaners take care of many of these tasks, each surface being cleaned responds best to a particular combination of cleaning agent, technique and tools. The combination, furthermore, is subject to change; it is affected by the type of stain or dirt, and even by the place in which the surface is located. Thus, a soot-stained brick fireplace is washed down with muriatic acid and a scrub brush, but an outside brick wall is pressure cleaned with a powerful jet of water. Similarly, window glass is cleaned in one way, but a totally different method applies to the glass prisms that dangle from a chandelier.

For each of the surfaces being cleaned in this chapter—wood floors, wood furniture, interior and exterior stonework, metals, plastics, glass, porcelain plumbing fixtures and wallpaper—there is one general rule of thumb. Always begin with the least abrasive or caustic cleaner, and move up to a stronger cleaner only when the mild one fails to do the job. Gentle cleaning prolongs the life of the finish on most household surfaces, eliminating the need to restore a finish harmed by too-rigorous cleaning.

Assembling a Battery of Cleaning Supplies

Modern standards of cleanliness, far exceeding those of a century ago, have spawned a staggering array of specialized cleaning compounds. Most of these cleaners fall into six general categories based on similarity of function (although the cleaners within any given category may differ markedly in composition and strength). A few cleaners, however, are one of a kind, designed to solve specialized problems. The characteristics of the six general categories are explained in the glossary below; the chart opposite lists chemicals that have special uses or unique cleaning action.

☐ ABRASIVES: Available as emulsions, powders and pastes, abrasives are gritty compounds containing insoluble mineral particles such as silica or pumice. They are sometimes mixed with soap, detergent, bleach or various other additives. Fine-grained abrasives are suitable for cleaning and polishing numerous metals, such as silver, pewter and aluminum, and are an ingredient in hand cleaners for removing heavy, oily dirt. Coarse-grained abrasives, commonly used in household scouring powders, clean and brighten hard surfaces, such as ceramic tile and porcelain plumbing fixtures.

Abrasive cleaners work through a combination of physical and chemical action. The initial cleaning effect is physical—they dislodge the dirt by scraping at it. Then the soap or detergent in the mixture combines with the dirt particles and lifts them from the surface being cleaned.

☐ ABSORBENTS: Named for their function, these powdered substances purge porous materials of stains and soil by soaking up fresh spills and still-moist grease. Their use must occasionally be followed by further treatment—scrubbing or laundering—to flush away any residue of the spot. Most absorbents are well-known household products normally purchased for other uses. Cornmeal, cornstarch, salt and talcum powder, for example, are excellent all-purpose absorbents, and cat litter is good for drawing oil from stained

asphalt and concrete. Less familiar are French tailoring chalk, which comes in a neutral color, and fuller's earth, a dark, crumbly clay; both are useful for blotting stains from colored fabrics on which white powders might leave telltale traces.

☐ BLEACHES: Bleaches use either chlorine or oxygen to break down stains organically. They are designed primarily to clean, brighten, deodorize and disinfect laundry. Chlorine bleach will also remove stains from sinks, tubs and tiles; lighten dark or discolored wood; disinfect swimming pools and strip mildew from exterior wood or masonry surfaces.

Chlorine bleaches contain calcium hypochlorite or sodium hypochlorite, which are powerful whitening agents. Oxygen bleaches, when added to water, form hydrogen peroxide, also a whitener, but less strong. Oxygen bleaches are safer to use on colored fabrics and, unlike chlorine bleaches, they will not harm fabrics that contain silk, wool or synthetic fibers.

Hydrogen peroxide, the active agent of oxygen bleaches, can also be purchased as a liquid and used as a mild bleach to remove spots from fabrics or in a strong solution of one part hydrogen peroxide, one part acetic acid and six parts water to remove stains from masonry.

☐ CLEANING FLUIDS: Most cleaning fluids consist of hydrocarbon derivatives of petroleum or natural gas. They act by dissolving grease, oil or the gummy residue left by adhesive tape. Most of them are toxic, and some of them—such as kerosene and benzene—are very flammable. See the box opposite for cautions regarding their use. Petroleum-base cleaning fluids are sold under various trade names and often identified on product labels as petroleum naphtha, petroleum distillate or petroleum hydrocarbon.

Less potent and also less widely available than the petroleum-base cleaners are the nonflammable cleaning fluids— trichloroethylene, perchloroethylene and trichloroethane. All three are compounds

of chlorine and either ethylene or ethane, both of which are derivatives of natural gas. They are sold under numerous trade names as well as their chemical names. Although they are not fire hazards, they are poisonous to breathe or swallow and must be handled with extreme care, in strict accordance with the manufacturer's instructions.

☐ DETERGENTS: Synthetic substitutes for soap, detergents clean by breaking up and dispersing soil particles so that they can be rinsed away. Detergents dissolve easily in hot or cold water, function in hard water as well as in soft, and leave behind no film or scum—all of which are advantages over soap. Further, they can be formulated—by the addition of more or fewer enzymes, foaming agents or other additives—to suit a particular cleaning task. These special-purpose formulations may be created to clean a specific material, to treat a certain kind of soil, to wash in cool water, to suit the type and degree of mechanical action, or to suit the ratio of wash water to soiled material.

In this book the two most frequently recommended detergents are a mild liquid detergent, commonly sold for washing dishes by hand, and a general-purpose household detergent, normally sold in powder form.

☐ SOAPS: Soap is a solidified emulsion of fats or oils in lye. It cleans by emulsifying other fats and oil with which it comes in contact, then carrying them away in rinse water. Some soaps are not effective in very hard or very cold water, and they can leave behind a chalky film on the otherwise clean surfaces. Soaps vary in performance according to the type of fat or oil they contain and the proportion of fat or oil to other ingredients. Some soaps contain oils that make them especially useful for washing wood without raising the grain or for washing leather without destroying its suppleness. There are also soaps that have additives, such as pumice or naphtha, meant to boost their cleaning power.

Chemicals with Special Properties

Exceptional chemicals and their uses. The cleaning agents in this chart either do not fall under any of the general categories in the glossary opposite or have specific applications. They are listed by their common names, along with symbols—identified at the top of the chart—that denote their dangerous properties. The sec-ond column gives their principal applications, and the third notes restrictions that should be observed. Constant for most of them are restrictions on strength. Most of these chemicals are powerful enough to damage some fabrics and surfaces if used at full strength. They should always be diluted with water at least to the proportions specified. Before using any of them, read and follow package directions. Also test them on an inconspicuous area of the material being cleaned. All of the chemicals may be purchased in their generic form from sources listed in the last column. Many are also available as active ingredients in brand-name products.

Cleaning agent	Applications	Restrictions and strengths	Sources
Acetic acid	Removes alkaline substances, perspiration, urine and metallic stains from natural fibers.	Do not use on acetate fibers or ammonia stains; dilute with 2 parts water.	Drugstores
Acetone	Removes airplane glue, paint, varnish, lacquer and fingernail polish from natural fibers, from wood, tile and vinyl floors, from wood furniture.	Do not use on acetate, triacetate or modacrylic fibers. Do not dilute.	Drugstores, hardware stores
Alcohol	Disinfects; cleans glass, removes stains of natural and man-made resins from all fabrics.	When used on glass, dilute 2 tablespoons in 1 quart water; otherwise, dilute with 2 parts water.	Drugstores, supermarkets
Ammonia	Cleans glass, ceramic tile, plastics and nonaluminum cookware; removes perspiration, urine and grease from all fabrics.	Do not use on wool; on silk, dilute with an equal amount of water; use at full strength on other fabrics.	Drugstores, supermarkets
Amyl acetate	Removes airplane glue, paint, varnish, lacquer and fingernail polish from acetate, triacetate and modacrylic fibers.	Do not use on wood or plastic. Use at full strength.	Drugstores
Borax	Disinfects; cleans grease, mildew and dirt from flat paint.	Dilute ⅔ cup borax in 1 gallon water. Do not use on enamel paints.	Supermarkets
Muriatic acid	Removes spattered mortar from masonry and tile, efflorescence from brick, and stains from plaster swimming-pool walls.	When used on masonry or tile, dilute with 15 parts water; on swimming pools, dilute with 4 parts water.	Hardware stores
Oxalic acid	Removes most inks from all fabrics; urine stains, most inks and water spots from wood floors; rust and copper stains from porcelain bathtubs and sinks; rust from masonry and stone.	When used on fabrics or wood floors, dilute 1 tablespoon in 2 cups water; on porcelain, masonry or stone, dilute 1 pound in 1 gallon of water.	Drugstores
Sodium bicarbonate	Cleans glass, tile, porcelain and china; deodorizes refrigerators and drains.	Dilute 4 tablespoons in 1 quart water.	Supermarkets
Trisodium phosphate	Cleans grease and dirt from porcelain, tile and flat paint; removes oil-base paint spatters.	Dilute ⅔ cup in 1 gallon water; do not use on enamel paints.	Hardware stores, paint stores

☠ Poisonous   ✋ Caustic   ⚗ Toxic   🔥 Flammable

Safe Handling of Cleaning Chemicals

All cleaning agents should be kept out of reach of children: Colorful or sweet-smelling poisons can easily be mistaken by them for food. And unless specifically directed to do so, never mix different cleaners: Some combinations, such as ammonia and chlorine bleach, form compounds that emit fatal fumes. In addition, when working with the following types of chemicals, observe the following specific precautions:

☐ CAUSTIC: Avoid splashing. Wear safety goggles, rubber gloves and clothing that covers all areas of the skin.

☐ FLAMMABLE: Do not smoke, and do not use near heat, sparks or flames. Extinguish pilot lights when working near a gas stove, clothes dryer or water heater. Do not dry any articles cleaned with a flammable agent in a clothes dryer.

☐ POISONOUS: If swallowed, do not induce vomiting; drink milk or water, and call a physician immediately.

☐ TOXIC FUMES: Work outside or in a well-ventilated area. If the area cannot be ventilated, wear a paper respirator and take frequent fresh-air breaks.

A Basic Kit for Cleaning

Like any other task, cleaning is made easier by the proper tools. The supplies shown here are standard for many kinds of cleaning and should always be kept on hand. Extraordinary cleaning tasks, such as buffing a floor *(page 19)* or scouring heavily soiled masonry *(page 26)*, may require the rental of specialized heavy-duty equipment.

Although most cleaning tools are relatively simple, there are some helpful guidelines for choosing them:

□ Clean, white cotton cloth is preferable to synthetics because it is absorbent; especially useful are terry-cloth toweling and cotton-knit fabric—an old T-shirt, for example.

□ Nylon-bristled brushes are preferred by most professional cleaners for every cleaning job, from scrubbing upholstery to scrubbing concrete; they are more durable than natural bristles and dry more quickly. The length of the bristles, as well as their diameter, determines their stiffness or softness. Some scrub brushes have threaded sockets for attaching long handles, making them more versatile. Toothbrushes and shoe-polish applicators, normally not intended for house cleaning, are ideal for scrubbing such inaccessible crannies as the interstices of wickerwork.

□ Steel wool and sandpaper are proven remedies for stubborn spots and stains in wood. They should be stocked in several grades, from #1 to #4/0 in steel wool; from 20- to 600-grit in sandpaper.

□ A flexible-bladed putty knife is useful for scraping candle wax and chewing gum from hard surfaces, and a razor-blade window scraper makes short work of paint spatters on glass. For mixing cleaning compounds, a polyethylene pail is preferable to a metal one; acids and solutions that contain chlorine bleach have a corrosive effect on metal surfaces. Rubber gloves and goggles should be worn when working with harsh cleaning compounds. A canister-type vacuum cleaner, which comes with a variety of specialized attachments—a duster, a crevice tool, and brushes for upholstery and floors—is useful for handling a broad range of cleaning tasks.

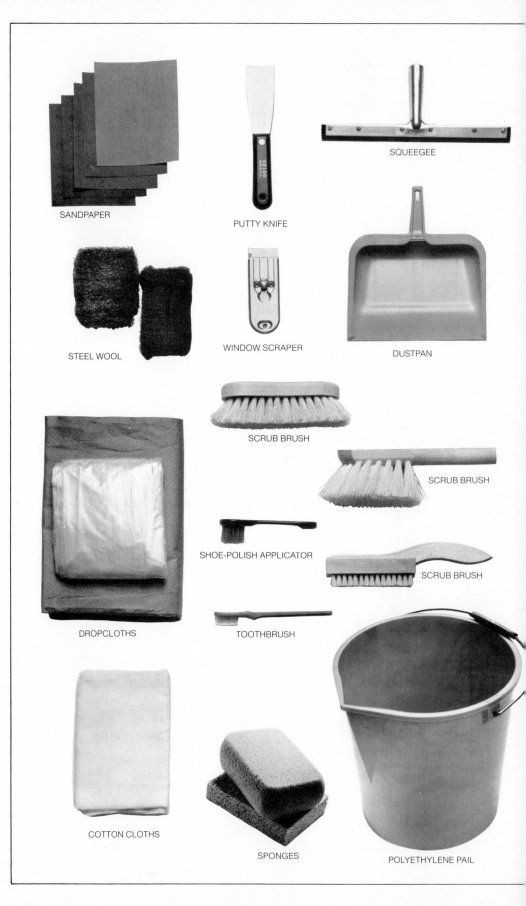

SANDPAPER

PUTTY KNIFE

SQUEEGEE

STEEL WOOL

WINDOW SCRAPER

DUSTPAN

SCRUB BRUSH

SCRUB BRUSH

DROPCLOTHS

SHOE-POLISH APPLICATOR

SCRUB BRUSH

TOOTHBRUSH

COTTON CLOTHS

SPONGES

POLYETHYLENE PAIL

WAX APPLICATOR

LONG-HANDLED SCRUB BRUSH

SPONGE MOP

BROOM

VACUUM HOSE

CREVICE TOOL

DUSTER

UPHOLSTERY BRUSH

FLOOR BRUSH

RUBBER GLOVES

GOGGLES

CANISTER VACUUM CLEANER

Reviving Protective Finishes on Wood

Wood is probably the most common material found in the average home, but its cleaning is usually indirect. The reason is simple: Most wood surfaces are protected by some sort of coating, ranging from clear varnishes on fine paneling to paints that mask the utilitarian woods of interior trim and exterior siding.

Painted wood surfaces are the simplest to clean: When they get dirty, they can be washed. Exterior painted surfaces can be scrubbed with a brush, using a relatively strong cleaning solution composed of chlorine bleach mixed with water and either trisodium phosphate (TSP) or borax (page 14). The TSP or borax removes dirt and chalky film; the bleach kills mildew. Interior painted surfaces can be washed with a cloth or sponge and a milder solution of TSP or borax mixed with water alone, 1 teaspoon of the cleaning agent to a quart of water. Only glossy enamels require special care: Because strong cleaners could dull their gloss, they are washed with a solution of 1 teaspoon of washing soda in a gallon of water. In all cases the cloth or sponge should be wrung out until almost dry.

The diverse clear finishes used on wood furniture and paneling can all be maintained by routine polishing and by quick cleaning of spills. Simply use a cloth dampened with a cleaning solution appropriate to the finish. When age, prolonged exposure to dampness, or high humidity causes the finish to fade or discolor, more rigorous cleaning techniques are required; and spots and blemishes need special treatment (chart, opposite). However, all of these techniques are designed to remove only discolorations that lie on or near the surface. When the cloudiness or blemish extends through the finish to the wood itself, the only solution is to strip the finish entirely and refinish the wood.

The four most common clear finishes are varnish, lacquer, shellac and oil—all of which are easily identified (box, opposite). Less common is french polish, a mixture of shellac and oil that is hand-rubbed to produce a deep, elegant luster. Varnish, lacquer and shellac finishes are often covered with an additional coating of liquid or paste wax for extra protection, especially on kitchen or dining-room tables, where hot or wet glasses and dishes may be placed on the furniture regularly. Whether waxed or not, these three finishes can be cleaned with a commercial cleaner/polish, which is usually sprayed on, then lightly rubbed with a soft, lint-free cloth.

Oil finish and french polish are best cleaned with a cloth dampened in boiled linseed oil. Prepare the cloth by pouring a small amount of oil into the center; then twist and wring the cloth to distribute the oil evenly. Use only commercially prepared boiled linseed oil; the term "boiled" is a misnomer that actually refers to the addition of chemicals that make the linseed oil dry faster. No heat is involved. If you try to boil raw linseed oil at home, it will not produce the same result—and the oil will catch fire long before it begins to boil.

Restoring a finish clouded by age or dampness usually means rubbing the surface with a substance matched to that finish. Oil is treated in one way, varnish, shellac and lacquer in another, and french polish in still a third. Except for the french-polish treatment, the de-clouding substances should be rubbed into the finish in the direction of the grain, and with care, so that you do not rub through the finish to the underlying wood. The french-polish treatment, like the finish itself, demands a circular motion. Practice the technique on scrap wood before using it on furniture.

For brightening a faded oil finish, combine equal parts of turpentine and boiled linseed oil. Wipe this mixture over the entire surface, then wipe it away immediately. Allow the surface to stand for two or three days, until it is completely dry, before polishing it with more of the same turpentine-and-oil mixture. (If you want to store the oiled cloth for future use, put it in a tightly sealed jar to eliminate the risk of spontaneous combustion.)

Treat faded varnish, shellac and lacquer finishes with a cloth dampened in lemon oil, available at paint stores. Wipe the entire surface with the cloth, re-moistening it as necessary, until the cloudiness disappears. If the surface appears dull after cleaning, apply a coat of paste wax and buff well.

Unfinished woods may be cleaned with the same measures commonly applied to finished woods. Unfinished exterior siding, chosen for its weather resistance, can be scrubbed and rinsed like painted surfaces. However, when cleaning unfinished interior wood, such as solid pine paneling, use a cloth barely dampened in the cleaning solution to prevent the water from spotting the wood and raising the grain.

Unfinished butcher-block wood surfaces in the kitchen are a special case, because they are wetted regularly with moist or juicy foods. Before they are ever used, they should be rubbed with vegetable oil to seal the wood pores against moisture. Wipe them clean after each use with a damp cloth and reapply oil occasionally. Chopping blocks that are badly stained or splintered can be restored by rubbing the surface down with #1 steel wool. The block should then be treated with several thin coats of vegetable oil, each rubbed into the wood with a pad of #3/0 steel wool before the next coat of oil is applied.

Remedies for Removing Spots from Woodwork

Stain	Treatment					
	Damp cloth	Trisodium phospate	Mineral spirits	# 3/0 steel wool	Rottenstone/ mineral oil	3/F pumice/ mineral oil
Alcohol	●			●	●	●
Built-up wax			●			
Grease		●	●			
Ink	●			●	●	●
Oil-base paint		●	●	●	●	●
Water-base paint	●	●	●	●	●	●
Water spots			●	●	●	●
White rings or spots	●			●	●	●

Lifting blemishes from finished wood. This chart lists the most common causes of spots and blemishes on wood finishes in the left-hand column and the remedies—indicated by dots—across the top from left to right in order of their strength. Always try the weakest remedy first, proceeding to the next one only if necessary. If the finish is dulled by the treatment, use the techniques described opposite to revive it.

A solution of trisodium phosphate—1 teaspoon per quart of water—should remove grease and oil-base paint from wood surfaces. Rub lightly with a cloth dampened in the solution, then wipe clean with a wet cloth and dry well.

To lift a spot from a wood surface by using mineral spirits, dip a clean cloth into the solvent and rub it over the spot; change to a fresh cloth whenever the old one becomes discolored.

To clean a wood finish with steel wool, rub the spot lightly, making short passes back and forth. If the grain is exposed, be sure to work in the direction of the grain.

When removing a blemish with rottenstone and mineral oil, first mix the two ingredients to a creamy paste. Rub the paste over the spot with a clean cloth or with # 3/0 steel wool, taking care not to rub through the finish. When the spot has disappeared, wipe off the paste with a cloth dampened with water and dry the surface with a soft cloth. For extremely stubborn spots, combine 3/F pumice and mineral oil; apply this mixture in the same way.

Identifying the Furniture Finish

The first step in choosing which of the cleaning or restorative techniques (opposite) to use on a wood surface is to determine—by a process of elimination—the type of finish used. Begin by rubbing an inconspicuous spot with a cotton-tipped swab dipped in denatured alcohol; a shellac finish will soften and begin to flow when moistened with alcohol. If the finish remains unaffected, dip a second swab in lacquer thinner and rub it over the surface; a lacquer finish will soften and then dry almost immediately. If neither of these tests dissolves the finish, rub a mixture of turpentine and boiled linseed oil vigorously over a small area; if this mixture can be rubbed into the wood, the finish is oil—if not, it is varnish. The information yielded by this test will also prove helpful when you want to refinish.

EAU CLAIRE DISTRICT LIBRARY

Brightening the Surface of a Faded French Polish

1 **Sanding down a dull surface.** To clean faded or blemished french polish, rub the surface gently with #4/0 steel wool or 320-grit sandpaper, using light, circular strokes. Rub only until the cloudiness or blemish disappears; do not expose the bare wood. If the treatment leaves the surface uneven, go over it again with the same abrasive to smooth out any depressions.

2 **Building up a french polish.** Soak a wad of clean lint-free cotton with shellac, and wrap it inside a lint-free cotton covering previously moistened with a few drops of boiled linseed oil. Rub this polishing pad over the wood with a circular motion, working from the center outward. When the pad begins to stick, add a few drops of linseed oil. Check the condition of the shellac inside the pad occasionally; add more as it becomes dry. Go over the wood at least six times, then discard the outer pad and continue rubbing the surface with the inner shellac-filled wad until the wood surface is dry.

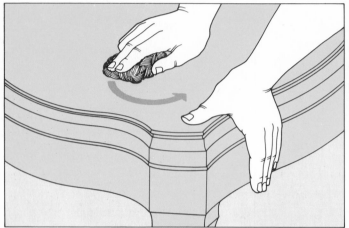

Restoring a Fresh-painted Look to Wood Siding

1 **Applying the cleanser.** Brush coarse dirt off the siding with a wadded cotton cloth. In a plastic pail, mix 3 quarts water, 1 quart chlorine bleach and ⅔ cup trisodium phosphate or borax. Using a long-handled, stiff-bristled brush, scrub the siding with long lateral strokes; work up from the bottom in 5-foot-wide strips. Wear goggles, rubber gloves and old clothes, and avoid spilling the caustic solution on yourself.

2 **Rinsing away the dirt.** Beginning at the bottom and working to the top, hose down the washed strip with a strong spray of clear water to remove the loosened dirt and the cleaning solution. Continue washing and rinsing adjacent strips of siding, always working from the bottom to the top. With each rinse, flush off the adjacent wall surfaces to prevent the loosened dirt from resettling on another part of the wall.

Caring For Wickerwork and Caning

Furniture made from woven reeds and grasses is often painted or finished with the same clear substances used on wood. However, such furniture poses special cleaning problems—partly because of the nature of the material, partly because of its openwork patterns.

Most woven furniture is made of rattan, a climbing palm with sturdy, polished stalks that is native to the East Indies. For furniture making, the stalks are processed to make three different fibers, all of which are cleaned in slightly different ways. The glossary of furniture fibers at right explains these cleaning methods as well as those for two related fibers often used in woven furniture.

Deep cleaning the crannies in wicker. After removing surface dirt, clean the interior parts of wicker and the intricate scrollwork with any small brush, such as a toothbrush, dipped in warm, soapy water. Shake the brush vigorously to throw off most of the water, then scrub with short, straight strokes, following the direction of the weave. Rinse by dipping the brush in clear water and again shaking it almost dry; then scrub out the residual soap.

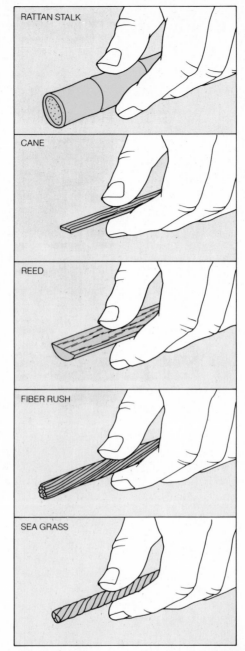

RATTAN STALK

CANE

REED

FIBER RUSH

SEA GRASS

Five wicker fibers. Rattan stalks in their natural form usually provide the structural framework of wicker furniture. They are sold in diameters ranging from ⅜ to 1½ inches. Clean rattan by scrubbing it with a soft-bristled brush dipped in warm, soapy water. Mist unfinished rattan once a year with a fine spray from the garden hose to keep it from drying out and getting brittle. Do not hose rattan that has been painted or coated with a clear finish, rattan used in combination with wicker fibers other than cane, or wood furniture accented with rattan. Moisten the rattan parts of combination furniture with a damp cloth to keep it from drying out.

Cane is the glossy covering that sheathes stalks of rattan. Most used for woven seats and backs for chairs, cane should be cleaned as rattan stalks are; take care not to harm the finish of the wood to which it may be joined. To moisten cane, use a fine spray from a house-plant mister.

Reed, the smooth core of the rattan plant, is highly absorbent and bends easily when soaked in water. It is widely used for the woven covering of all parts of wicker furniture. Besides the half-round section shown at left, center, it is also cut into rods and flat strips of various widths and thicknesses. Reed should be washed with as little water as possible—a damp cloth will usually do—and should not be hosed or misted.

Fiber rush is a machine-twisted cord of kraft paper fashioned to resemble natural rush. It may be as thick as ⁷⁄₃₂ inch and is used primarily in woven chair seats. The individual strands will unravel when soaked, so fiber-rush wicker furniture should be cleaned only with a damp cloth and should never be sprayed with water.

Sea grass, or Hong Kong grass, is made of strands of dried sea grass twisted together. It is normally sold in ³⁄₁₆-inch-wide strands and used, like fiber rush, for weaving chair seats. Sea grass resembles fiber rush in its tendency to unravel when saturated. It and similar dried grasses should be wiped clear with a damp cloth and should never be sprayed with water.

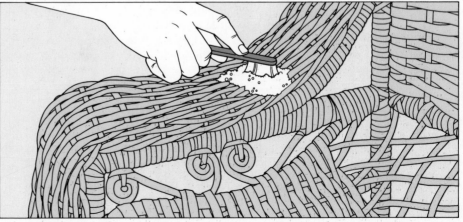

Cleaning and Repolishing Wood Floors

The rich, warm glow of a polished hardwood floor is produced as much by its finish and layers of wax as by the wood itself. These coatings protect the porous, absorbent wood from wear, and they seal it against dust and spilled liquids as well. But the daily grind takes its toll: Spots and discoloration mar the clear film of wax, and heavy traffic may even wear through the wax and finish to the wood itself. Quick attention to problems, plus regular cleaning and waxing, is the key to keeping a wood floor beautiful.

Most of the wear on a floor affects only the topmost layer—the wax. The preferred wax for wood floors is buffing wax, a mixture of wax and solvent—usually naphtha. Sometimes, however, you will inherit a floor on which a self-polishing wax has been used. Technically, these nonbuffing waxes are made with acrylic polymers rather than wax, and they are, strictly speaking, floor polishes.

Acrylic floor polishes are available in two forms: water-base and solvent-base. Water-base polishes are not recommended for wood floors; they leave spots as they dry. Yet they have one advantage: When they fade, they can be restored with buffing wax. Solvent-base polishes cannot; when they fade, they must be stripped off and replaced.

Buffing waxes are also available in two forms, as pastes or liquids, but both are based on solvents and differ only in the amount of solvent they contain. Paste waxes, which are thicker, tend to be more durable and are a good choice for old floors because they fill in small cracks. But liquid buffing waxes are easier to apply, and for most floors they are perfectly adequate.

To prolong the life of the wax, vacuum the floor weekly, before dirt and dust are pressed into the surface, and wipe up spills promptly with a damp cloth. When the surface begins to dull, the gloss can usually be restored by buffing—either by hand or with a buffing machine. Because each buffing removes a little wax, you will eventually have to rewax the floor—but this will serve a dual purpose. The solvent in the new wax will dissolve the old, forming a single protective coating, and it will clean as it polishes. Before rewaxing, be sure to vacuum the floor thoroughly; otherwise, any surface dirt will be dissolved into the new wax.

If your floor has a coat of discolored or badly soiled wax or polish, you should remove it before rewaxing. Strip solvent-base wax as shown on page 17. To remove water-base polish, work on a small section at a time, using a sponge mop to wet the floor with a solution of 1 cup of ammonia, ¼ cup of powdered floor- or wall-cleaner containing trisodium phosphate, and ½ gallon of water. Allow the solution to soak for two to three minutes, then scrub the floor with a stiff-bristled brush to loosen the dissolved polish. Remove the polish and the ammonia solution with clean cloths before swabbing the floor with clear water, again using the sponge mop. Use water sparingly and wipe up all excess moisture after rinsing each section.

Under the wax coating of most floors is a permanent finish, applied when the floor was installed. The most popular of these finishes are the penetrating sealers, thin varnishes that soak into the wood grain, filling its pores and in effect becoming part of its structure. Surface finishes, such as polyurethane varnish, lacquer or shellac, lie on top of the floor, providing a protective film for the wood.

All floor finishes, of which penetrating sealers and polyurethane varnishes are by far the most common, can be patched in worn areas with new finish of the same type *(page 18)*. A penetrating sealer will have left the natural texture of the wood exposed, but if a surface finish was used you can test it for type by using the method described on page 13.

On some floors, a stain is applied before finishing. Worn spots on such floors will have to be restained after you have sanded them and before you apply the new finish. You will have to match the color and type of patching stain to those of the existing stain, which may be water- or oil-base. Since oil and water do not mix, you can test your stain by applying a small amount of oil stain—the most common—to an inconspicuous spot. If the new stain beads up rather than sinking in, the old stain is water-base.

To get the color right, test the stain on a scrap of similar flooring purchased from a building supplier (95 per cent of all hardwood floors are oak). Brush the stain on the scrap, let it stand for about three minutes, then wipe off the excess with a dry cloth. If the result is too light, apply additional coats, wiping each one off after about three minutes, until you achieve a matching color.

Although wax can be applied and buffed by hand with an applicator similar to a sponge mop, a floor polisher does a much more even job and is obviously faster. Professional floor polishers, usually with a single brush 12 to 19 inches in diameter, are available from rental agencies and some supermarkets. The brushes on these machines can be changed, but the standard brush supplied for applying wax to floors is one with stiff bristles. It is used in combination with a soft-bristled polishing brush and a felt buffing pad, laid under the brush and gripped by the bristles. Smaller buffing machines, often with two counter-rotating brushes, are lighter, more maneuverable and ideal for less ambitious jobs, such as small rooms or hallway floors.

A Choice of Weapons against Blemishes

Stain or mark	Cleaning method
Alcohol	Rub with a cloth dipped in liquid or paste wax.
Black heel marks, caster marks	Rub with #3/0 steel wool dipped in floor wax; buff or let dry, according to label directions.
Burns	Rub with #3/0 steel wool.
Chewing gum, crayon, candle wax, tar	Apply ice to harden; scrape off with dull knife. Remove residue with #3/0 steel wool dipped in mineral spirits or trichloroethylene.
Dark spots (ink, urine, etc.)	Rub with #1 steel wool dipped in mineral spirits. Sand with medium, then fine sandpaper. Apply a 1:32 solution of oxalic acid and water.
Dried milk or food	Rub with damp cloth, wipe dry.
Mold, mildew	Rub with cloth dipped in chlorine bleach; wipe with cloth dipped in clear water; dry thoroughly.
Oil, grease	Rub with lye soap, then rinse. Saturate cotton with hydrogen peroxide and place over stain; then saturate a second layer of cotton with ammonia and place over the first.
Scuffing, scratching	Buff affected area. Rub with #3/0 steel wool dipped in paste wax; wipe off excess wax, buff.
Water spots	Rub with #2/0 steel wool. Sand lightly with fine sandpaper. Rub with #1 steel wool dipped in mineral spirits.

Cleaning hardwood floors. Materials that commonly blemish the wax on hardwood floors are listed in the left-hand column of the chart at left. The methods for dealing with them are given in the right-hand column; they are listed in order of effectiveness. Try the gentlest method first, using the subsequent ones only if the first proves ineffective. Wear rubber gloves to protect your hands from steel wool and harsh cleaning solutions. When using steel wool, take care not to remove the underlying finish; if rubbing creates a thin spot, patch it (*page 18*) so that the subsequent rewaxing will result in an even shine over the entire floor.

Stripping Off Layers of Built-up Wax

Loosening old wax. Open all doors and windows for ventilation, then tie a pad of #3/0 steel wool to a long-handled wax applicator or sponge mop (*inset*). Pour mineral spirits over a 2-foot-square area; rub briskly back and forth with the steel wool in the direction of the floor-boards (*above, left*); on parquet floors, work parallel to the direction of one of the wood elements. As the wax dissolves, wipe it up immediately with a lint-free absorbent rag (*above, right*). Continue cleaning small sections until you have covered the entire floor, changing the steel wool and the wiping rag as they become clogged with dirt and wax.

Remove residual wax by rubbing lightly with a dry pad of #3/0 steel wool after the floor dries. Sweep up or vacuum up remaining wax powder.

Patching a Worn Spot in a Wood Floor

1 **Sanding off the old finish.** Use a cloth moistened with mineral spirits to remove all wax from the surrounding area. Fit an orbital sander or a sanding block with 220-grit sandpaper and sand the spot down to the bare wood, working from the center outward. Sand the edges of the spot to smooth them into the surrounding finish. Sweep up or vacuum up the sanding dust. If the sanded area's color does not match the rest of the floor, apply stain (page 16) and let it dry.

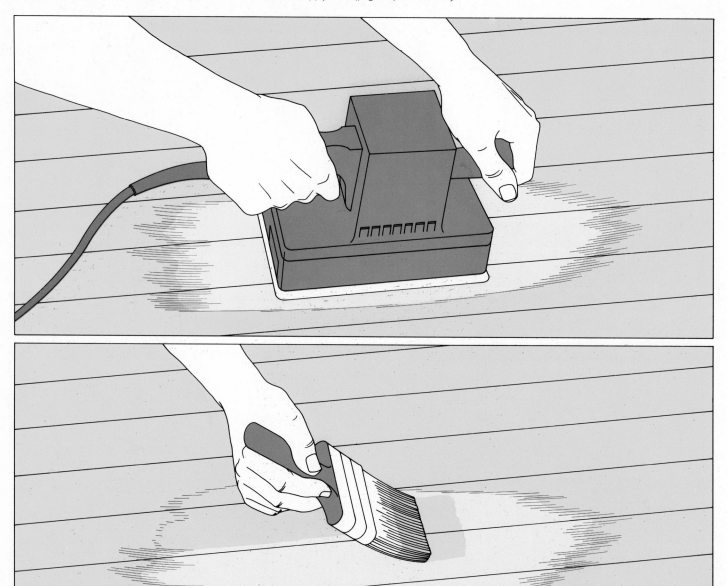

2 **Recoating the spot.** Working with the grain of the wood, use a 3-inch paintbrush to apply a very thin layer of finish over the sanded spot, brushing in smooth, even strokes to avoid air bubbles. Feather the new finish into the old by starting at the center and lifting the brush at the edge of the spot. Allow the new finish to dry; then apply additional coats in the same manner, allowing each coat to dry before applying the next one. Rewax the spot after the final coat dries.

Waxing and Buffing
with a Floor Polisher

Waxing the edge of the floor. Dust or vacuum the floor to pick up loose dirt. Then use a folded lint-free cotton cloth to spread a thin coat of paste or liquid wax—just enough to cover the surface—along the edges of the floor and in the corners, coating a strip about 6 inches wide where the floor polisher will not reach.

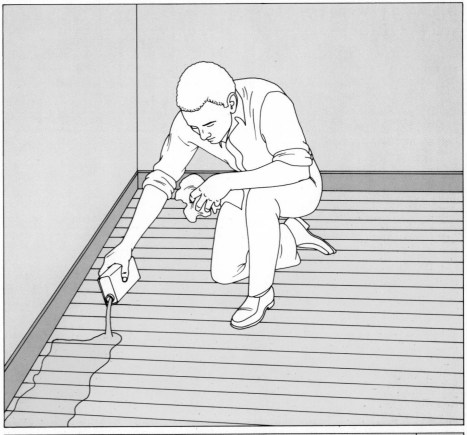

Waxing and buffing. When using liquid wax, pour a saucer-sized pool of wax on the floor near one wall. Position the polisher over the wax, switch it on, and use it to spread the wax over an area about 3 feet square. Move the machine from side to side in the direction of the floorboards. To change direction effortlessly, tilt the machine slightly forward or backward; the edge of the brush on the low side of the machine will grip the floor and move the machine. When using paste wax, smear a thin layer of wax directly onto the bristles and spread it as for liquid. Continue applying wax to roughly 3-foot sections until the entire floor is covered.

After the wax has dried about 30 minutes, attach the soft-bristled polishing brush to the machine and buff, again working on small sections in a side-to-side pattern. Buff the floor a final time with a lamb's-wool buffing head or with a felt pad placed under the brush. This will brighten the shine and eliminate any swirl marks that may have been left by the brush.

Removing Grime from Brick, Concrete and Stone

Masonry is subject to two very different standards of cleanliness. Because of its strength and durability, it is often the material of choice for surfaces begrimed by the dirtiest dirt there is—the oil and grease of garage floors, the soot of fireplace interiors. No one expects these utilitarian surfaces to be spotless, but they do have to be cleaned occasionally—if only for safety's sake. At the opposite end of the cleaning spectrum are masonry surfaces whose decorative purpose entitles them to the same loving attention as fine wood—marble mantels, slate entry floors, patterned brick patios.

As it happens, the cleaning methods for both types of masonry are essentially the same: Decorative surfaces merely call for a little more patience. At the start of the cleaning process, a bit more elbow grease is substituted for strong chemicals, which are a last resort. In the final stages, more effort goes into erasing the last lingering shadows of a spot or stain.

Whatever the masonry surface, the cleaning power of a good natural-bristled scrub brush and a standard all-purpose household cleaner should not be underestimated. A surprising number of spots and stains will yield to such routine treatment. If this fails to dislodge the dirt, try a heavy-duty household cleaner or scouring powder. Be warned, however, that these stronger cleaners and powders may dull the stone's polished surface, which will later have to be restored.

Some stains and blemishes, of course, require more abrasion than a scrub brush can supply. When brick is speckled with paint or excess mortar, or discolored by the traceries left by ivy, you will have to resort to sanding—but not with sandpaper. Instead, use broken brick, whose gritty residue will be invisible.

Efflorescence, the white powdery deposit left by salts leached out from the interior of bricks when they are exposed to moisture, also requires special treatment. It must be removed with muriatic acid *(opposite),* a diluted form of hydrochloric acid. When the stain is gone, the acid in turn must be neutralized with an alkali—an ammonia solution, usually—and the wall then has to be flushed with clear water.

When you work with muriatic acid or with any other strong cleaning solution or solvent, be sure to wear protective clothing, and follow all the safety precautions described on page 9.

Other cleaning regimens are less hazardous. A sprinkling of cat litter is helpful for soaking up oil and grease spills from a garage floor, and the remaining stain can be removed with a strong detergent. Lumps of spilled plastic that have hardened can be reduced to ash with a blowtorch, then swept away.

For large outdoor areas of masonry, such as a brick-walled house or a concrete driveway, you can rent a powerful machine called a pressure washer *(pages 26 and 27),* which delivers a stream of water or detergent at pressures sufficient to blast out all but the most deeply ingrained dirt. The washer is powered by either a gasoline engine or an electric motor, but the gas-powered washer is much stronger and is preferable for large cleaning jobs.

For stubborn stains that have worked into the pores of other masonry surfaces, a poultice may be preferable. Like the old-fashioned mustard plaster that was thought to draw poisons from the body, a cleaning poultice holds a strong chemical solvent in contact with the masonry long enough to penetrate and dissolve the stain. Meanwhile, the absorbent powder in the poultice soaks up the dissolving stain so that it can simply be brushed away. The powder in the poultice can be talc, whiting (also known as calcium carbonate) or hydrated lime—whichever is most readily available. The solvent, however, must be matched to the stain. On page 23 you will find a list of the common masonry stains, along with a poultice recipe for each one.

After the dirt or stain has been removed, you may also have to remove the effects of the cleaning process. Concrete and brick usually require nothing more than a thorough rinsing. Marble and slate may require buffing with a polish. One of the polishes recommended is tin oxide cream, widely used by jewelers to polish gemstones; the others are jeweler's rouge, a fine abrasive, and its slightly coarser relative, stone-polishing compound. All three are available at stores that carry supplies for lapidary work. Tin oxide cream is usually applied and rubbed by hand; jeweler's rouge and stone-polishing compound are applied and polished with a buffing attachment on an electric drill.

Finally, to protect newly cleaned masonry against soil, you may want to coat it with a silicone-base sealer, obtainable at most paint and hardware stores. Such sealers are best applied to smooth surfaces, such as marble, in several thin coats in succession. On rougher surfaces, such as brick and concrete, they are usually sprayed on with a pressurized sprayer in a single coat. The silicone sealer will impart a slightly unnatural gloss to the surface of the masonry, which is not to everyone's taste.

Asphalt-surfaced driveways and walkways also are often sealed after cleaning. The sealant is a coal-tar pitch emulsion, which not only fills hairline cracks but restores the blacktop's sooty blackness. The emulsion, which is available at building-supply stores, is applied with a combination brush and squeegee made specifically for this job. The squeegee is used to spread the coating, the brush to smooth out irregularities.

Dislodging Surface Deposits from Masonry

Sanding surface deposits from brick. Break a matching brick into fragments, and choose a fragment that will comfortably fit your hand. Working slowly and pressing lightly, rub the broken face of the fragment over the deposits in a back-and-forth motion. Avoid using the outside faces of the fragment; in firing, these faces become harder than the brick core, and they could scratch the brickwork.

Dissolving efflorescence. Before scrubbing the wall, protect the surface beneath the wall by covering it with a plastic dropcloth. Then protect yourself by donning safety goggles, a cap, heavy rubber gloves with cuffs, and old clothing—including a long-sleeved shirt. Thus insulated, mix one part muriatic acid to 10 parts water in a plastic pail. Pour the acid into the water, rather than vice versa. Pouring the water into the acid could cause it to foam up, dispersing droplets of acid into the air.

After soaking the masonry with plain water, scrub the diluted acid onto the wall with a natural-bristled scrub brush. When the acid stops bubbling, wash down the wall with a solution of one part ammonia to two parts water. Finally, rinse the wall thoroughly with plain water.

When working indoors, open all the windows and wear a respirator in addition to the goggles and gloves. If your nose or eyes begin to sting, leave the room immediately and splash your face with cold water. Do not return to the task until the stinging subsides.

Soaking up grease and oil. Flood the masonry surface with mineral spirits or paint thinner to dissolve heavy deposits. Then cover the stained area with an absorbent material such as cat litter or fuller's earth, a claylike substance available at drugstores. Let the absorbent material stand on the stain several hours or overnight, until it has soaked up the loosened grease and oil. Then sweep the absorbent material into a dustpan and scrub away any residual stain with a solution of ½ cup trisodium phosphate in 1 gallon of hot water. If oil or grease has gone deep into the masonry, use a benzene poultice (*opposite*).

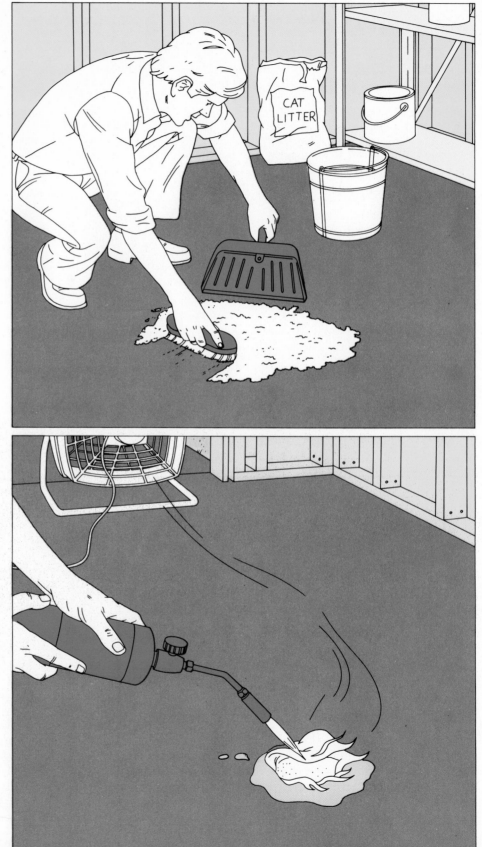

Burning off hardened globs of plastic. To remove hardened drippings of plastic-base paint, cement or caulking compound, hold a propane blowtorch approximately 6 inches above the masonry surface. Play the flame slowly back and forth until the plastic chars and turns to ash. Be sure to provide adequate ventilation, since the burning plastic will give off acrid black smoke: If you are working indoors, open at least two windows for cross ventilation and set a fan in one of the windows to speed the air flow.

Drawing Out Deeply Embedded Stains

Substances that penetrate deep into masonry leave persistent stains that require the special treatments listed below. In most cases the instructions call for a poultice (below, right), which is simply a thick paste made by mixing a strong cleaning agent with an absorbent powder. The treatments, organized alphabetically according to stain, specify the most effective cleaning agent for each of the stains.

Any time you are using these strong cleaning agents, whether in liquid or in poultice form, be sure to wear rubber gloves to protect your hands, and make certain your work area is well ventilated. Solvents such as benzene, acetone, trichloroethylene or muriatic acid may require special precautions; if you are unfamiliar with a particular cleaning agent, see pages 8 and 9 for any special safety considerations.

☐ ASPHALT AND TAR: Scrape away excess material with a putty knife, then scrub the stain with scouring powder and hot water. If this fails to dislodge the stain, apply a poultice impregnated with benzene. After the poultice is removed, scrub the stain again.

☐ BLOOD: Wet the stain with water, then cover the dampened area with a thin, even layer of sodium peroxide powder. Take care not to let the powder come into contact with your skin; it is extremely caustic. Dampen the powder with a little more water, and let the mixture stand for a few minutes. Then add more water and scrub the area with a stiff brush. Finally, brush on vinegar to neutralize any alkaline residue left by the sodium peroxide, and rinse once again with water.

☐ CAULK, CHEWING GUM: Scrape and scrub off as much of the material as possible, then apply a poultice impregnated with denatured alcohol. After the poultice is dry, brush it away and wash the surface with trisodium phosphate and hot water.

☐ COFFEE AND TEA: Make a poultice impregnated with one part glycerin, two parts alcohol and four parts water, and apply it to the stain. Repeat the application up to three times if necessary. If the stain is still visible after the third application, switch to a poultice based on chlorine bleach diluted to one-quarter strength.

☐ GREASE: Scrub the stain with a solution of trisodium phosphate and hot water; then apply a poultice impregnated with oil-dissolving solvent, obtainable at an auto-supply store, or with benzene or trichloroethylene, which are available at paint stores.

☐ INK: Although some inks, such as printer's ink and India ink, can be removed from masonry surfaces by scrubbing them with strong soap or scouring powder, the marks left by the inks in felt-tipped pens must be bleached away. Because pen makers have differing ink formulations, you will have to use a trial-and-error process to determine which bleaching compound works best: Try poultices made with diluted chlorine bleach or bleaching powder; with mildew removers that contain potassium hypochlorite; or with calcium hypochlorite, which is available at swimming-pool-supply stores. Some indelible inks contain silver salts, which leave black residues. To remove the residue, apply a poultice made with household ammonia; repeat the application as necessary.

☐ NONFERROUS METALS: To remove the blue or green stains that can be left by copper, brass or bronze, make a poultice with sal ammoniac and household ammonia. To remove the white powdery stains left by corroding aluminum, use the same treatment as for efflorescence (page 21).

☐ PAINT: Blot fresh paint spills with rags or paper towels; work gently, without wiping, which could spread the paint and drive it farther into the pores of the masonry. After the spill has been blotted up, scrub out remaining stains of latex-base paints with scouring powder and water; remove remaining stains of oil-base paints with mineral spirits. To remove paint once it has dried, use commercial paint remover; then scrub the remaining stain with a one-to-10 solution of muriatic acid (page 21).

☐ TOBACCO: Apply a poultice of scouring powder and hot water; when the mixture dries, scrape it off and rinse the area well with additional hot water.

Applying a poultice. To use a poultice, mix just enough liquid cleaning agent into talc, whiting or lime to make a thick paste. Spread the paste about ¼ inch thick over the stain, and cover it with plastic film, sealed around the edges with masking tape. Leave the poultice in place until it dries, then scrape it away. Rinse the area well. Most poultices can be rinsed off with plain water, although some will require several washings. If special washes or rinses are needed, they are included in the recipe for the poultice.

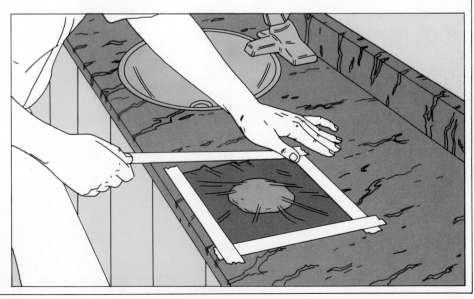

Restoring the Polish of Dressed Stone

Polishing with jeweler's rouge. Hold a bar of jeweler's rouge or stone-polishing compound against the revolving buffing attachment of an electric drill *(below, left);* press the bar against the edge of the cloth-covered wheel hard enough to charge the wheel liberally with polish, but not so hard as to mat the fibers. Then hold the charged buffing wheel lightly against the surface of the stone and work it slowly back and forth until the surface is smooth *(below, right).* Wash the polished surface with very hot, soapy water to remove any residual wax.

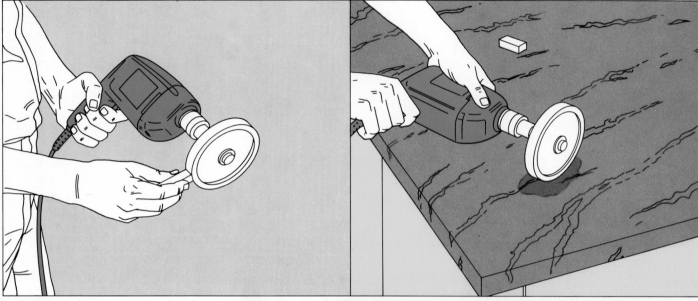

Sanding out scratch marks. Wrap a sanding block with ultrafine (600-grit) wet-or-dry sand paper, moistened with water. Press the sanding block against the damaged area and rub hard, in circular strokes, until the surface is smooth. To restore the gloss, sprinkle powdered tin oxide—available from lapidary-supply stores—onto the surface. Add just enough water to make a thick paste. Flip the sandpaper smooth side out and wrap it over the sanding block; resume rubbing until the stone is glossy. Finally, wash the surface with warm, soapy water, rinse it, and polish it with jeweler's rouge *(above).*

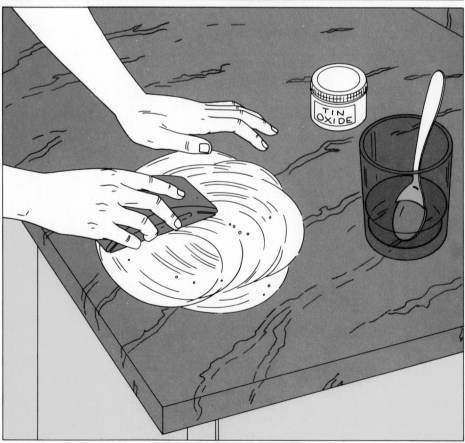

A Protective Coating That Deflects Soil

Sealing smooth surfaces. Use a paint roller with a short nap—¼-inch nap works best—to apply a thin film of silicone sealer to the stone surface. Along the edges, use a cloth pad saturated with sealer. Do not apply too much sealer at one time—thin films dry harder and wear better than thick ones. Allow the sealer to dry for 45 to 60 minutes, then apply a second thin coat.

Sealing rough surfaces. For outdoor surfaces, fill a tank-type garden sprayer with silicone sealer and work the pump up and down several times to pressurize the tank. Holding the sprayer nozzle 12 to 18 inches away from the masonry, lightly fog the entire surface to provide a base for the sealer. Then, starting at the top, work the sprayer back and forth in a gradually descending pattern until the entire surface is flooded with as much sealer as the stone can absorb. On indoor surfaces, use a sponge applicator.

To clean a tank-type garden sprayer, pump turpentine through it to flush out the sealer. Then flush the turpentine out with water.

Refinishing a blacktop driveway. After cleaning the surface, use driveway-patching compound to fill any holes and cracks more than ⅛ inch wide. Then, beginning along one edge of the driveway, pour a thick ribbon of coal-tar pitch emulsion, 3 feet long, onto the old surface *(above, left)*. Spread the emulsion all the way across the surface in a 3-foot-wide swath, using the squeegee side of a combination brush-and-squeegee tool *(above, right)*. Flip the tool over to the brush side and use the bristles to smooth any ridges in the coating.

Repeat this procedure, coating the surface in 3-foot sections until the entire driveway is covered—one 5-gallon pail of emulsion will coat about 400 square feet. Clean the recoating tool immediately with warm, soapy water. Keep traffic off the recoated surface for 24 hours.

Blasting Off Dirt with Water

Gasoline-powered pressure washers—which are widely available at tool-rental agencies—can dramatically speed cleaning exterior masonry surfaces. A brick house wall, which could take a full day's scrubbing with a brush and detergent, can be blasted clean with a pressurized jet of plain water in less than two hours, and there are similar time savings in pressure cleaning driveways, patios and sidewalks. And you can spread out the rental charges by using the machine to clean your garden tools, lawn-mower undercarriage, barbecue grill and trash cans.

The heart of a pressure washer is a powerful centrifugal pump. Driven by a two- to five-horsepower gasoline engine, the pump sucks water from an outdoor faucet and blasts it out through a spray wand and nozzle at pressures up to 2,000 pounds per square inch. At such pressures, the water loosens and washes away dirt, grime, sea-spray salt and even peeling paint. For less demanding chores and for rinsing, the machine comes with other nozzles that deliver a wider spray at lower pressures.

Although most pressure washers operate similarly, different models vary in the exact ways that hoses are attached and engine controls are set. Before leaving the rental agency, ask for a demonstration of how to use your particular machine. When you get the machine home, practice starting the engine and spraying the water by shooting it into the air. Grasp the spray wand firmly before squeezing the trigger so that the sudden recoil does not jerk the equipment out of your hands. Take care never to point the nozzle at yourself or anyone else: At the machine's highest pressure, the jet of water could cause severe injury, especially at close range.

Once you feel confident with the machine, prepare the surrounding environment for the drenching mist that will soon envelop it. Swaddle any nearby bushes or flowerbeds with plastic dropcloths, and protect exterior light fixtures, electrical receptacles and vents with plastic bags and tape *(top right)*. Finally, don full-length rain gear to shield yourself from the mist.

Pressure Washing a House Exterior

1 Battening down the house. Before you start a pressure washer, tape heavyweight plastic bags around outdoor light fixtures to protect them from water damage. Seal exterior electrical outlets and soffit vents under the eaves with overlapping strips of plastic tape. Make sure that all of the doors and windows are securely closed, and protect any nearby shrubs or flower beds by draping them with large plastic bags or with dropcloths.

2 Connecting and venting the lines. Connect the washer's water-intake line to a garden faucet, adding an extra length of garden hose if necessary. Turn the faucet all the way on. Without starting the engine, point the spray wand toward the ground and squeeze the trigger to vent air from the lines. When a steady stream of water flows through the wand, release the trigger and snap the smallest-diameter spray nozzle onto the wand.

3 **Starting the engine.** Extend the water-discharge line at least 10 feet from the machine and lay the wand on the ground. Point the nozzle away from the machine and keep the trigger closed. Flip the choke lever to CLOSED or ON and pull the starting rope. As soon as the engine catches, flip the choke lever to OPEN or OFF to bring the engine to full speed.

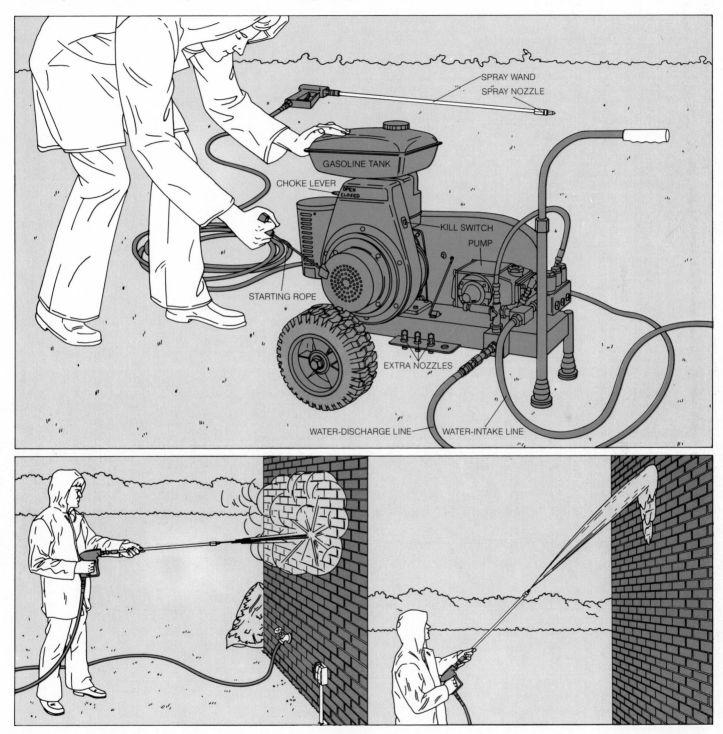

SPRAY WAND
SPRAY NOZZLE
GASOLINE TANK
CHOKE LEVER
OPEN CLOSED
KILL SWITCH
PUMP
STARTING ROPE
EXTRA NOZZLES
WATER-DISCHARGE LINE
WATER-INTAKE LINE

4 **Washing and rinsing a wall.** Point the wand directly at the wall, holding the nozzle about 18 inches away from the surface. Pull the trigger (*above, left*) and, working slowly in long vertical swaths from the ground to the eaves, blast away loose dirt. Avoid spraying directly into the joints at window frames or doorframes; water could be driven into the house.

When the washing is done, release the trigger and flip the KILL switch on the cowling to turn off the engine. Remove the washing nozzle and snap on a larger-diameter rinsing nozzle. Vent the system for air bubbles as in Step 2 before restarting the engine. Then rinse away loosened dirt, moving the wand across the wall in gentle horizontal sweeps, starting at the top and working down (*above, right*).

Dealing With Atmospheric Assaults on Metal

Metal surfaces are prized for their durability, but they are no more immune to dirt and grime than the most delicate upholstery fabric. And in some circumstances, metals are vulnerable to atmospheric corrosion as well. Without the protection of paint, oil or lacquer, many metals are rusted or tarnished by oxygen and airborne salts and acids. The methods used to clean metals depend on the character of the metal and on whether it is covered by a protective coating.

Metal surfaces normally left uncoated—a stainless-steel sink or an aluminum doorframe, for example—shed everyday dirt readily with nothing more than a thorough washing with mild liquid detergent and water. Even when the surface oxidizes, the solution usually is simple. The white powder that forms on aluminum frames and screens can be washed off with detergent and water or baking soda and water. Rust on iron, a more insidious form of oxidation, can be banished with steel wool or a wire brush, but then requires coats of primer and paint to prevent a recurrence.

The more delicate, decorative metals—such as copper, brass and pewter—need gentler treatment. Smudges and light tarnish can usually be removed with a commercial metal cleaner or with one of the recipes in the box on page 30; these are applied with a soft cloth and allowed to dry, then rinsed or simply rubbed off. For heavier tarnish on copper or brass exposed to the weather, you will need a special stripping solution *(page 33, top)*.

Metal cleaners, whether commercial or homemade, usually contain a polishing agent to restore the metal's luster. Polishing, unlike cleaning, involves abrasion: Some of the metal surface is actually rubbed away to leave a shiny new finish. Metal-polishing abrasives are extremely fine-grained—pumice, tripoli, rouge and whiting are the most common. They come in powder, paste and bar form and are available in hardware stores; the first two are most used for preliminary polishing, the latter two for buffing to a high sheen. Polishing abrasives are applied with a soft buffing wheel mounted on an electric drill or on a bench grinder.

With decorative metals, the final step to polishing often is coating the metal with a clear protective finish. Lacquers are popular, and they come in aerosol sprays or in a liquid form that can be brushed onto the metal surface. Lacquers have two main disadvantages: They tend to darken with age, and metals will often tarnish despite their presence. A good alternative to lacquer is tung oil, which can be buffed to a lustrous finish that does not darken with age. If properly applied *(page 33, bottom),* tung oil dries to a durable, invisible film that is highly resistant to water, alcohol, acids and heat.

Another unavoidable problem with the paints and lacquers that protect many metal surfaces from dirt and corrosion is that they often require, paradoxically, gentler treatment than the metals they cover. They cannot be rubbed with abrasives or cleaned with the harsh chemicals used to remove tarnish. With age, they are prone to chipping, scratching and peeling. When this happens, paints and lacquers can become cleaning problems themselves; they will have to be removed with paint and lacquer strippers, available in hardware stores.

If you are cleaning large areas of metal outdoors—a chain-link or wrought-iron fence, for example—you can rent a sandblaster; its high-velocity jet of sand will take off even the most stubborn layers of old paint or rust. Sandblasters are available at tool-rental stores and are normally powered by air compressors that run on ordinary household current. When using a sandblaster, be sure to wear a face mask and a respirator as well as sturdy gloves, long pants and a long-sleeved shirt. Dropcloths are also a must, to protect nearby foliage and windows and to make cleanup easier.

Sometimes a straightforward metal-cleaning task is complicated by the size, shape or location of the surface to be cleaned. Horizontal venetian blinds, for example, are difficult to wash and rinse thoroughly when they are hanging in place. But the job becomes much simpler if you hang the blinds on a clothesline. Similarly, the nooks and crannies of ornamental metalwork are easier to clean if you think small and use a toothbrush and toothpicks to reach them.

The metal-cleaning methods described on the following pages are shown in typical situations, but most of the techniques apply to a wide variety of metal surfaces. The chart on the opposite page lists the typical metals found in most households and gives the appropriate cleaning solutions for each one, as well as specific techniques and special tips for dealing with that particular metal.

Cleaning Coated and Uncoated Metals

Metal surface	Cleaning solution	Cleaning technique	Special tips and cautions
Painted metals Indoor (appliances, radiators, doors)	Mild liquid detergent and warm water	Vacuum to remove dust, then wash with cloth or sponge dampened in solution; rinse; dry with soft cloth.	Avoid cleaners containing abrasives or ammonia. Commercial appliance polish protects painted surfaces.
Outdoor (railings, gates, fences)	Mild liquid detergent and warm water	Wash with soft-bristled brush dampened in solution; rinse.	Remove rust and old paint with an electric drill fitted with a wire-brush attachment *(page 32, top)*; for heavy jobs, use sandblaster *(page 32, bottom)*. Protect cleaned metal with rust-resistant primer and paint.
Lacquered metal	Mild liquid detergent and warm water	Wash gently with soft cloth dampened in solution; rinse; dry with soft cloth.	Avoid cleaners and metal-polishing compounds containing abrasives or ammonia. Remove old lacquer with hot vinegar, used at full strength, or commercial lacquer thinner.
Unfinished metals Aluminum	Mild liquid detergent and warm water; for tough dirt, baking soda and water	Wash with soft cloth or brush dampened in solution; rinse; dry with soft cloth.	Avoid abrasive pads and cleaners containing abrasives.
Brass, bronze, copper	All-purpose metal cleaner (homemade); commercial compounds; mild abrasive polishes	Apply cleaners with soft cloth, allow to dry, buff with soft cloth. Apply polishing abrasives with buffing-wheel attachment of electric drill, bench grinder or polisher.	Remove especially heavy tarnish with stripping solution *(page 33, top)*.
Chrome	Mild liquid detergent and warm water; for mineral deposits, full-strength vinegar	Wash with cloth or sponge dampened in solution; rinse; dry with soft cloth. For mineral deposits, rub with a soft cloth dampened with vinegar. On heavy deposits, leave vinegar-soaked cloth for several hours.	Avoid abrasive powders and pads.
Pewter	Paste of rottenstone and olive oil (for dull finishes); paste of whiting and denatured alcohol (for bright finishes)	Apply paste with soft cloth, allow to dry; buff with soft cloth. Then wash with mild liquid detergent and warm water; rinse; dry with soft cloth.	Avoid harsh abrasives. For tough spots, rub gently with fine steel wool dipped in olive oil.
Silver	Mild liquid detergent and hot water; commercial silver polish	Wash, rinse and dry silver; polish with soft cloth or chamois; rub polish off with soft cloth or chamois. Wash, rinse and dry again.	A small toothbrush is useful for crevices, chased surfaces, beaded edges. Wash off all traces of polish.
Stainless steel	Mild liquid detergent and hot water	Wash with soft cloth dampened in solution; rinse; dry with soft cloth.	On brushed finishes, rub out scratches with fine steel wool, working with the grain. On highly polished finishes, avoid abrasive pads and scouring powders.
Outdoor metals Window screens Aluminum	Water; for mineral deposits, a solution of 2 teaspoons cream of tartar, 1 gallon boiling water	Hose off screen with water. Brush screen with soft-bristled brush and cleaning solution; rinse; air dry.	Cover aluminum screens with thin coat of kerosene before installing.
Copper	Water	Hose off; brush with soft-bristled brush.	Apply spar varnish to screen before installing.
Siding (aluminum)	Mild liquid detergent and warm water; for mildew, mix 1/3 cup liquid detergent, 2/3 cup TSP, 1 quart chlorine bleach, 3 quarts water	Hose down siding; then scrub with cleaning solution and soft-bristled brush; rinse.	Avoid cleaners containing abrasives or ammonia. Divide into 6-foot-square areas to prevent cleaning solution from drying.

Restoring metal surfaces. Metal surfaces differ in their cleaning needs, depending on whether they are painted, lacquered or left unfinished and on whether they are indoors or out. The chart above is designed to help you match the procedure to the surface. Most cleaning jobs can be taken care of with liquid detergent or with an all-purpose metal cleaner you can mix yourself *(page 30, box)*, although you can, if you prefer, use commercial products made for specific metals. Cleaning tips and cautions unique to certain metals are listed in the last column.

Formulas for Homemade Metal Cleaners

Unfinished household metals that are dirty or tarnished can be buffed to shiny perfection with mildly abrasive cleaning solutions. Below are three recipes for metal cleaners—one an all-purpose cleaner for brass, bronze, copper or stainless steel; one specifically for brass and copper; and one designed for touching up copper kitchenware. It is a good idea to wear plastic gloves while you do the buffing, to prevent skin oils from smudging the newly cleaned surface. The gloves are obtainable in drugstores.

□ ALL-PURPOSE METAL CLEANER: Combine in a clean glass jar: ¼ cup water, ¼ cup household ammonia, ½ cup isopropyl alcohol (70 per cent) and 1 cup diatomaceous earth (available at swimming-pool-supply stores). Stir the ingredients until the mixture is approximately the consistency of heavy cream;

if the mixture seems too thin, add more diatomaceous earth; if it is too thick, pour in additional water. To use the cleaner, spread it on the surface of the metal with a clean, soft cloth and allow it to dry completely. Then buff off the residue with another soft cloth.

□ PASTE FOR BRASS AND COPPER: Combine in a clean glass jar: ¼ cup salt, ½ cup cornmeal and ¼ cup white vinegar. Stir the mixture into a paste. To use the cleaner, rub it lightly over the metal surface with a water-dampened cloth or sponge, then rinse the metal with more water and a clean cloth or sponge. Dry the metal with a soft cloth.

□ QUICK COPPER CLEANER: Cut a lemon in half and sprinkle the cut surfaces liberally with salt; then rub the salted lemon over the tarnished copper. Rinse the treated area with water and dry the metal with a soft cloth.

Cleaning Horizontal Venetian Blinds

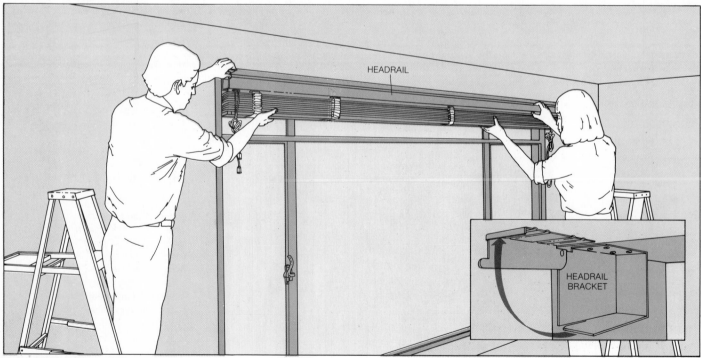

HEADRAIL

HEADRAIL
BRACKET

1 **Taking down a blind.** Dust or vacuum the slats while the blind is hanging in place, then raise the blind to the top and tie up the cords at both ends to keep them out of the way. Lift the front covers on the headrail brackets (*inset*) and, with a helper, grasp the ends of the headrail and slide it forward out of the brackets.

2 **Washing the blind outdoors.** To prepare the blind for scrubbing, suspend it from a length of sturdy rope or nylon cord strung between two anchoring points, such as trees. Be sure that the rope is high enough for the fully extended blind and that it has enough slack to make a loop over each end of the headrail. With a helper, loop the rope at each end of the headrail and slide the rail into the loop. Then untie the cords and drop the blind. First, hose it down with water. Then scrub both sides of the slats with a soft-bristled brush and a solution of mild liquid detergent and warm water. Rinse with the garden hose, and allow the blind to dry completely.

If you cannot hang a venetian blind outside for cleaning, you can lay a small blind in a bathtub for washing and rinsing.

LOOP

Washing Vertical Venetian Blinds

Washing the blind in place. Spread a plastic dropcloth over the floor beneath the blind; spread newspapers on top of the plastic to absorb dripped water. Close the blind, turn the slats perpendicular to the window and, after a preliminary dusting, use a soft, absorbent cloth dampened in a solution of mild detergent and warm water to wipe both sides of each slat from top to bottom. Be sure to squeeze excess moisture from the cloth so that liquid will not drip into the tracks. Rinse each slat in the same manner.

An Abrasive Brush
for Stubborn Dirt

Brushing dirt and rust away. To remove encrusted dirt or rust from a painted or unpainted metal surface, fit a wire-brush attachment to an electric drill and, wearing goggles, lightly abrade the metal surface. Then, if the metal surface was painted, repaint it; ask a paint dealer to recommend an appropriate paint. The metal surface shown here is coated with stove blacking, applied with a soft cloth and buffed, when it is dry, with a shoe brush.

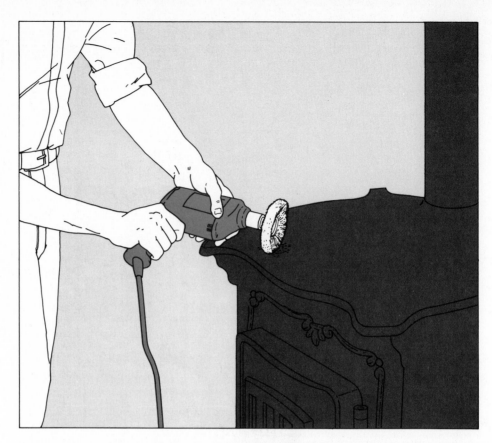

Sandblasting Deposits
of Soil from Metalwork

Blasting off dirt, rust and old paint. Place a dropcloth beneath the metal to be cleaned and over nearby shrubs and windows; then fill the sandblaster canister, following the manufacturer's instructions. Grasp the sandblaster firmly—one hand supporting the underside and the other on the handle-and-trigger assembly. Hold the nozzle 1 to 2 feet away from the metal surface and pull the trigger. Direct the jet of sand up, down and sideways over one area of the metal surface until it is clean. Refill the canister with fresh sand as necessary.

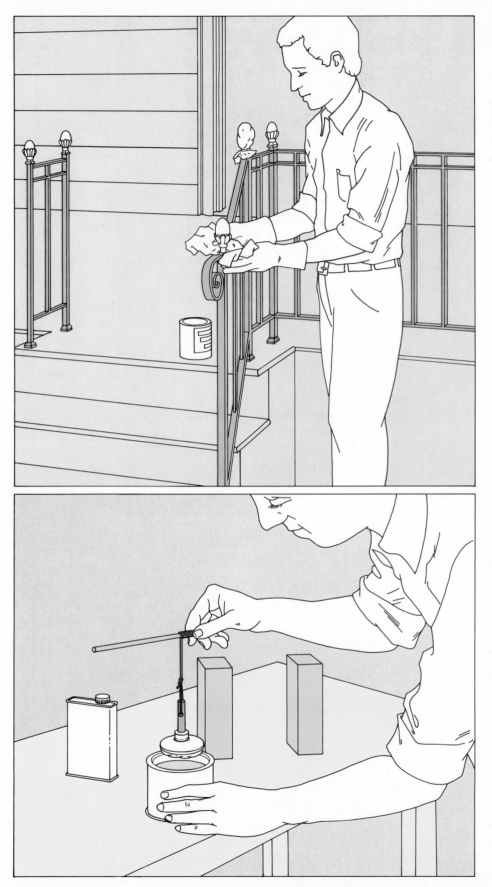

A Cure for Heavy Tarnish on Brass Hardware

Soaking off heavy tarnish. For brass that is badly tarnished, prepare a stripping solution by combining 1 quart of water, 1 cup of vinegar and ¼ cup of salt. Soak the tarnished object in this solution overnight, either by immersing it in a glass container or, if the object cannot be moved, by wrapping it with a clean cloth saturated with the solution. To slow evaporation, enclose the wrapping in a layer of plastic, and tie the entire package with white string. Remove the wrappings the following day, and apply brass cleaner (page 30, box). Protect the finish, if desired, with tung oil (below).

Sealing brass with tung oil. In lieu of lacquer, which darkens with age, dip brass hardware in tung oil to prevent tarnishing. First, remove old lacquer with a clean cloth dipped in lacquer thinner; wear rubber gloves to protect your hands from the harsh chemicals in the thinner. Then polish the brass object and warm it in the sun, or place it in a 150° F. oven for about 20 minutes.

Immerse the warmed brass in a container of tung oil, suspending it from a string wrapped around a dowel, which in turn is supported between two pieces of scrap wood. Allow the brass to remain in the oil for about two minutes, until the oil has seeped into all the crevices of the design. Air dry the brass object, still suspended, for about 15 minutes, until the oil has set. Then buff off excess oil with a soft, lint-free cloth, wearing gloves to protect the oiled surface from smudges. Allow the brass object to dry for about four hours in a dust-free area.

Larger brass objects can also be coated with tung oil: Simply rub the oil over the surface, using a clean, lint-free cloth.

Keeping Up the Appearance of Plastics

One of the great advantages of plastics in the home is that they are easy to clean. The smooth, nonporous surfaces of vinyl tile floors, laminated countertops, acrylic storm windows and fiberglass bathtubs usually require nothing more elaborate than a sponging with mild detergent and warm water to remove dust and everyday stains.

For stubborn stains, you may have to use stronger detergents, mildly abrasive powders or a nylon scrub pad. You may even have to resort to caustic cleaners or abrasives, but in general these should be avoided; they can actually damage plastic surfaces. Further steps to be used against stains will depend on the nature of the plastic (box, below).

Minor scuffs and scratches may complicate the cleaning process by trapping dirt. One way to avoid this problem is to coat scratch-prone surfaces with protective finishes, such as automobile wax for countertops and acrylic floor wax for vinyl floors. But wax build-up on floors may cause stickiness or yellowing, making it necessary to remove and replace the finish from time to time.

Scuffs and scratches—if they are not too deep—can be smoothed or filled in by the techniques described opposite. Sometimes these repairs are done with special patching compounds. Such repairs should always be followed by waxing and buffing of the entire surrounding surface, so that the restored area will be as inconspicuous as possible. Holes in vinyl upholstery can be filled by similar techniques (page 37).

Characteristics of Four Typical Plastics

Of the many plastics found in the home, four types predominate: acrylics, fiberglass, laminates and vinyls. This guide tells how they are used and provides some cleaning do's and don'ts.

□ ACRYLICS: Familiar as the clear, shatterproof plastic commonly sold as Plexiglas or Lucite, this plastic is also available in an opaque marbleized form called Corian. Acrylics are found in storm windows, shower doors, shelving and picture frames.

Acrylic surfaces are easily scratched and should be cleaned only with a sponge or a soft cloth dampened with a solution of one tablespoon of mild detergent to 6 cups of warm water. Grease and oil stains can sometimes be removed by light rubbing with kerosene or naphtha, which should be rinsed off immediately afterward with soap and water. Avoid cleaning fluids that contain alcohol, acetone, benzene or carbon tetrachloride, which may soften or cloud an acrylic surface. Most scratches can be removed by the techniques shown opposite, top.

□ FIBERGLASS: A light but exceptionally strong material, fiberglass is made by impregnating glass fibers with liquid resin. It is molded into a variety of shapes, including bathtubs, shower stalls, sinks and patio roofing.

Fiberglass is easily cleaned with the same detergent solution used for acrylic. Tough stains usually respond to gentle rubbing with a paste of nonabrasive cleansing powder and water. Paint spatters can be removed with turpentine or paint thinner. Both should be used sparingly and washed off as quickly as possible with a mild detergent. Surfaces that have become dull can often be restored by rubbing and buffing them with a compound made for buffing automobiles.

□ LAMINATES: Manufactured under a variety of names—including Formica, Micarta, Wilsonite, Arborite and Nevamar—laminates are widely used to cover countertops, tables and cabinets.

A sponge or a cloth moistened with mild detergent will take care of most soil, and a nonabrasive powdered cleanser such as baking soda can also be used, but sparingly. Mix the powder with water into a paste before using.

You may be able to disguise knife scratches with a coat of paste wax; a scratch too big to be disguised can be filled by the technique shown opposite, bottom. Colored plastic fillers for laminates are available from countertop fabricators. Be sure to specify the trade name and the designated color of your countertop—or bring along a scrap—to get an exact match.

□ VINYLS: This versatile family of vinyl chloride derivatives is found in plumbing pipe, resilient floor covering, the flexible webbing of garden furniture, and such soft fabrics as shower curtains and artificial upholstery leather.

Most vinyls can be cleaned with the same detergent solution used for acrylic. Regular vinyl flooring should be finished with a protective coat of acrylic wax. No-wax vinyl, manufactured with a glossy polyurethane finish, requires only dusting and occasional damp mopping with specially formulated detergents that will not discolor the clear finish. Vinyl shower curtains and tablecloths can be cleaned in a washing machine, using the slowest wash and rinse cycles and a warm-water setting. Remove them without spin drying, and hang them up to air dry after shaking off excess water.

Repair kits are available for patching holes in vinyl fabrics. For flooring, you can manufacture your own patching material as shown on page 36.

Polishing Out Scratches on Acrylic

1 **Removing scratches from a storm window.** Lay the storm window on a work surface padded with a soft cloth. Rub deep scratches with a sanding block fitted with 400-grit wet-or-dry sandpaper (*below, left*). Wet the paper and work gently in back-and-forth strokes, carrying the treatment several inches beyond the scratches. To fill shallow scratches, apply a thin, even coat of automobile paste wax, then buff the surface lightly with a soft cloth (*below, right*).

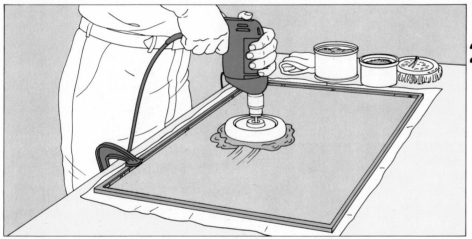

2 **Restoring the window's luster.** Clamp the window against the work surface, and buff the entire pane with a fine buffing compound such as jeweler's rouge. Use an electric drill fitted with a 4-inch buffing wheel covered with a muslin buffing disk, and work in small, overlapping loops. When the sanding marks and wax-filled scratches are no longer detectable, wash away the buffing compound with soap and water. Then cover the buffing wheel with a clean wool buffing disk and use it to rub a coat of automobile paste wax onto the surface. When the desired luster is achieved, wipe the acrylic with a clean, damp cloth to remove dust-attracting static charges.

A Quick Fix for Countertop Scratches

Using plastic seam filler. Squeeze a small quantity of filler onto a scrap of plastic or a plastic plate, and work it with a clean putty knife until it begins to thicken. Wipe the scratch with a cloth moistened with the solvent that comes with the filler, then press the paste into the scratch with the putty knife. Immediately wipe away excess filler with the solvent-dampened cloth. If the filler shrinks as it hardens, wait an hour and repeat the process.

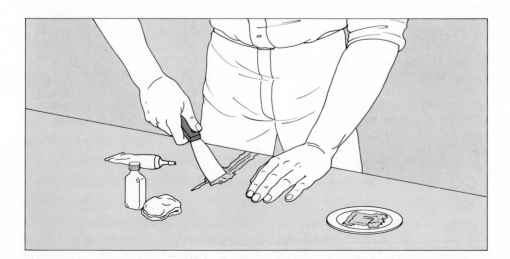

Mixing a Soft Patch for a Vinyl Floor

1 Preparing the paste. Take a scrap of vinyl that matches the floor covering, fold it right side out, and scrape the surface with a utility knife, catching the powdery shavings in a bowl. If the vinyl is patterned, be sure to scrape from an area that matches the color of the damaged area of the floor. Refold and scrape until you have collected sufficient powder for the patch. Add a few drops of clear nail polish and stir with a polished putty knife until the mixture thickens to the consistency of putty.

2 Spreading the paste. Mask the scarred area with 1-inch tape, placing the tape as close to the damage as possible. Press the paste firmly into the masked opening with the putty knife. Scrape off the excess, and smooth the patch. Let the paste set for half an hour. Then remove the tape and buff the patch with #2/0 steel wool. Apply a coat of acrylic floor wax or clear nail polish to the patch, if necessary, to match the glossy finish of the surrounding floor.

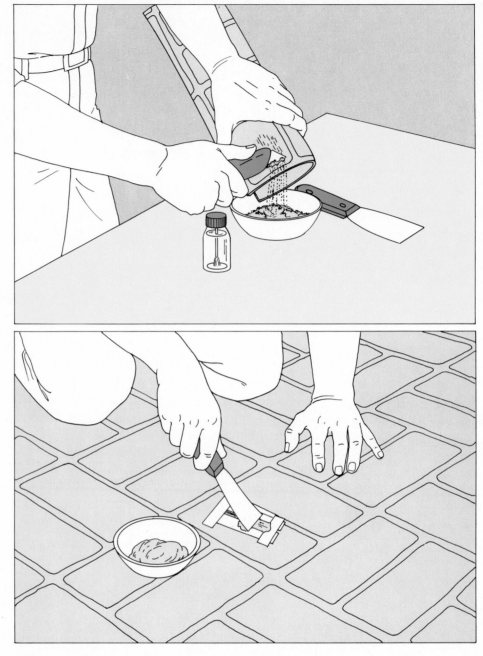

Cleaning Linoleum, a Vinyl Look-alike

Linoleum, an older nonplastic flooring material still found in some houses, can be mistaken for vinyl, but it is cleaned differently. Made of linseed oil, ground cork and burlap, linoleum tends to grow brittle and crack with age, and since production of it stopped in 1974, existing linoleum floors must be treated gently. They should be cleaned with a mop dampened with warm water and a mild detergent, then damp mopped with clean water to rinse off the detergent. When thoroughly dry, the clean linoleum can be given a thin coat of acrylic floor wax. Do not use varnishes, which tend to yellow, or polyurethane coatings, which do not bond well with linoleum. Both are difficult to remove.

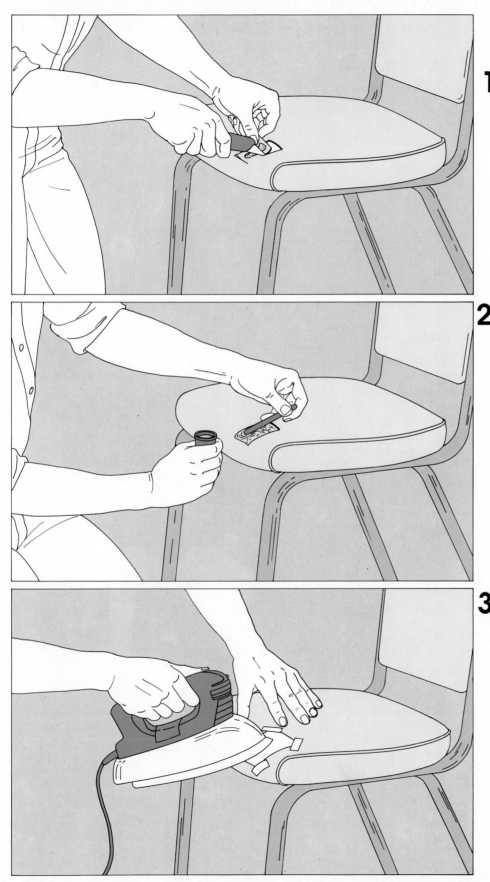

Filling a Hole in Vinyl Fabric

1 Trimming the damage. With scissors or a utility knife, trim around the damaged area to remove frayed edges and leave a neat outline. If there is no backing material beneath the vinyl, cut a piece of adhesive tape slightly larger than the trimmed opening; work the tape into the opening, adhesive side up.

2 Applying the patching compound. Using a tongue depressor or a coffee stirrer, fill the opening with the matching color vinyl compound that comes in a vinyl-repair kit. Work from the center outward, smoothing the thick compound so that it is level with the surrounding vinyl surface.

3 Bonding the patch. Select a graining paper from the repair kit that matches as closely as possible the texture of the vinyl fabric. Place the graining paper over the compound-filled opening, textured side down, and anchor it at the corners with masking tape. Using the tip of an iron heated to the cotton setting or a soldering iron at low heat, press the paper against the patching compound; move the iron steadily in a circular motion for one minute, making sure that it does not scorch the paper or touch the surrounding vinyl fabric. Let the bonded paper set for at least three minutes; then peel it off. Polish the patch with a clear vinyl finish, sold at automotive-supply stores for finishing vinyl tops and interiors.

Making Cloudy Glass Perfectly Clear

Washing glass can be one of the easiest of chores and often one of the most time-consuming. If the area is small, as with a tabletop or a mirror, cleaning is a simple matter of spraying on a commercial window cleaner and wiping it off with a lint-free cloth. Even a delicate crystal chandelier comes clean easily with a spray sold by lamp-supply stores *(opposite, bottom)*. This product spares you the tedium of dismantling and washing the fixture, crystal by fragile crystal.

Washing the windows in an average house is a much more formidable task, involving hundreds of square feet of glass. And, of course, every window has two sides—one of which is often hard to reach. In addition, the presence of storm windows doubles the work. Little wonder that cleaning women traditionally announce that they "do not do windows."

With the right tool, however—the squeegee used by professional window washers—the job is not all that difficult. A good-quality squeegee has two rubber blades locked in a metal housing. The blades have knife-sharp edges, which is what makes them so effective; professional window washers, who are rather particular about their squeegees, replace the blades for every house.

Squeegees come in various lengths. Choose one wide enough to cover 60 to 70 per cent of the window, so that only two vertical strokes are necessary to cover the entire surface *(below)*. Very large windows are squeegeed with a continuous sideways motion, without lifting the blade from the glass *(opposite, top left)*.

Corners and edges missed by the squeegee are cleaned with a chamois or a soft lint-free cloth, such as an old cotton T-shirt or cotton knit underwear. Discarded newspaper, crumpled up, does an excellent job of wiping glass dry without leaving streaks.

Many sorts of cleaning liquid can be used. All the traditional grease-cutting agents—rubbing alcohol, vinegar, baking soda, borax, even baby powder—are effective when mixed with water. Professional window washers generally prefer ammonia or trisodium phosphate. For a 2½-gallon bucket, they recommend 6 ounces of ammonia or 1 tablespoon of trisodium phosphate. To make the squeegee glide more easily, they sometimes add ½ teaspoon of automatic-dishwasher detergent. In freezing weather, they also add automobile window-washing solvent, mixed as specified on the label.

The toughest job, say professionals, is

removing screen rust—tiny specks of oxidized aluminum deposited on the glass by rain filtering through old aluminum screens. This gritty residue must be removed before the window can be squeegeed. Oven cleaner, sprayed on a very fine steel-wool pad and rubbed on the glass immediately, will remove these stubborn particles. Paint spatters, another common problem, must also be removed in advance: Just scrape the window with a razor blade or with a wallpaper-trimming knife.

Washing the outside of upper-story windows is customarily done by leaning out the window or using an extension ladder. But both approaches are risky. A less hazardous alternative is a pair of telescoping poles that extend to reach 30 feet above the ground. Available at stores that specialize in janitorial supplies, the poles can be fitted with a sponge, a squeegee, a chamois or a scraper.

Skylights can be cleaned only by climbing on the roof. Although some are glass, many skylights are made of plastic, which is softer than glass. Before you wash a skylight, dust off loose dirt; it could scratch a plastic surface during cleaning. Then sponge on the cleaner and wipe it dry with a chamois.

Getting Windows Clean with a Rubber Squeegee

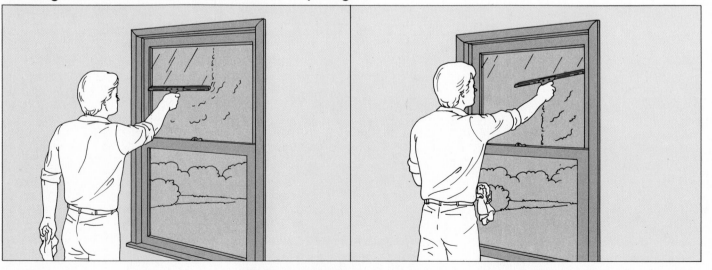

Cleaning small windows. Sponge on just enough cleaning liquid to wet the entire window, then pull the squeegee straight down over half of the window *(above, left)*. To clean the other half of the window, slightly angle the blade of the squeegee as you descend, so that the excess cleaning liquid is forced into the lower corner *(above, right)*. Then, using a chamois or a lint-free cloth, wipe off the edges of the glass and remove any drips from the window sill.

A clean sweep for large windows. After sponging cleaning liquid onto the glass, squeegee the window in a continuous side-to-side motion (*arrows*). Begin by placing the squeegee against the upper edge of the window, with the blade vertical. Pull it toward the opposite edge and, as the blade approaches that edge, reverse direction by pivoting the squeegee. Without lifting the blade from the glass, continue sweeping back and forth, from edge to edge, until you reach the bottom of the window. Then turn the blade so that it is horizontal, to carry the liquid down to the window's lower edge. Wipe off all the edges and the sill with a chamois or a lint-free cloth.

Extension poles for high windows. To reach windows between 7 and 30 feet above the ground, use adjustable aluminum extension poles, twisting the collars of the poles (*inset*) to lock them at the desired length. Use two poles, if possible, fitting one with a sponge attachment, the other with a squeegee, and enlist the aid of a helper to handle one of the poles. With a single pole, you will have to change fittings constantly, and the liquid may dry in the time it takes to switch from sponge to squeegee.

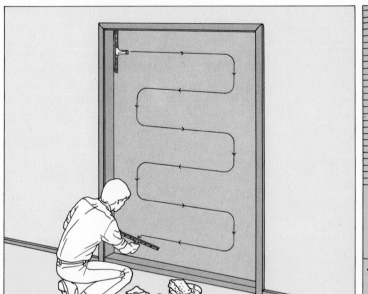

COLLAR

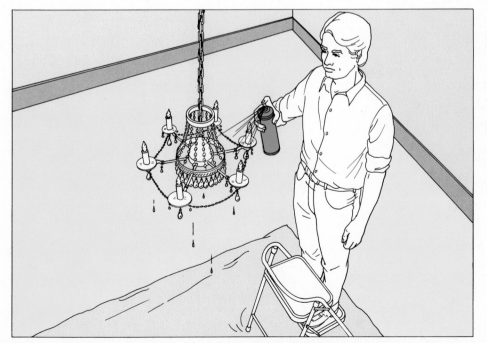

The Quick Way to Clean A Crystal Chandelier

Spraying dirt off glass crystals. Move furniture out from under the chandelier, and spread a plastic dropcloth over the floor. Turn off the electricity to the chandelier at the light switch and allow the light bulbs to cool; then tighten the bulbs in their sockets. Working from a ladder or step stool placed to the side of the fixture, spray a chandelier cleaner onto the glass pendants until the liquid begins to drip. Allow the chandelier to dry before removing the dropcloth.

Cleaning Porcelain Plumbing Fixtures

The most-cleaned surfaces in a house—kitchen sinks, toilets, bathtubs, bathroom floors and walls—are often manufactured of ceramic tile, porcelain or porcelain enamel, all of which resist stains. Regularly wiped down with an all-purpose cleaner or a mildly abrasive scouring powder, ceramic and porcelain surfaces will normally remain sparkling. But even these materials, with their glasslike surfaces, cannot shed every kind of discoloration. Grout—the porous material between tiles—is even more vulnerable.

When routine cleaning measures fail, you will need to resort to one of the heavy-duty regimens listed below. To get rid of one common and particularly persistent stain—iron—you may even prefer to substitute prevention for cure. Iron that has been dissolved in water leaves rusty stains on plumbing fixtures and, after a time, deposits fine sediment that leaves pepper-colored stains. You can treat these problems by installing a filter in the water line. Small filters—12 to 15 inches high—that depend on activated charcoal, or fabric cartridges such as the one opposite, can remove small amounts of iron and sediment. Larger filters that employ manganese-treated sand as a filtering medium remove much more.

Both types of filter have an inlet and an outlet hole and are installed by cutting into the main water line where it enters the house. To join them to the line, you will need the appropriate fittings—soldered ones for copper plumbing systems, threaded ones for galvanized-steel systems. The larger filters also may require an electrical hookup if they have an automatic flushing system to clean themselves out periodically; the electrical hookups differ widely, however, so you will have to follow the instructions for the particular model you have purchased.

Before buying a filter, have a water-quality technician test your water and recommend the appropriate size and type of unit; water-softener dealers who sell water-conditioning equipment will often do such analyses without charge.

Combating Discoloration with Chemicals

With luck, you may never have to deal with the staining problems listed below. But accidents do happen. Except where otherwise noted, the cleaning solutions recommended can be used on both glazed and unglazed surfaces, including grout. Unglazed surfaces that are light in color, however, are liable to take on the color of the cleaning solution. If you are in doubt, test the solution on a small patch before undertaking an entire project. After finishing with any cleaning substance, rinse the area with plain water and dry it off with toweling or absorbent cloth.

□ COFFEE: Dampen a cloth with warm water, dip it in baking soda and scrub the mixture over the stain.

□ FRUIT JUICE, TEA: Wash the area with a solution made of 1 tablespoon trisodium phosphate and 1 quart hot water. Rinse, then follow with a solution of 3 tablespoons laundry bleach in 1 quart of warm water.

□ GREASE: Using a stiff-bristled brush, scrub the affected area with a strong solution of heavy-duty household detergent or a solution made of ½ cup trisodium phosphate and 1 gallon of very hot water. Repeat if necessary.

□ HARD-WATER SCUM: Scour the area thoroughly with a solution made of equal parts of vinegar and warm water using a nylon scouring pad.

□ MILDEW: Mix ½ cup laundry bleach with 1 quart water and apply with a sponge. If the mildew remains, use a commercial mildew remover that contains sodium hypochlorite and sodium carbonate. Wear gloves and keep the room well-ventilated.

□ OIL: Mix a thick paste of household scouring powder and water. Apply the paste to the stain, and allow it to stand overnight. Then wet the dried paste with water and scrub vigorously with a stiff-bristled brush.

□ PAINT: Remove fresh oil-base paint with a cloth dipped in turpentine or paint thinner. Wash away the residue with a solution of ¼ cup trisodium phosphate mixed with 1 gallon of warm water. Remove fresh water-base paint with a cloth dampened with warm water and mild household detergent, such as dishwashing liquid. Scrub the area with a soft-bristled brush.

Dry paint, both oil-base and water-base, can be removed with a solution of ½ cup trisodium phosphate and 1 gallon of warm water. Or—if it has hardened into thick droplets—scrape off the paint carefully with a single-edged razor blade.

□ RUBBER HEEL MARKS: Dab the marks off with a cloth that you have dipped in cleaning fluid or mineral spirits.

□ RUST: To remove a light stain, rub it with a cut lemon, then wash the area with mild household detergent, such as liquid dishwashing detergent. Remove a darker stain by using a solution of one part oxalic acid (page 9) to 20 parts water. Wash the solution off with clear water immediately. Repeat the procedure if necessary.

To remove heavy deposits of rust around the drain of a bathtub or a sink, scrub with a solution of ½ cup naphtha-soap chips, ½ cup mineral spirits and 1 gallon of hot water, using a stiff-bristled brush or #2 steel wool.

□ SOAP SCUM: Mix a paste of cream of tartar—obtainable in bulk at drugstores—and hydrogen peroxide. Scrub on the paste with a stiff-bristled brush. (This method is also effective for mercurochrome and merthiolate stains.)

□ UNKNOWN STAIN: On glazed surfaces, apply a stiff paste of whiting (calcium carbonate) and household ammonia; let it stand for one hour, then wash it off with soapy water. On porous surfaces, mix household scouring powder with water to make a slurry, and mop it over the area. Let the solution stand for approximately five minutes, and then scrub the surface vigorously with a stiff-bristled brush.

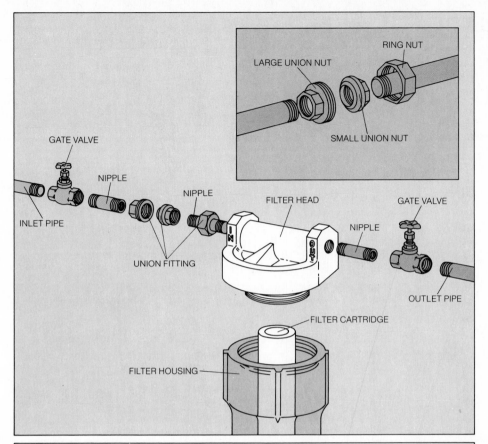

Fitting a Water Filter into an Existing Line

In galvanized piping. Turn off the main water supply and open several faucets around the house to drain as much water as possible from the line. Cut through the pipe where the filter will be mounted, using a hacksaw. Dismantle the section of pipe back to the nearest fitting on each side of the cut. Remove the fittings, exposing male threads—or add nipples to achieve the same result. Attach a gate valve to each pipe end. On the outlet side of the filter, add a nipple to the gate valve, then turn the filter head onto the valve. On the inlet side of the filter, add nipples to the gate valve and to the filter head; then join the two nipples with a three-part union fitting.

To assemble the union fitting, first screw the large union nut onto one nipple (inset). Then slip the ring nut over the second nipple, and screw the small union nut onto the second nipple. Finally, join the large and small union nuts and screw the ring nut over them. Tighten all the threaded joints with two open-end or adjustable wrenches, using one wrench to hold the pipe steady and the other to tighten the joint.

In copper tubing. Turn off the main water supply and, using a hacksaw or a tube cutter, cut out a section of pipe where the filter will be mounted. The length of the cutout section should equal the length of the filter head plus the necessary fittings—two male threaded-copper adapters, a nipple, a three-part union fitting and two brass gate valves. Solder one end of the valves to the cut pipe ends, the other end of the valves to adapters. Screw the outlet hole of the filter head onto the threaded end of the adapter on the outlet side of the assembly. Screw a nipple onto the inlet side of the filter head, and join the nipple to the other adapter with a three-part union fitting as above.

To solder together sections of copper pipe, clean the pipe ends with emery cloth and coat them with soldering flux. Fit together the pipe sections, and tape a heatproof pad to the wall behind the pipe to protect the surface. Heat both sections evenly with a propane torch, then touch the heated joint with solder (inset); it should flow quickly around the joint. If the solder does not flow, apply the heat for a longer time; but never apply the flame directly to the solder.

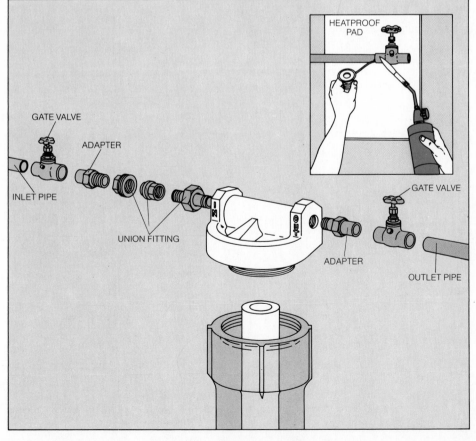

First Aid for Dingy Walls and Ceilings

Thanks to the law of gravity, the surfaces of walls and ceilings escape the daily spills and footprints that leave their mark upon floors and carpets. But walls and ceilings are by no means immune to dirt. Furniture that touches a wall, the smoke of an after-dinner cigar, or even a child's head rested repeatedly against a favorite spot during bedtime stories can all smudge, scuff or film these surfaces with the kind of dirt that vacuuming or dusting cannot remove.

The type of covering on a wall or a ceiling will dictate the method used to clean it. Flat and enamel paints and vinyl- or plastic-coated papers are washable to some extent and can be cleaned with the solutions listed in the box opposite. Depending upon how they are made, wallpapers may be categorized as scrubbable or washable. If you do not know which kind of paper you have, it is best to begin with a weak solution and gentle sponging action. Paints vary in quality; the better ones usually last longer and will withstand a greater number of washings. The approximate life expectancy of many paints appears on the label.

Before you begin, consider the whole wall or ceiling and what the effect of cleaning just one spot will be. A highly visible smudge that needs to be scrubbed may leave a clean mark on an otherwise dingy wall. And, depending on the color and quality of the paint, some of the pigment may come off on the rag. Faced with the task of washing the whole wall in order to dispose of the smudge, you may instead prefer to live with it.

If you do decide to wash an entire wall or ceiling, a few preliminary steps will make the job easier. Pull all of the furniture away from the walls, and cover it and the floor with dropcloths. Take down pictures, curtains and drapes; tape plastic wrap over metal fixtures such as chandeliers or wall sconces to protect them from damage by chemicals in the cleaning solution. Then thoroughly vacuum the walls, ceiling, baseboard, and door and window trim, paying special attention to corners and to the grooves and patterns in fancy woodwork. Use the vacuum attachments, such as the crevice tool and dust brush.

For the actual washing, you will need a stepladder with a shelf wide enough to accommodate two buckets—one for the cleaning solution, the other for rinse water. If the existing shelf is too small, extend it by clamping a board to it. Use separate sponges for washing and rinsing, and wear rubber gloves for protection.

All wall surfaces should be dusted and vacuumed before a thorough cleaning, but wall coverings that are too delicate to be doused with water and cleaning solutions will require extra care and, often, unusual recipes. Wood paneling requires the special techniques described on pages 12-13, and nonwashable wallpapers can stand only gentle dusting and an occasional spot cleaning. Many such papers, especially those found in older houses, were made before colorfast dyes were available; thus, the patterns may be destroyed by moisture. A number of special coverings, including grass cloth, burlap and foil, are essentially nonwashable—but you may vacuum them. Acoustic tile is cleaned with the methods used for nonwashable papers.

Before cleaning a nonwashable wallpaper, it is also wise to consider your options. As with washable surfaces, you may decide that it is easier to live with a few scuffs and smudges than to attempt to remove them—especially since you cannot disguise the cleaned spot by washing the surrounding wall surface. And with particularly fragile papers, such as screen- or hand-printed ones, you run the risk of rubbing off the surface if you wipe or brush too vigorously.

Several techniques, though, are generally safe for all but the most delicate papers. An artgum eraser, the pale brown, crumbly type that is available in stationery stores, will often lift light dirt and smudges from a wall. A doughlike wallpaper cleaner, available at most hardware and home-decorating stores, works in a similar fashion.

You can also make your own cleaning paste at home. In a large saucepan, combine 1 cup of salt, 1½ ounces of potassium alum (available at pharmacies) and 2 cups of water. Heat the mixture over low heat, stirring constantly until all of the solids are dissolved; remove the mixture from the stove, add 1 tablespoon of kerosene, and stir. Transfer the mixture to a basin and slowly stir in 5 cups of flour. When the mixture becomes too thick to stir, knead in the remaining flour by hand. This recipe makes 1¼ to 2 pounds, but you may double the amounts given. Store the mixture in a tightly sealed jar, and use it as a poultice to clean large sections of wallpaper. But test it first in an inconspicuous area to be sure that it does not damage the paper.

Another stain-removing measure, also to be tested in a hidden area before use, involves applying a paste made by mixing petroleum-base cleaning fluid (page 8) with an absorbent—fuller's earth for dark surfaces, whiting or cornstarch for light surfaces. The paste should be allowed to dry, then brushed off. Finally, the area should be rubbed with a soft, clean cloth dipped in borax. A third means of spot cleaning wallpaper is to use a chemically treated synthetic sponge, sold at hardware and home-decorating stores.

One wall-cleaning method is designed to deal with a specific problem. If wallpaper is so badly soiled that it must be removed, you will most likely be confronted, once the paper is off, with a bare wall or ceiling covered with deposits of old paste. Unlike the paper it once anchored, the paste can be attacked vigorously. Use a special wallpaper-paste solvent to prepare the surface for whatever new treatment you plan (page 45, bottom). The solvent, which is available at paint, wallpaper and hardware stores, must be mixed with water according to the manufacturer's instructions.

Washing Solutions for Paints and Wall Coverings

The solutions below are effective for removing dirt and various stains from walls and ceilings with washable finishes. In general, the stains that respond to washing are mildew, ink and substances with a greasy base—crayon, lipstick or food splatters. To remove mildew, add 1 cup of chlorine laundry bleach to 1 gallon of warm water, and sponge the surface. Wipe off with a clean, wet sponge.

FLAT PAINTS. For washing entire walls and ceilings, mix 2 tablespoons trisodium phosphate or powdered household detergent into a gallon of lukewarm water. For greasy stains, use a stronger solution of trisodium phosphate or a mixture of enzyme detergent and water. SEMIGLOSS AND GLOSSY PAINTS. When washing entire walls and ceilings, use a solution of 1 teaspoon washing soda per gallon of lukewarm water. Use the

same solution for washable stains, except on painted wood, such as a baseboard or a doorframe (page 12). WASHABLE AND SCRUBBABLE PAPERS. To wash entire walls and ceilings, work as for flat paint, above; do not let water get behind seams. Rinse each section, then pat dry. For ink or grease, use a one-to-10 solution of enzyme detergent and water, or rub with a cloth dampened with isopropyl alcohol.

A Systematic Approach to Scrubbing Walls

Washing an entire room. Set up a stepladder tall enough for you to reach the ceiling without extending your arm fully. Place two buckets— one containing cleaning solution (box, above), the other rinse water—on the ladder shelf. If necessary, clamp a 1-by-8-inch board onto the shelf to support the buckets. Immerse a sponge in each bucket. Wring out the cleaning sponge until it no longer drips, and gently scrub the ceiling with circular strokes. Cover as wide an area as you can safely and comfortably reach. Then wipe off the cleaner with the rinsing sponge—also

wrung out until it is drip-free—and move the ladder to an adjacent area. Continue in this manner until you have scrubbed the entire ceiling. Change the cleaning solution and the rinse water as needed—for ordinary soil, usually after you have covered about 100 square feet.

To clean the walls, begin by washing and rinsing particularly dirty areas—over heat registers, near light switches, and around the perimeter of spaces occupied by picture frames. Then, starting in a corner and directly above the base-

board, wash and rinse a 3-foot-wide strip up the wall all the way to the ceiling, working in overlapping vertical and horizontal strokes. Immediately rinse the strip, working now from ceiling to floor in order to wipe away streaks and drip marks before they have a chance to dry. Continue in this fashion, cleaning adjacent strips until you have circled the entire room.

When the walls of the room are finished, clean the wooden baseboards and the framing around doors and windows.

Picking Up Dirt from Nonwashable Wallpaper

A gentle rubdown for wallpaper. Soak a light-colored cotton terry-cloth towel in turpentine, and wring it dry. Air-dry the towel completely, then wrap it around the head of a dry sponge mop, securing it with string or masking tape (if using tape, make sure it does not touch the wallpaper during cleaning). Wipe the towel-wrapped mophead across the ceiling in long, parallel strokes; using similar parallel strokes, wipe the walls from ceiling to floor. When the towel looks dusty, turn it inside out or replace it with a fresh towel. If stains remain, use one of the techniques shown below and opposite to remove them.

When a papered room has a painted ceiling, wash the ceiling first (*page 43*). Near the edges of the ceiling, work with a barely damp sponge to avoid lifting or staining the edges of the wallpaper. Then wipe down the walls as above.

A cleaner that rolls dirt away. Knead a grapefruit-sized lump of cleaner dough (*page 42*) between your hands until it is malleable. Shape the dough into a cylinder and press it firmly against the soiled wallpaper with one palm; roll it slowly up and down (*above, left*). When the surface of the cylinder is coated with dirt, knead and fold the soiled surface into the center (*above, right*). Then form a new cylinder and again roll it over the dirty wallpaper.

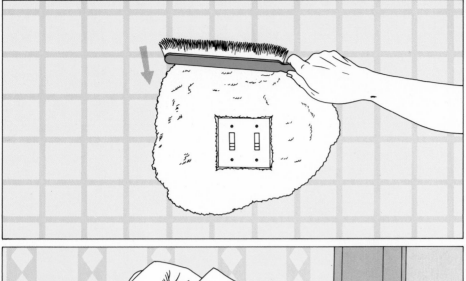

A poultice for stubborn stains. Apply a ⅛-inch-thick layer of cleaning paste (*page 42*) on the soiled area with the palm of your hand, and allow it to dry. When the surface is chalky to the touch, after about 30 minutes, remove the paste with a clean, medium-hard-bristled brush. Use a series of swift, firm downward strokes to dislodge it. A paste brush or a new dustpan brush is excellent for this purpose. Repeat the application if the stain remains.

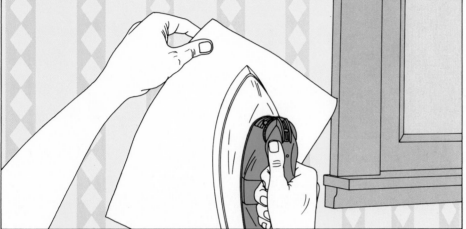

Blotting out grease stains. Hold a piece of clean blotting paper over the stain and press an iron, on a low setting, firmly against the paper for about 2 seconds. Repeat the process, using a clean section of the paper each time, until all traces of grease have been removed.

If blotting paper does not absorb all the grease, rub gently with a piece of cheesecloth that has been sprinkled with turpentine or benzene.

Removing Remnants of Wallpaper

Dissolving wallpaper paste. Wearing gloves to protect your hands (and goggles to protect your eyes if your are working on the ceiling), mix the solvent in a bucket (*page 42*) and dab it over a 4-foot-square area (*above, left*) with a household sponge. Let it work for 15 minutes; then scrape off the paste with a putty knife; deposit the waste material in a tin can or jar (*above, right*), preferably one large enough to hold a sizable quantity. Repeat the process, section by section, until the entire surface is cleared of paste residue. Then wash the room (*page 43*).

Caring For Textiles

An unlikely grouping. A garden hose and a scrub brush—tools more commonly associated with cleaning brick paving—lie ready to launder a densely piled Oriental-style rug. In fact, the soft bristles of the brush and copious amounts of cool water, augmented by a mild detergent, are the safest method for floating out deeply embedded dirt without harming the brilliant colors of the rug *(pages 62-63)*.

By some quirk of fate, the softest furnishings in a house—its carpets, curtains and upholstery—often seem to get the hardest use. They also tend to have their own distinctive cleaning requirements, caused in part by their diversity. Household textiles come in a multiplicity of weaves, textures and fibers, each with properties that affect how the textile responds to soil and how the soil is removed. Cotton fiber, for example, is prized for its absorbency, a quality that unfortunately allows it to soak up stains as readily as it soaks up dyes. The same is true of silk, but silk fibers are so finespun that cleaning them generally calls for the most delicate handling. As for synthetics, although they are by nature resistant to soil, they can also hold on to it tenaciously, and spilled coffee and cream on a nylon carpet may call for special handling.

There is a logic to tackling such cleaning problems, however, and it begins with recognizing the fiber. Despite their diversity, most household textiles tend to fall into groups *(pages 48-49)*. Carpeting, for example, is often nylon; and, although there are dozens of different formulations for nylon carpeting yarn, all of them are cleaned in the same way. Similarly, the weave and texture of the fabric may dictate how roughly or gently it must be handled, but dirt that settles on the fabric is inevitably trapped in the interlocking warp and weft of its yarns and must be released by agitation. Indeed, routine cleaning of rugs, carpets, drapes and upholstery can be accomplished with a surprisingly small number of strategies. There are, for example, only two ways to wash tacked-down carpeting, whatever its composition. And a single method of laundering removable rugs—with a scrub brush and a garden hose *(opposite)*—applies equally to expensive Oriental rugs and machine-loomed copies of them.

Even stains yield to a logical approach. All of them are the result of chemical action, which other chemicals can usually counter. The trick lies in applying the chemicals in a certain order and in combining them with suitable cleaning regimens—most of which are simply the routine brushing, sponging, wiping and blotting used for everyday cleaning. Like most cleaning, the stain removal usually starts with the gentlest combination of chemicals and mechanical action and works up to the bigger guns only when necessary. The chart on pages 56-59, which looks formidable but is as easy to use as a telephone book, is designed to guide you through this step-by-step process. Under the listings for more than 100 common stains and the major categories of washable and nonwashable fabrics, you will find what stain-removal measures to try first, what to move on to when these measures fail and, as a last resort, the methods to use when the stain is particularly persistent.

Matching Care to Fiber Content

The fibers in a fabric are an important clue to its care, but in modern fabrics they are not always easy to identify. Wool, silk, cotton and linen have more or less recognizable attributes, but synthetic fibers hide their origins under myriad disguises. The chart at right lists the 16 most common natural and synthetic fibers used for home-furnishing fabrics. It is intended to help you determine when those fibers are present in a fabric and how they affect the fabric's care.

Clues to a fabric's fiber content are surprisingly numerous. Most fabrics today are blends of fibers and must be so labeled. The use of a fabric is also a clue. With upholstery, for example, you can probably rule out the presence of such fibers as modacrylics, which are not strong enough to stand up to the constant abrasion such fabrics must take. Brand names are also a help in running fiber content to ground: If you see the word Creslan on a drapery fabric, you know it contains acrylic, and Antron is simply another name for nylon.

When you are dealing with a fabric that is a blend of fibers, very likely you will have to choose between different methods of care. Always choose the one that is gentlest. Celanese, for example, is a blend of nylon and acetate fibers. Nylon can be machine washed and machine dried; acetate must be dry cleaned or hand washed and drip dried. To avoid damaging its acetate fibers, Celanese must be treated like acetate.

In caring for fabrics, you will have to consider more than fiber content alone. The weave of a fabric, as well as the dyes and finishes used, will also enter into the equation. Fabric-care labels, affixed by law to all fabrics since 1972, simplify this task. But when labels are absent, common sense usually comes to the rescue.

A gauzy curtain fabric, for example, should be washed gently, whatever its fiber content. And crinkled fabrics such as cotton crepe and plissé must be ironed at a medium setting to protect their texture. Keep in mind, too, that some glazed finishes can be damaged by strong cleaning agents; always pretest an inconspicuous area of the fabric.

A Guide to Cleaning Household Fabrics

Fiber	Trademarks	Uses
Acetate	Acetate, Ariloft, Celanese, Chromspun, Estron, Lanese, Loftura	Bed linens, drapes, upholstery
Acrylic	Acrilan, Bi-Loft, Creslan, Fina, Orlon, So-Lara, Zefran	Blankets, carpets, drapes, upholstery
Anidex	Anim-8	Lace, upholstery
Cotton		Bed linens, carpets, drapes, towels, upholstery
Flax (linen)		Table linens, upholstery
Glass	Fiberglas, Beta Glass, PPG, Vitron	Curtains, drapes
Modacrylics	Acrilan, SEF, Verel, Dynel	Awnings, blankets, carpets, drapes, synthetic furs
Nylon	A.C.E., Anso, Antron, Ayrlyn, Blue "C," Cadon, Cantrece, Caprolan, Celanese, Courtaulds Nylon, Crepeset, Cumuloft, Eloquent Luster, Eloquent Touch, Enka 10-10, Enkaloft, Enkalure, Lusterloft, Natura Luster, Qiana, Shareen, Silver Label, Softalon, Ulstron, Ultron, Viva La Crepe, Zeflon, Zefran	Bed linens, carpets, drapes, tarpaulins, upholstery
Olefin	Herculon, Marquesa, Marvess, Patlon, Polyloom, Vectra	Carpets, carpet linings, upholstery
Polyester	A.C.E., Avlin, Blue "C," Caprolan, Crepesoft, Dacron, Encron, Fortrel, Golden Glow, Golden Touch, Hollofil, Kodel, KodOfill, KodOsoff, Plyloc, Polyextra, Silky Touch, Spectran, Strialine, Trevira, Twisloc	Bed linens, carpets, curtains, cushion stuffings, drapes
Rayon	Absorbit, Avril, Absorb, Beau-Grip, Coloray, Enkaire, Enkrome, Fibro, Rayon by Avtex, Zantrel	Bed linens, carpets, drapes, table linens, upholstery
Saran	Lus-trus, Saran 25S, Velon	Awnings, carpets, outdoor upholstery
Silk		Bed linens, carpets
Spandex	Glospan, Lycra, Numa, Unel	Bed linens, upholstery
Triacetate	Arnel	Drapes, upholstery
Wool		Blankets, carpets, upholstery

Characteristics	Recommended care
Weak but elastic fiber. Resistant to shrinking, wrinkling, mildew. Susceptible to alkalies, organic solvents such as benzene and toluene, abrasion.	Dry clean or hand wash in warm water. Do not presoak colored fabrics. Drip dry; do not wring or twist. Iron while damp, on wrong side, at low setting.
Medium-strength fiber; retains shape well, dries quickly. Resistant to most chemicals, oil, sunlight.	Hand wash delicate weaves; machine wash others in warm water. Use fabric softener with every fourth washing to prevent static cling. Machine dry at low heat; iron at medium setting.
Very elastic fiber; retains elasticity after repeated washings.	Machine wash in warm water; use chlorine bleach. Machine dry at low heat. Iron at medium setting.
Strong fiber; easy to dye. Susceptible to shrinkage; weakened by prolonged exposure to sunlight.	Machine wash woven fabrics in hot water; machine dry at warm setting. Use chlorine bleach. Hand wash knitted fabrics; dry flat. Iron at high setting.
Strong fiber. Resistant to heat. Susceptible to wrinkling unless specially treated.	Machine wash white fabrics in hot water; use chlorine bleach. Machine dry at high heat. Iron at hot setting. Dry clean or machine wash colored fabrics in warm water. Iron at medium setting.
Strong fiber. Resistant to stretching, heat, mildew, chemicals, sunlight.	Hand wash in hot water (wear rubber gloves). Drip dry; no ironing necessary.
Strong fiber but soft to the touch; colorfast. Resistant to flames, acids, alkalies. Susceptible to shrinkage.	Machine wash in warm water; use fabric softener. Machine dry at low heat; iron at low setting. Dry clean synthetic furs.
Extremely strong, elastic, nonabsorbent fiber.	Machine wash in warm water; wash colored fabrics separately. Use chlorine bleach for white fabrics. Use fabric softener with every fourth washing to prevent static cling. Machine dry at low heat; iron at medium setting.
Strong, lightweight fiber. Resistant to dirt, mildew. Susceptible to heat.	Dry clean or machine wash in lukewarm water. Machine dry at low heat—do not use gas-fired commercial dryers. Do not iron 100% olefin; iron blends at low setting.
Strong, nonabsorbent fiber. Resistant to dirt; easy to dye.	Dry clean or machine wash in warm water; use fabric softener. Wash colors separately. Machine dry at low heat; iron at medium setting.
Weak but absorbent fiber; soft to the touch; easy to dye.	Dry clean or hand wash in lukewarm water. Do not twist or wring; iron while damp, on wrong side, at low setting.
Strong, elastic fiber. Resistant to water, sunlight, chemicals.	Wipe with detergent and water or with chlorine bleach and water. Do not iron.
Strong fiber; easy to dye. Resistant to moths and mildew. Susceptible to water stains, sunlight, perspiration.	Dry clean or hand wash gently in cold water. Do not bleach; do not twist or wring. Iron at low setting.
Very soft, elastic fiber. Resistant to sunlight, body oils.	Dry clean or machine wash in lukewarm water. Do not use chlorine bleach; whiten with oxygen bleach. Machine dry at low heat. Iron at low setting.
Weak fiber. Resistant to shrinkage, fading, wrinkling.	Machine wash in warm water; use chlorine bleach. Machine dry at low heat. Iron at high setting.
Strong fiber; easy to dye. Susceptible to shrinkage, moths.	Dry clean or hand wash in lukewarm water. Do not use chlorine bleach. Do not wring or twist. Dry flat; iron at low setting, with steam.

A Methodical Approach to Removing Spots

Even in the best-ordered household, accidents will happen. A guest will emphasize a point with a glass of red wine in hand, and splash the drapes. A rapt child reading a book will rest a peanut-butter-and-jelly sandwich on the arm of the living-room couch. Fabrics and carpeting prone to stains are often chemically treated to repel them. But even those without protection can usually be rescued: Almost any stain will yield to some cleaning method.

A prime consideration in dealing with a stain is its age. Stains you treat immediately are the easiest to remove. Often you can draw off a spill by a simple process called wicking (opposite, right) or by blotting with an absorbent powder (opposite, left). Stains that you discover later require more complicated treatment, especially if they have penetrated the fiber and have set.

To remove an older stain, you must identify the substance that caused it, select an appropriate cleaning agent (a choice that will depend on the nature of the fabric as well as the source of the stain) and choose a cleaning procedure that is compatible both with the fabric and with the stain.

These multiple choices may seem bewildering, but in fact they are made in a fairly methodical way. Identifying a stain, for example, is usually a matter of examining how it looks, feels or smells. Even an old stain of unknown origin will usually yield to this sort of scrutiny. And the choice of cleaning agent is immediately narrowed by the fabric itself. The fabric chart on page 48 shows, for example, when a particular chemical is likely to damage the fabric's structure and whether the fabric is washable.

Choosing a cleaning agent is further simplified by the fact that stains tend to fall into three main categories. Nongreasy stains such as coffee, fruit or food coloring are normally dissolved in a water-

An Emergency Cleaning Kit for Accidents

A well-stocked kit of spot- and stain-removing compounds is the best defense against the accidents that endanger household fabrics. Having the right solution on hand, and a sponge to apply it, will allow you to catch most spills before they have a chance to set.

Label and fill several small, tightly capped glass bottles or jars with white vinegar, glycerin, ammonia, acetone, hydrogen peroxide, amyl acetate, isopropyl alcohol, chlorine bleach, peroxygen bleach, and dye remover; all of these are available in drugstores or hardware stores. Portion-sized bottles of club soda and white wine are also handy: The effervescence of club soda will often bubble a fresh stain out of a fabric, and white wine will sufficiently dilute a red wine stain to allow the entire spot to be rinsed away with water.

For dusting spills, fill a small plastic bag with cornstarch, cornmeal or talcum powder, and a second bag with fuller's earth, an absorbent clay available at pharmacies or garden-supply stores. Fuller's earth, because it is dark colored, is best for dark fabrics.

The kit should also include a mild, colorless liquid detergent made for fabrics; a powdered enzyme detergent, which is useful for food stains; and some dry-cleaning fluid. All three are available at hardware or grocery stores.

Some stains require treatment with special solutions, called spotters, which should be mixed beforehand and also kept in the kit. A combination of one part liquid detergent with one part glycerin and eight parts water produces a wet spotter for washable fabrics; the glycerin, acting as a lubricant, helps loosen certain stains. For a dry spotter, add one part coconut oil or mineral oil to eight parts dry-cleaning fluid; the oil acts as a lubricant and also helps slow the cleaning fluid's evaporation.

Add a pair of rubber gloves; a roll of white utility paper or several clean, absorbent white cloths; a small sponge; a spoon; an eye dropper; and two small, soft-bristled nylon brushes—one for detergent, one for dry-cleaning fluids. Label both brushes. Include copies of the stain and fabric charts on pages 56 and 48, for quick checking of cleaning solutions and application techniques.

Caution: 1) Many cleaning solutions are flammable. Store them and use them in well-ventilated areas, never near pilot lights or open flames. 2) The fumes of dry-cleaning fluids are toxic and can burn skin and eyes; avoid inhaling them, and wear rubber gloves and safety goggles. Work with small quantities. 3) Never combine two different dry-cleaning fluids, and never use two cleaning agents on a stain without rinsing out the first agent completely.

base cleaning solution. Greasy stains such as oil, butter and petroleum products are removed with solvent-base solutions. The third group, a combination of greasy and nongreasy elements, such as coffee with cream, need to be treated twice—once to remove the greasy element, and a second time to deal with the nongreasy one.

The type of stain also dictates the cleaning procedure to be used. Cleaning agents are applied and stains are lifted by a variety of means—soaking, sponging, flushing, tamping and scraping—used alone or in combination. Each of these techniques is illustrated on the following pages, and the chart on pages 56-59 indicates which are appropriate to each stain, as well as the order in which they

should be performed. To some extent, however, the choice of technique will depend on the location of the stain. Flushing and soaking would be inappropriate to a stain on the arm of a couch. Both techniques could saturate the lining and backing materials, which could discolor the surface fabric.

You will find a well-stocked cleaning kit invaluable (box, opposite), since the faster you take action against a stain, the better your chances of removing it. Once you have chosen a cleaner, take a moment to test it to be sure it will not damage the fabric (page 52). Even water ought to be tested if the fabric is particularly delicate or if it seems likely to shrink or bleed.

Testing is especially important when

the spot is of unknown origin and you have to experiment with various kinds of cleaning agents. Most often, such stains are treated as the third type, the combination stains.

The actual work of lifting a stain requires patience and gentleness rather than skill. Detergents and chemical solvents need time to act, and several light applications usually produce better results than one heavy one. Avoid vigorous scrubbing, which could weaken the fabric's structure; as a further safeguard, work on the reverse side of the fabric whenever possible.

Always begin at the center of a stain and work out to its edges. And when the job is complete, flush or sponge out the cleaning compound.

Using Powder or a Wick to Remove Fresh Stains

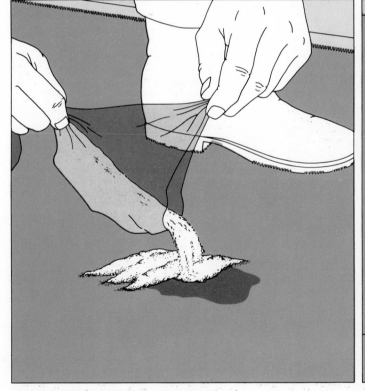

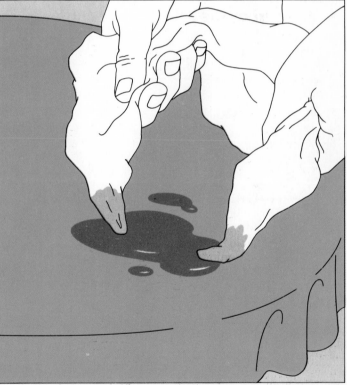

Blotting up grease with powder. Immediately after a spill, cover the entire spot with a ¼-inch-thick layer of absorbent powder (box, opposite). Leave the powder in place for one minute; then either shake it out over a piece of newspaper or gently scrape it off with a spoon, taking care not to rub the powder into the fabric. Repeat with fresh layers of powder as long as the powder continues to absorb traces of the spill.

Wicking out fluid. While the spill is still wet, lightly touch the tip of a crumpled absorbent white cloth or paper towel to the spot. The liquid will be drawn into the cloth or paper by capillary action. Do not use pressure; this could force the liquid into the fibers or spread the stain.

Spots caused by substances other than liquids must be lightly scraped with a dull knife to remove the solid matter. They can then be diluted with an appropriate cleaning solution (chart, pages 56-59) and drawn out as described above.

Checking Out the Cleaning Action

Performing a spot test. After choosing a cleaning agent (chart, pages 56-59), use an eye dropper to apply several drops of the cleaner to an inconspicuous area of the fabric, preferably on the reverse side. Leave the solution for one minute, then blot it with a clean white cloth, pressing firmly for 30 seconds. Check to see that the cloth has not picked up color from the fabric, and check the fabric for bleeding, bleaching or fiber damage. If none is visible, rinse the test area with water and use a fresh section of the white cloth to blot up the moisture. If the cleaner does damage the fabric, rinse it out quickly with water, blot out the moisture and try a different solution. Continue to experiment as necessary, but always rinse out one cleaner before trying another to prevent the solutions from interacting.

Once you have determined that a cleaner is safe, test its effectiveness by applying several drops to the center of the stain. Let the solution soak in for one minute, then blot it gently with a clean white cloth. If none of the stain is lifted from the fabric, try a different cleaner.

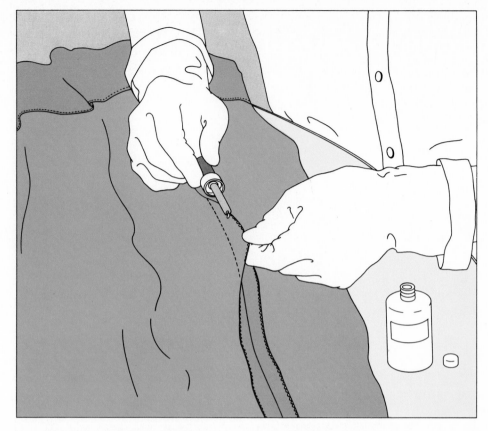

Flooding Stains from Washable Fabrics

Driving out a stain with water. Stretch the stained area of the fabric, drum-fashion, over a large container, such as a heat-resistant bowl or pot, and secure it around the rim with clean white twine. Place the container in the bathtub or outside, and prop up one side of the container with scrap wood so that the stretched fabric slants slightly away from you. If the fabric can withstand boiling water, pour boiling water through the stain from a height of 2 to 3 feet. Repeat as often as necessary until the stain is completely gone. For delicate fabrics or for stains that would be set by hot water, flush in the same way with cool or lukewarm water.

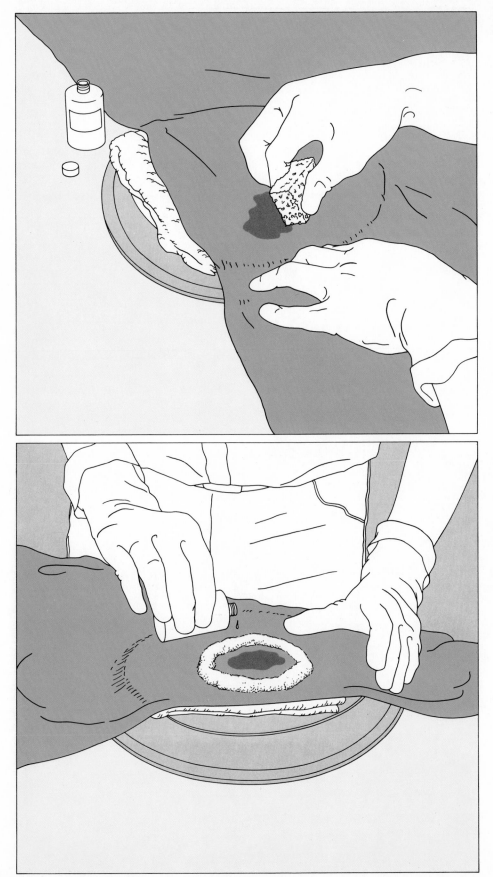

Sponging and Flushing: Two Ways to Attack a Stain

Sponging out a spot. Pad the stained area of the fabric by placing it right side down over several layers of absorbent white cloth laid on top of a flat, nonabsorbent work surface—such as the bottom of a glass baking dish. Dampen the corner of a household sponge with the chosen cleaning solution (*chart, pages 56-59*) and blot lightly, working outward from the center of the spot to slightly beyond its edge, to prevent the appearance of a ring. Adjust the position of the padding frequently to keep a clean area always under the stain.

If you cannot pad the stained area—when working on upholstery, for example—simply sponge the surface of the stain as above, taking special care to squeeze the sponge almost dry so that you do not saturate any lining or backing with the cleaning solution.

Flushing a stain away. Lay the stained fabric right side down over several layers of absorbent cloth. Sprinkle a ¼-inch-thick ring of absorbent powder around the stain, ½ inch beyond its edge. Trickle small amounts of cleaning solution onto the spot, and wait for the cloth below to absorb the liquid. Then change the position of the absorbent cloth to provide a clean padding beneath the stain, and repeat the process.

Unlike sponging, flushing cannot be adapted to upholstery, and it cannot be used on any fabric that cannot be laid over absorbent padding.

Softening a Stubborn Stain

1 Presoaking to loosen the stain. Sandwich the stained area of fabric between two ½-inch layers of absorbent white cloth, dampened with cleaning solution. Then place the layers between two sheets of foil on top of a firm surface, and weight the entire assembly with several heavy books. Allow the fabric to soak up to 24 hours, adding more cleaning solution as needed to keep the stain moist. Each time you add more cleaner, change the white cloth to keep the softened stain from seeping back into the fabric.

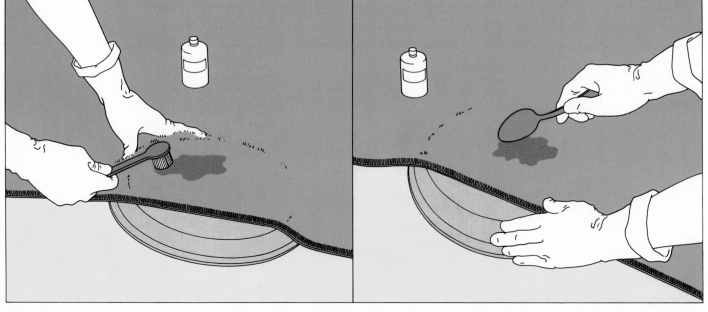

2 Tamping the stain out of the fabric. When the stain is loosened, lay the still-wet fabric on a hard, flat nonabsorbent surface such as a glass baking dish, and gently tap the fabric with a clean, short-bristled brush moistened with the same cleaning solution used in Step 1. Hold the brush so that the bristles are perpendicular to the fabric, the tips flat against the stain *(above, left)*. Blot the fabric occasionally with a clean,

absorbent white cloth, and keep tapping with the fluid-moistened brush until the stain is gone.

Another way to loosen a set stain is to sprinkle the spot lightly with cleaning solution, then scrape very gently with the edge of a stainless-steel spoon, using ¼-inch strokes *(above, right)*, and work outward in a spiral pattern, blotting occasionally with an absorbent white cloth.

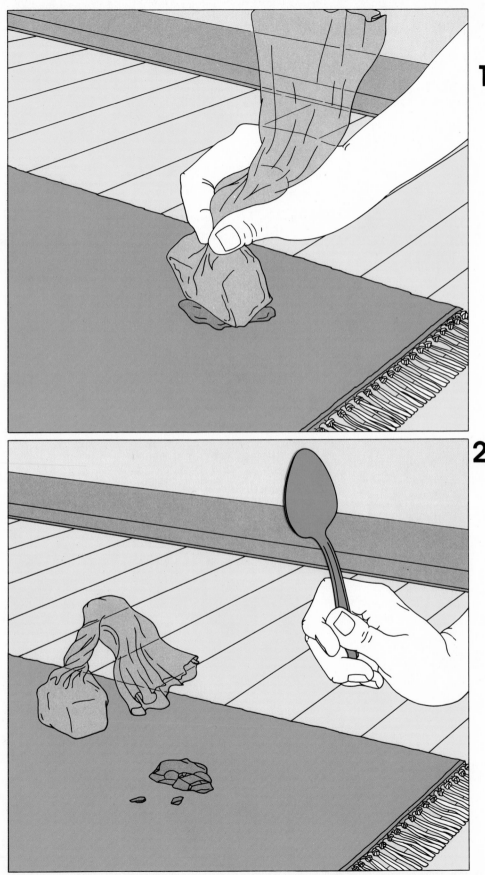

A Chilling Technique for Removing Chewing Gum

1 **Hardening the gum with ice.** With a single-edged razor blade, shave away as much of the gum as possible from the top of the fabric. Then put an ice cube in a plastic bag and press the ice against the gum, holding it there until the entire wad is brittle.

2 **Lifting the gum from the fabric.** While the gum is still frozen, slide the edge of a stainless-steel spoon between the gum and the fabric and pry the gum loose. If the gum sticks, rap it sharply with the spoon's edge, and chip it away in pieces. Re-ice the gum to keep it brittle. When the gum is removed, treat the remaining stain as sugar *(chart, pages 56-59)*.

Procedures for Stain Removal

The chart on these and the following pages gives instructions for removing almost any spot or stain from almost any fabric. Listed across the top are 119 types of stain; cleaning solutions appear on the left, grouped according to application techniques. For illustrations of these techniques, see pages 50-55.

To use the chart, first determine whether the stained fabric is washable—usually, the information can be found on a care label. Next, locate at the top of the chart the substance that caused the stain. Cleaning steps for that stain are indicated in the column below. Perform them in descending order and according to the notation system detailed in the legend. When you see a number, skip it until you have completed all of the lettered steps. The numbers refer to second and third treatments. If the spot remains after you have completed the first course, perform the steps marked "2"; then, if the spot is still visible, the steps marked "3."

Mud, for example, should be sponged with cool water on both washable and nonwashable fabrics, then soaked either in wet spotter with vinegar on nonwashables or in detergent with vinegar on washables. After that, the next five steps are identical for both types of fabric, as is the second course of treatment—soaking in enzyme detergent.

The cleaning solutions listed are described on page 50. When the recommended treatment is a combination of spotter or detergent with ammonia or vinegar, use ½ teaspoon of ammonia or vinegar for every ½ cup of spotter or detergent. Bleaching agents—chlorine, peroxygen, hydrogen peroxide and dye remover—should be mixed with equal parts of water. When the chart recommends using dry spotter mixed with amyl acetate, combine three parts spotter and one part amyl acetate.

Be careful with strong chemicals. To avoid unwanted chemical reactions, let dry-cleaning fluids dry before proceeding with further treatment. Chlorine and peroxygen bleach should be left no longer than two minutes before rinsing; hydrogen peroxide and dye remover can be left for up to 15 minutes.

	Legend	
Washable fabrics	W	
Nonwashable fabrics	N	
All fabrics	W/N	
Second treatment	2	
Third treatment	3	

Application technique	Acids	Adhesive tape	Airplane glue	Alkalies	Asphalt	Bath oil	Beer	Berries	Blood	Bluing	Butter	Candle wax
Sponge												
Cool water	W/N			W/N		W/N	W/N	W/N	W/N	W/N		
Ammonia												
Glycerin												
Enzyme detergent												
Acetone			W/N									
Dry-cleaning fluid		W/N			W/N						W/N	W/N
Soak												
Dry spotter		W/N	W/N		W/N					W/N		
Wet spotter				W/N								
Wet spotter with ammonia						N			N			
Wet spotter with vinegar							N	N	N			
Detergent with ammonia						W			W	2		
Detergent with vinegar							W	W	W			
Enzyme detergent						2	2	2	2			
Flush												
Dry-cleaning fluid		W/N	W/N		W/N					W/N		
Cool water	W/N			W/N		W/N	W/N	W/N	W/N	W/N		
Sponge, tamp or scrape with spoon												
Dry-cleaning fluid			W/N		W/N						W/N	W/N
Dry spotter with amyl acetate												
Wet spotter		W/N										
Wet spotter with ammonia						N			N	N		
Detergent												
Detergent with ammonia						W			W			
Detergent with vinegar				W/N								
Alcohol							W/N	W/N	W/N			
Amyl acetate			2									
Ammonia	W/N											
Flush												
Dry-cleaning fluid			W/N		W/N						W/N	W/N
Cool water		W/N		W/N		W/N	W/N	W/N	W/N			
Alcohol									W/N			
Sponge												
Chlorine bleach										W/N	W/N	
Peroxygen bleach			W/N					W/N	W/N			
Hydrogen peroxide						W/N			W/N			
Dye remover												
Sponge rinse												
Cool water						W/N	W/N	W/N	W/N	W/N	W/N	W/N
Cool water with vinegar	W/N		W/N	W/N								

Candy	Carbon paper	Catsup	Cheese	Chlorine	Chocolate, cocoa	Coffee	Corn syrup	Cough syrup	Crayon	Cuticle remover	Deodorant	Dye: red	yellow	other	Egg white	Egg yolk	Epoxy cement	Excrement	Eye liner, shadow	Fingernail polish	Fish slime	Flavoring extract	Floor wax	Food color: red	yellow	other	Fruit juice, jam	Gentian violet	Glue: white	hide	Grass	Gravy	Grease	Hair spray	Hand lotion	Ice cream	Ink: ballpoint	felt pen, india	stamp pad: red
W/N				W/N		W/N	W/N	W/N			W/N	W/N		W/N	W/N			W/N			W/N	W/N		W/N		W/N	W/N	W/N		W/N									W/N
																																					W/N		
	W/N									W/N										W/N									W/N										
		W/N	W/N		W/N				W/N				W/N			W/N	W/N		W/N				W/N		W/N						W/N	W/N	W/N	W/N	W/N	W/N		W/N	
	W/N	W/N	W/N		W/N				W/N	W/N			W/N			W/N			W/N	W/N			W/N		W/N				W/N			W/N	W/N	W/N	W/N	W/N		W/N	
																						W																	
N											N	N			N			N			N			N						N									N
2						N	N	N			2	2	2	N										2	2	N	N	N											2
W		2			2						W	W		2	W	2		W			W			W		2		2		W		2				2			W
						W	W	W						W												W	W	W											
		3	2		3	2	2	2							2	3		2			2						2			2		3				3			
	W/N	W/N	W/N		W/N				W/N	W/N			W/N			W/N	W/N		W/N	W/N			W/N		W/N				W/N		W/N	W/N	W/N	W/N	W/N	W/N		W/N	
W/N		2	2		2	W/N	W/N	W/N			W/N	W/N		W/N	W/N	2		W/N			W/N	W/N		W/N		W/N	W/N	W/N		W/N		2				2	W/N		W/N
	W/N									W/N										W/N									W/N										
									W/N				2						W/N			W	W/N		2								W/N	W/N	W/N		W/N		
														N	N			N			N					N		N		N									
		W/N	W/N		W/N										W	W/N		W			W									W		W/N				W/N			
																															2								
W/N						W/N	W/N	W/N			W/N	W/N	3	W/N								W/N		W/N	3	W/N	W/N	W/N			3								W/N
	2									2			W/N							2					W/N						W/N								
																																					2		
	W/N									W/N			W/N							W/N					W/N						W/N								
W/N		W/N	W/N		W/N	W/N	W/N	W/N	W/N		W/N	W/N			W/N	W/N	W/N	W/N	W/N		W/N	W/N	W/N				W/N			W/N	2	W/N	W/N	W/N	W/N	W/N	W/N	W/N	W/N
														W/N												W/N		W/N			3								
W/N		W/N	W/N			W/N						W/N	W/N						W/N				W/N	W/N	W/N	W/N	W/N	W/N									W/N		W/N
	W/N						W/N	W/N		W/N	W/N			W/N		W/N				W/N																W/N			
					W/N																																		
				W/N																																			
W/N		W/N	W/N	W/N		W/N	W/N	W/N			W/N	W/N		W/N		W/N			W/N				W/N	W/N		W/N	W/N	W/N			W/N					W/N	W/N		W/N
	W/N				W/N					W/N			W/N							W/N					W/N														

Legend (Application technique):
- Washable fabrics — **W**
- Nonwashable fabrics — **N**
- All fabrics — **W/N**
- Second treatment — **2**
- Third treatment — **3**

Stain / Application technique	Ink: stamp pad: yellow	other	Insecticides	Jelly, jam	Lacquer (furniture)	Lard	Lipstick	Maple syrup	Margarine	Mascara	Mayonnaise	Meat juice	Mercurochrome	Mildew	Milk, cream	Mimeograph fluid	Molasses	Mucus	Mud	Mustard	Nose drops	Oil: cooking	lubricating	Paint, oil- or water-base	Pencil	Perfume	Permanent-wave solution
Sponge																											
Cool water	W/N		W/N				W/N					W/N					W/N	W/N	W/N						W/N	W/N	
Ammonia												2															
Glycerin																											
Enzyme detergent																											
Acetone					W/N											W/N											
Dry-cleaning fluid	W/N		W/N			W/N	W/N	W/N	W/N	W/N	W/N	W/N		W/N	W/N				W/N	W/N	W/N	W/N	W/N	W/N			
Soak																											
Dry spotter	W/N		W/N		W/N	W/N	W/N	W/N	W/N	W/N	W/N	W/N		W/N	W/N	W/N			W/N	W/N	W/N	W/N	W/N	W/N			
Wet spotter																										W	
Wet spotter with ammonia					2								N				N										
Wet spotter with vinegar	2	N	N				N					2					N	N									N
Detergent with ammonia		2								2	2	W		2			W										
Detergent with vinegar		W	W				W									W	W										W
Enzyme detergent			2				2					3	3		3		2	2	2								2
Flush																											
Dry-cleaning fluid	W/N		W/N		W/N	W/N	W/N	W/N	W/N	W/N	W/N	W/N		W/N	W/N				W/N	W/N	W/N	W/N	W/N	W/N			
Cool water	W/N		W/N				W/N				2	2	W/N		2		W/N	W/N	W/N						2	W/N	W/N
Sponge, tamp or scrape with spoon																											
Dry-cleaning fluid					W/N											W/N						W/N					
Dry spotter with amyl acetate											W/N																
Wet spotter	2		W/N			W/N		W/N	W/N												W/N		W/N	W/N			
Wet spotter with ammonia		N					W/N									N								W/N			
Detergent																											
Detergent with ammonia										W/N	W/N				W/N		W										
Detergent with vinegar						2							2						W/N								
Alcohol	3	W/N	W/N			3	W/N					W/N	3			W/N		W/N						W/N	W/N		
Amyl acetate	W/N		2													2											
Ammonia																											
Flush																											
Dry-cleaning fluid	W/N		W/N									W/N	W/N						W/N								
Cool water			W/N	W/N	W/N	W/N	W/N	W/N	W/N	W/N	W/N	2	W/N				W/N	W/N	W/N	W/N	W/N	W/N	W/N	W/N		W/N	
Alcohol		W/N										3														W/N	
Sponge																											
Chlorine bleach	W/N	W/N	W/N				W/N		W/N			W/N	W/N		W/N		W/N										
Peroxygen bleach				W/N			W/N			W/N	W/N				W/N	W/N										W/N	W/N
Hydrogen peroxide																								W/N			
Dye remover																											
Sponge rinse																											
Cool water		W/N		W/N			W/N	W/N	W/N	W/N	W/N	W/N			W/N		W/N		W/N					W/N	W/N	W/N	
Cool water with vinegar	W/N				W/N							W/N			W/N												

Stain removal chart — column headings (left to right):

1. Perspiration
2. Rouge
3. Rubber cement
4. Rust
5. Salad dressing
6. Scorch
7. Shaving cream
8. Shellac
9. Sherbet
10. Shoe dye: black
11. brown
12. Shoe polish: white
13. other
14. Smoke, soot
15. Soft drinks
16. Solder
17. Starch
18. Sugar, caramelized
19. Suntan lotion
20. Tar
21. Tea
22. Tobacco
23. Tomato juice
24. Tomato paste
25. Toothpaste
26. Typewriter ribbon: nylon
27. carbon
28. Urine
29. Varnish
30. Vegetables
31. Vegetable soup
32. Vinegar
33. Vomit
34. Walnut
35. Watercolor paint: red
36. yellow
37. other
38. Whiskey
39. Wine
40. Unknown stains

	Persp	Rouge	Rub. cem	Rust	Salad dr	Scorch	Shav cr	Shellac	Sherbet	Dye blk	brown	Pol wht	other	Smoke	Soft dr	Solder	Starch	Sugar	Suntan	Tar	Tea	Tobacco	Tom jc	Tom pst	Tooth	TW nyl	carbon	Urine	Varnish	Veg	Veg soup	Vinegar	Vomit	Walnut	WC red	yellow	other	Whisk	Wine	Unknown
						W/N		W/N		W/N				W/N		W/N	W/N	W/N		W/N	W/N	W/N			W/N			W/N		W/N		W/N	W/N	W/N		W/N	W/N	W/N		
	W/N																									W/N														
														W/N												W/N		W/N												
		W/N	W/N	W/N	W/N			W/N		W/N			W/N	W/N	W/N					W/N		W/N		W/N			W/N						W/N							W/N
		W/N	W/N	W/N	W/N			W/N		W/N			W/N	W/N	W/N		W/N			W/N		W/N		W/N	W/N	W/N							W/N							W/N
	N						N			N			N			N		N	N		N	N	N		N		N		N		N	N	W/N 2	2	N	N	N	2
	2		2			N		W		2			W			W			2			W		2		W		2	W	W	2							
	W					W				W			W			W W		W W W		W					W		W W		W W W									
			3	2	2							2		2 2 2			2 2 2 3	2			2 3 2 2								2 2										
		W/N W/N W/N W/N			W/N		W/N		W/N W/N W/N			W/N			W/N			W/N		W/N W/N W/N		W/N	W/N W/N					W/N						W/N				W/N
	W/N		2		W/N		W/N		W/N		W/N		W/N W/N W/N W/N		W/N W/N W/N W/N 2	W/N			W/N		W/N 2 W/N W/N W/N N W/N		W/N W/N W/N															

Rejuvenating Soiled Rugs and Carpets

Even with frequent vacuuming, rugs and carpets eventually lose their bright colors and springy nap. Deep cleaning will restore them, and in fact most rug and carpet manufacturers recommend just such a cleaning at least once a year. The cleaning method will vary with the degree of soil and with the construction of the floor coverings. Almost any rug or carpet—whether it is made of natural or synthetic fibers—can safely be deep cleaned, with the possible exception of a fragile antique or a delicate silk oriental. These you may prefer to entrust to a professional's care.

Before you undertake deep cleaning, you should examine your carpet to help determine the best cleaning method. Although most carpets can be cleaned by any of the methods shown on the following pages, some carpets (box, right) may be so constructed that one method may be more suitable than another.

Conventional tufted rugs and carpets are often backed with jute, a natural fiber that may shrink when saturated with water. For area rugs this may not be a problem, since the shrinkage will be uniform and a slight change in rug size is usually unimportant. Older area rugs may even be shrink-resistant, having already shrunk in previous washings. The classic way to clean such a rug is to take it outdoors, scrub it by hand and then rinse it with the garden hose.

More typical indoor cleaning methods avoid the problem of shrinkage by using little or no moisture and by removing most of the moisture immediately, along with the loosened dirt. This also speeds drying time and prevents excess water from dissolving colors in the backing or the underpad, which could rise through the carpet to stain the surface.

For light soil or with dyes that are not colorfast, the preferred method is dry cleaning with a solvent-impregnated absorbent powder. The powder is brushed into the pile with a special powder-brushing machine and allowed to remain there until it has absorbed the grease or dirt; then it is vacuumed out. A rug cleaned with an absorbent compound has the added advantage of being ready for use immediately.

For heavier soil the two common methods are steam cleaning and rotary shampooing. Steam cleaning is oddly misnamed; it does not use steam, which would damage most carpet yarns, but tap water—hot for synthetics, cold for wool. Shampooing is done with a mixture of detergent and water. Steam cleaning is the gentler of the two. It is the better choice for long-pile carpet or loosely twisted yarn that might be damaged by the vigorous brushing action that accompanies shampooing. On the other hand, shampooing is usually more effective for really deep-seated dirt.

In steam cleaning, one of the hoses of the cleaning wand sprays a pressurized mist of cleaning solution into the pile; the other hose almost immediately extracts it. The solution is pumped to a receiving tank, which should contain a small amount of a special defoaming agent to reduce the sudsing that may occur if shampoo has previously been used for cleaning.

In shampooing, the cleaning solution is dispensed sparingly onto the carpet and whipped into a lather by the rotary action of one or two brushes. Before the foam can penetrate the fiber too deeply, it is removed by a second machine, a wet vacuum, which sucks up water as a dry vacuum sucks up dirt.

Steam-cleaned and shampooed carpets and rugs must be allowed to dry for several hours before they are walked on or furniture is placed on them. In humid weather, the drying time may extend up to 48 hours. A pile-brushing machine can hasten the process by raising the pile and thus improving the circulation of air through the yarn.

Steam cleaners and rotary shampoo machines use mild carpet detergents, similar to those made for hand washing of woolen clothing. They should be mixed with water according to the label instructions; to avoid inaccuracy caused by foaming, measure water and detergent into separate graduated buckets, then pour the water into the detergent.

Before using any cleaning agent, even plain water, check it for compatibility with your rug or carpet. Even mild detergents can sometimes cause dyes to dull and bleed. Rug and carpet manufacturers often label their products with the cleaning agent to be used. In the absence of such a label, you can test the cleaning agent on an inconspicuous spot or, alternatively, unravel a few strands of yarn from a scrap of the same carpet and soak them for a few hours in the cleaning agent you plan to use. Allow the test fibers to dry before you compare them with the untested fibers.

In preparation for the cleaning, remove as much furniture as possible and wrap the legs of the remaining pieces with aluminum foil, to prevent wood and metal casters from staining the damp carpet and to protect the furniture from the cleaner. A preliminary brushing with a pile-brushing machine will help to lift compacted pile and expose deeply embedded dirt. The carpet should also be vacuumed, on both sides if possible, and any stains should be removed (pages 50-59) to prevent them from spreading during the cleaning process.

Carpet-cleaning machines can be rented from equipment-rental agencies and sometimes from local dry cleaners and supermarkets; the same sources also carry the specialized cleaning agents formulated for use with the machines. Although the design varies widely among manufacturers, the machines operate on the same principle; be sure to ask the supplier for any special instructions that apply to the machine you rent.

If you expect to clean your carpets frequently, you should consider buying one of the light-duty machines made for home use. Or you might decide to rent a machine that combines several operations. A steam cleaner, for example, may also function as a wet vacuum and a pile brush. Some of the shampooing machines can also be used for wet vacuuming, and some pile brushes have a suction action like that of a vacuum cleaner. Such dual-purpose machines can often save you time and money.

A Cross-Sectional Look at Tufted Carpeting

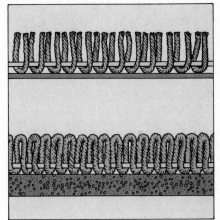

Tufted carpets, the most common type, are made of woolen, cotton or synthetic yarn—called the pile—that is stitched into a backing. Conventional carpets are backed by a thin sandwich of latex between two layers of woven fiber; the carpet is laid over a separate pad. Cushion-backed carpet has foam padding that is bonded directly to its back; cushion-backed carpet is frequently affixed to the floor with cement.

Either carpet type may have a looped-pile surface (the exposed ends of the tufts are left as closed loops) or a cut-pile surface, so called because the tufts have been trimmed, leaving a surface of cut ends. Most pile also exhibits a specific nap, or pile direction, created when the fibers are pressed down as the newly made carpet is rolled. You can tell pile direction by stroking the carpet: stroking against the pile direction will raise the nap. One purpose of brushing a carpet after cleaning is to restore this nap.

Brushing Pile before and after Cleaning

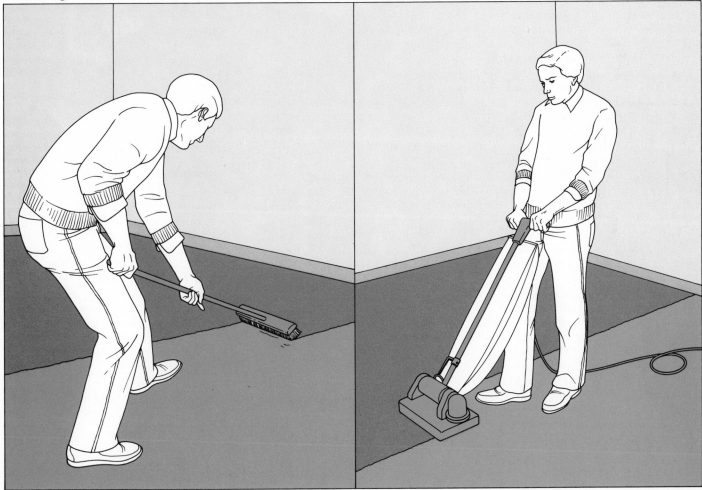

Hand and power brushing. A stiff-bristled deck brush or a power pile-brushing machine is used before cleaning to lift the pile of the carpet; it loosens the dirt and allows the cleaning agent to penetrate the pile. After cleaning, brushing the pile restores a uniform nap to tufts that have been left in a swirling pattern by the cleaning brushes; this brushing step also removes footprints and speeds drying.

The deck brush (above, left) is best for carpets and rugs with relatively long tufts. Determine the nap direction by brushing the pile until the tufts stand upright. Then pull the brush toward you in this direction in overlapping strokes, working across the entire carpet until the pile is uniform. The power pile brush (above, right) is suited for cut-pile or low-shag carpets. Starting opposite the door, alternately push and pull the machine in overlapping passes parallel to the wall, working across the carpet to the door.

Hand Washing an Area Rug

1 Preparing the rug. Indoors, vacuum both sides of the rug and test it for colorfastness; outdoors, clean an area of concrete patio or driveway large enough to accommodate the rug. Lay the rug face down on the work surface and wet it down thoroughly, using either a garden hose or buckets of water.

2 Scrubbing the backing. Dilute a mild carpet detergent as directed on the container. Starting near the center of the rug and using a soft-bristled brush (commonly sold for polishing shoes or general-purpose cleaning), scrub in wide, circular strokes, lathering an area about 2 feet square. After you have completed several overlapping areas, rinse away most of the lather. Continue this scrubbing and rinsing, working from the center out to each of the edges in turn. Change the detergent mixture when the suds become gray or when sediment has accumulated in the bottom of the bucket.

3 Cleaning the fringe. With the rug still face down on the work surface, slide one hand, palm up, under several inches of fringe and brush the strands with a combing motion, beginning at the edge of the rug and working out. When you have completed the fringe along one edge, rinse it before proceeding to the next.

For a section of fringe that is extremely dirty, use a slightly stronger detergent mixture and rub the fringe back and forth between your hands before you comb it out. Again, begin at the edge of the rug and work outward.

4 Rinsing the rug. When you have scrubbed the entire backing and the fringe, rinse it a second time, beginning at the middle and working out to each edge, driving the suds in a line ahead of the water jet *(top right)*. Continue rinsing until no more suds appear. Then turn the rug right side up and scrub it as in Steps 1 and 2. Rinse it as above, but during this rinse, have a helper remove some of the water with a wooden squeegee— a short, smooth piece of 1-by-4 attached to a handle *(bottom right)*. Pull the squeegee from the middle of the rug toward the edges, stopping short of the fringes. If the rug is too small for you to press out water with a squeegee, blot up the water with terry-cloth towels.

To dry the rug, hang it on a clothesline if it is small, or lay it, face up, on a sunny area of a dry lawn. While the pile is still slightly damp, brush it as described on page 61. Do not leave the rug exposed to the sun for more than two days, or its colors may fade, and move it occasionally to avoid damaging the grass.

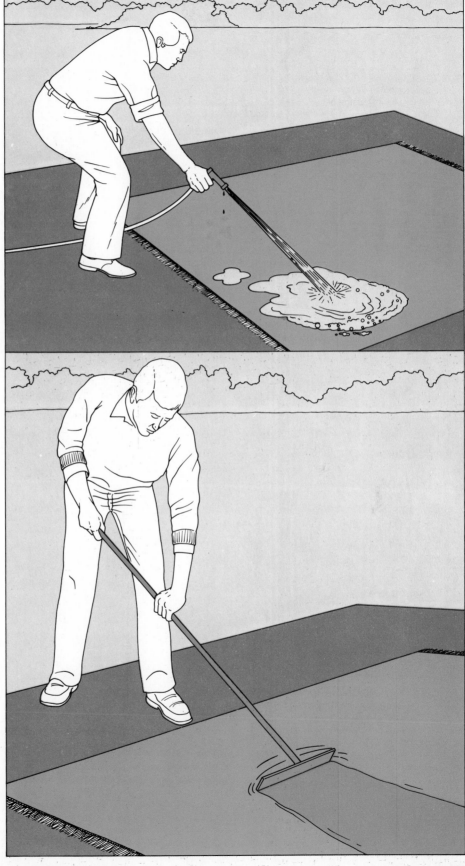

Dry Cleaning with Powder

1 **Powdering the carpet.** Spread solvent-impregnated powder, a cup at a time, over the surface of the carpet. Hold the cup about 1 foot above the carpet and use a throwing motion to distribute the powder evenly and heavily, but avoid mounds. Unless the manufacturer's instructions specify otherwise, use 5 pounds of powder for every 100 square feet of carpet.

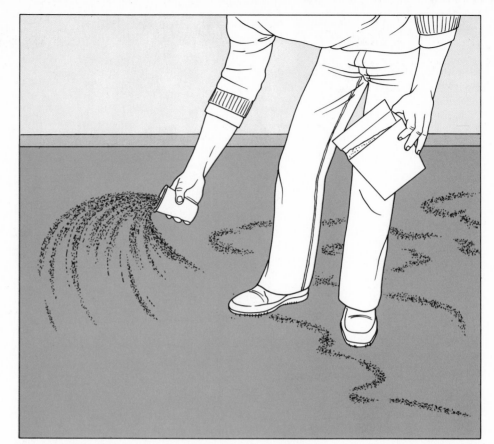

2 **Brushing in the powder.** Use a powder-brushing machine to work the powder down into the pile. Starting at a corner of the carpet, pull the machine backward along one edge, then push it forward in a slightly overlapping strip. Continue working back and forth in this manner, each time overlapping the previous strip, until you reach the opposite edge. Go back over the carpet at least twice in this same pattern of overlapping strips. Then turn the machine 90° and repeat the pattern. Finish the brushing with a final sweep back and forth across the carpet between the original two edges, but in the direction opposite to the first brushing. As you work, sprinkle additional powder on any area not thoroughly coated.

Allow the powder to dry for about two hours, or until it changes color from light brown to almost white. To remove the powder, vacuum the carpet very slowly, working in the same pattern that you used to brush the powder in.

Shampooing with Dry Foam

1 **Setting up the machine.** Using the proportions specified on the container label, measure carpet-cleaning detergent into one bucket and water into another. Pour the water into the detergent and transfer the mixture to the tank of the shampooing machine, filling it about three quarters full. As you mix and pour, work on a throw rug to prevent the carpet from getting wet.

Depress the foam lever on the machine several times to start the flow of cleaning solution. Then turn on the brush control and allow the brush to rotate on the throw rug until the bristles are damp and the foam thickens. If necessary, hold down the throw rug with your foot to keep it from spinning with the brush.

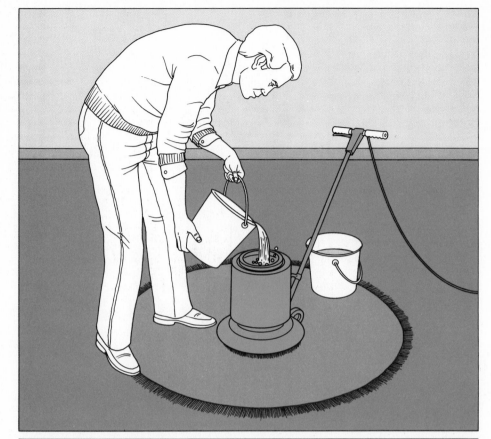

2 **Operating the machine.** Begin shampooing along a wall opposite an entrance. Face that wall and pull the shampooing machine slowly from left to right in overlapping parallel strips until you reach the opposite wall. Release just enough foam to dampen the carpet without soaking it, regulating the flow by depressing the foam lever at intervals rather than continuously. Refill the detergent tank as needed, each time resting the machine on the protective throw rug.

As you work across the rug, have a helper follow you with a wet vacuum to remove the foam before it has a chance to soak into the yarn. If you are working without a helper, stop when you have shampooed an area of about 100 square feet, and run the wet vacuum over the area.

For heavily soiled carpets, repeat the shampooing and vacuuming, working at a slightly different angle, but still between the same two walls. On the second pass, move more quickly and dispense much less detergent. When the shampooing is done, restore the nap with a deck brush or a pile-brushing machine (*page 61*).

A Pressurized Spray That Flushes Out Grime

Extracting dirt with water. Fill the detergent tank with cleaning solution and connect the pressure and extraction hoses to the machine, according to the manufacturer's instructions. If the carpet has previously been cleaned with shampoo, pour an inch of defoaming liquid into the receiving tank of the machine.

Starting on the far side of the room, opposite the door, clean an area of carpet about 3 feet square. Hold the cleaning wand with the suc-

tion nozzle flush against the carpet, and move it back and forth across the square in a zigzag pattern. On the backward stroke, squeeze the grip lever to spray cleaning solution; release the lever on the forward stroke, allowing the continuous vacuum action to extract dirt-filled water. Make no more than three passes to avoid overwetting the carpet. Then change the direction of stroke slightly and go over the square again. This time, use only the extractor on both the forward and the backward strokes.

Clean adjacent areas of carpet in the same manner, slightly overlapping the edges of the squares and working back and forth across the carpet in parallel lines until you have reached the opposite side of the room. Refill the detergent tank when it is empty, using a fresh mixture. Do not reuse the extracted solution; even if it looks fresh, it contains dirt particles that can clog the nozzle of the machine. When the entire carpet has been cleaned, brush the still-damp pile to raise the nap (page 61).

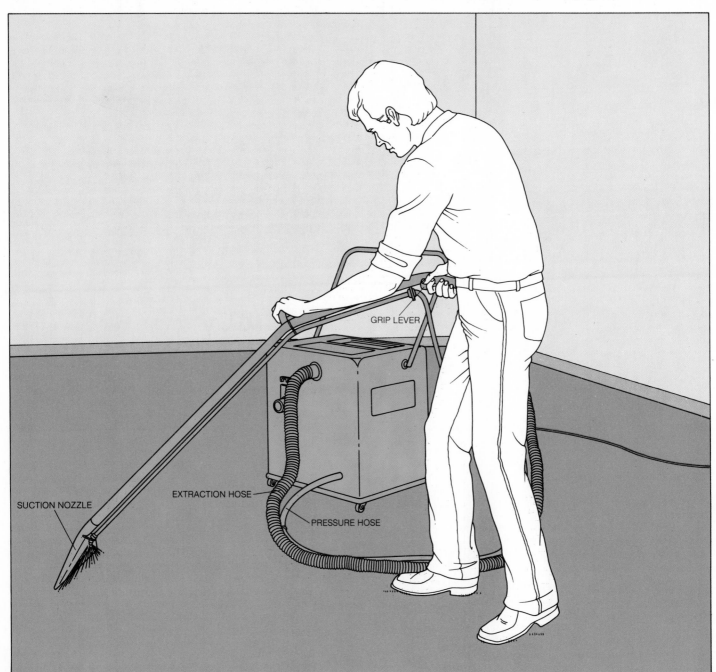

SUCTION NOZZLE

EXTRACTION HOSE

PRESSURE HOSE

GRIP LEVER

Repairing Cigarette and Cinder Burns

1 **Sanding the charred fibers.** Fold 150-grit sandpaper over the end of a thin strip of wood, and rub it over the charred area to remove the burned fibers. Sand the fibers away from the burned area. Vacuum up the sanding dust; then wash the area with a mild detergent and a soft flannel cloth until the burn marks are no longer visible and only a bare area remains.

2 **Reweaving damaged pile.** Thread a curved upholstery needle with a strand of yarn that matches the pile in color and thickness. Insert the needle under a strand of the backing material *(inset)*, and pull the needle up. Then pass it under the strand a second time, forming a loop. Continue looping the yarn through the backing in the bare area, matching the loops you make to the spacing and height of the loops in the undamaged part of the carpet. For cut-pile carpets, make the loops slightly higher than the surrounding pile; then use scissors to clip them to the height of the adjacent pile.

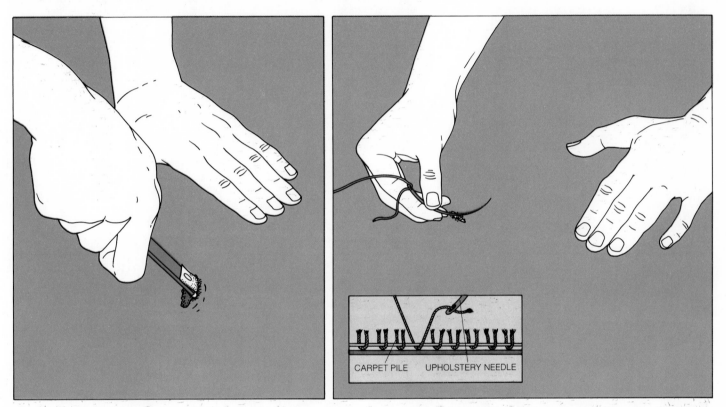

CARPET PILE   UPHOLSTERY NEEDLE

Tricks for Keeping Carpets Fresh

There are any number of ways to keep rugs and carpets looking fresh between deep cleanings. Perhaps the most novel method, used in cold climates, is to drag both sides of the rug through fresh snow. The snow's gentle abrasive action makes an almost perfect restorative for flattened nap and dulled colors.

Other methods of lengthening the intervals between heavy cleaning are more prosaic. Doormats and area rugs protect wall-to-wall carpeting from dirt brought in from outdoors and spills around a coffee table. Weekly vacuuming prevents dirt from becoming embedded, and stains and spots removed as soon as they happen *(pages 50-59)* are much less likely to set.

If you make a practice of shifting heavier pieces of movable furniture an inch or so each week, you can prevent the pile beneath the legs from being permanently crushed. When such depressions cannot be brushed out, lift tufts with the edge of a coin; then hold a steam iron set at medium heat 3 or 4 inches above the indentation to restore the crushed yarn to its upright position.

Shampooing Fabric-covered Furniture

Most people are meticulous about cleaning rugs and carpets but tend to overlook the textured and piled fabrics that cover upholstered couches and chairs. These fabrics, too, are dust traps. Furthermore, the grime that works its way into the arm or headrest of a couch can be as deep-seated and concentrated as any that scuffs into a rug. Upholstery should be vacuumed weekly to keep it bright and fresh-looking, and once a year it should be shampooed or—in rare instances—professionally dry cleaned.

The cleaning methods are similar, but do not embark on either one without first identifying the fabric content and determining whether it is washable and colorfast. The manufacturer's label, sewn to the underside of the cushions or stapled to the frame of the couch or chair, will usually say what the fabric is made of and how it should be cleaned. If it does not, consult the fabric chart on pages 48-49 for help in making an educated guess and selecting a suitable cleaning method.

Before cleaning, remove and vacuum loose cushions and pillows, then vacuum the chair or couch itself, using the upholstery brush and the crevice tool in seams and around cording and buttons, where dust collects. Do not, however, remove zippered cushion covers or slip covers for washing separately in the washing machine. Although designed for easy removal, these covers should be cleaned in place. Washed in the machine, they tend to shrink or stretch out of alignment.

Most washable fabrics can be cleaned with a weak solution of warm water and mild, nonalkaline detergent; a dash of ammonia or white vinegar added to the solution will enhance the detergent's brightening effect. Test the cleaning agent on an inconspicuous part of the upholstery to make sure that it is compatible with the fabric and dyes.

The basic tool for shampooing is a supply of clean white terry-cloth toweling, absorbent enough to retain cleaning solutions and abrasive enough to remove dirt without damaging delicate fabrics. Heavily soiled areas, such as arms and headrests, may require the firmer abrasion of a nylon- or natural-bristled scrub brush to remove gummy deposits of body oils and dust. Whichever tool is used, overwetting must be avoided. For this reason, detergent-base cleaning solutions should be whipped to a dry foam and applied with toweling or brushes that are moistened—but not wet.

Allow yourself several hours to shampoo a chair, a full day or more for a couch; but do not expect to do the whole job at once. Because of the constant wringing and rubbing involved, cleaning a large piece of furniture can be an arm-wearying process. And if you tire before the work is complete, the cleaned area may stand out in glaring contrast. To prevent both fatigue and unsightly contrasts, clean one panel at a time.

1 Preparing the cleaning solution. Mix 1 gallon of lukewarm water with 1 tablespoon of white, powdered laundry detergent and 1 teaspoon of household ammonia or white vinegar. Pour a small amount of the detergent mixture into a bucket; then, using an ordinary kitchen egg beater or an electric hand mixer, whip the ingredients into a stiff foam; there should be little or no liquid at the bottom of the bucket. Alternately, use an electric blender to create the foam.

Test the cleaning solution on an inconspicuous area of the upholstery—the underside, a hem or a seam allowance (*page 52*).

2 **Wiping out light soil.** Fold a clean white terry towel into a convenient working size, and dip it lightly into the foam. Wring it thoroughly, until no more moisture can be squeezed out. Wipe one complete panel of the upholstery with firm, parallel strokes, either horizontal or vertical; overlap the strokes slightly. Occasionally dip the towel into the foam to recharge it, each time wringing it out as above. As soon as the working surface of the towel appears dirty, refold it to expose a clean section. As the foam begins to dissolve, whip it again.

Repeat the entire process, going over the panel in the opposite direction. Then remove the foam by wiping the entire panel with a clean terry towel moistened in fresh water and wrung dry. Work in parallel strokes in the original direction; rinse the towel often, and each time wring it dry.

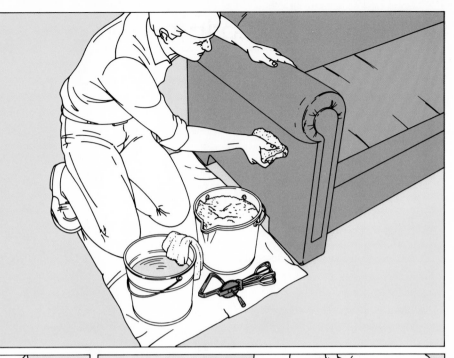

3 **Brushing out heavy soil.** Immerse a soft-bristled nylon scrub brush in boiling water for a few seconds to soften the bristles. Blot dry with a clean terry towel. Dip the brush in the foam mixture, and shake most of the foam back into the bucket. Using light pressure, scrub the upholstery in a circular pattern, working over about a square foot at one time. Repeat, scrubbing adjacent areas; as you work, overlap the areas slightly. Recharge the brush with foam as necessary, and when the bristles begin to stiffen, immerse them again in boiling water. If the foam begins to dissolve, rewhip it. Remove the foam with a clean terry-cloth towel moistened in fresh water, as in Step 2.

4 **Restoring the nap.** When the fabric has dried completely, run your hand back and forth to determine the direction of the nap. Then, using a clean, dry terry towel, raise the nap by wiping the fabric in the appropriate direction. For best results, flatten your hand, with fingers extended, and stretch the towel across the palm, holding the ends taut with your free hand. Work in smooth, overlapping strokes until the original appearance is restored.

Some napped fabrics, such as plush, can also be restored with light vacuuming. Run the upholstery attachment over the fabric in overlapping strokes, working in one direction only.

3

Lightening the Big Loads

Super suction. A wall-mounted inlet of a central vacuum-cleaning system, connected through a long hose to a wand and one of several cleaning heads, provides up to six times the dirt-lifting suction of a conventional upright or canister cleaner. Three to five inlets, linked by a concealed network of plastic pipe to a powerful remote motor and a collection bag, make it possible to clean the house more quickly and thoroughly than with a portable machine.

Some cleaning jobs seem formidable. Ridding a house of the flotsam and jetsam left behind by a flood is enough to dishearten the most dyed-in-the-wool optimist. But even the weekly tedium of vacuuming a house or the daily chore of testing the water chemistry in a swimming pool can be daunting. And by a curious sort of role reversal, some of the most onerous cleaning jobs are connected with the very amenities that make a modern house such a comfortable place to live and work.

For example, a typical kitchen, with its assortment of labor-saving appliances, also harbors two of the most time-consuming cleaning jobs—defrosting a refrigerator *(page 81)* and degreasing an oven *(page 84)*. And although frost-free refrigerators and self-cleaning ovens can eliminate both of these tasks, human hands are still required for cleaning the drain pan under the refrigerator and the drip pan under the top of the range—and to neglect either job is to invite strange and disagreeable odors.

Washers, dryers and dishwashers also collect dirt in hidden places and require occasional cleaning. So, too, do the hidden filters of air conditioners, central heating and cooling systems, range hoods, exhaust fans and electronic air cleaners *(pages 90-91)*. Fortunately, most manufacturers design their products to facilitate cleaning: Appliances often have removable parts that provide quick access to easily cleaned metal, plastic or porcelain interiors.

One major chore is cleaning the backyard swimming pool, the prized recreation center for many suburban families. Both the pool and its contents must be carefully and continuously cleaned in order to keep the water sparkling and safe. The regimen begins with an annual scrubbing of the pool itself and continues throughout the season with regular skimming and vacuuming to remove bugs, leaves and litter in the water, as well as the sludge and grime that can settle on the bottom *(page 95)*.

The underwater vacuum cleaner used for pools is one of several adaptations of the familiar home vacuum cleaner that are available to handle unusual cleaning problems. One of the most useful of these specialized cleaners is the heavy-duty shop vacuum, built to suck up wet or dry loads, indoors or outdoors. It is invaluable when disaster strikes and a water-soaked room or basement must be cleaned *(pages 100-101)*. A second adaptation, the built-in central vacuum system *(pages 73-79)*, is superior to any portable unit when it comes to the swift cleanup of anything from a dusty wood floor to a shag rug covered with spilled cat litter. Strategically located inlets, linked to a powerful motor and an enormous collection bag, are connected by plastic pipe that can be retrofitted into existing walls.

Retrofitting a Vacuum System into the Walls

A central vacuum-cleaning system may seem a luxurious addition to a home, but in fact it offers a host of practical advantages. Its powerful 2- to 3-horsepower motor delivers up to six times the suction of a typical portable vacuum cleaner; thus it cleans deeply embedded dirt far more efficiently. Yet despite this added power, it seems quieter because the motor is located away from the inlets—in a garage, a basement or a utility room.

The remote location of the motor unit and its huge 5- to 10-gallon collection bag (the bag needs to be replaced only a few times a year) also means that dirt and dust are carried far from the living area of the house. In addition, the exhaust air—with its residual dust—is commonly vented to the outdoors through a pipe inserted in an exterior wall. A muffler, similar to an automobile muffler but smaller, may be added to the exhaust pipe to baffle most of the high-pitched noise created by the rushing air and keep the system from annoying neighbors.

The job of vacuum cleaning is performed in the same way—and with virtually the same attachments—as with a portable canister-type cleaner. The hose, however, plugs into permanently mounted inlets in the floor or on the walls at strategic locations. Most central vacuum systems come with lightweight hoses 24 to 33 feet long so that several rooms can be cleaned from each inlet. As few as three inlets will serve in many houses; rarely are more than five needed. (If the person who normally cleans is confined to a wheelchair or is painfully arthritic, use wall-mounted inlets and place them higher than normal so that the vacuum hose can be inserted with a minimum of bending and reaching.)

Connecting the inlets to the central motor unit is a network of concealed semirigid, thin-walled, 1½- to 2-inch plastic pipes, which are assembled with parts that resemble plumbing fittings and are sealed together with pipe cement. The network consists of a main trunk line, which usually runs horizontally the entire length of the house, and shorter feeder lines branching off from it to connect the main trunk to the inlets.

Installing these pipes in an existing house can present some thorny prob-

lems, but none that is insurmountable. If the attic floor or basement ceiling is unfinished, the task is greatly simplified: Simply lay the trunk line on top of ceiling joists in the attic or suspend it beneath floor joists in the basement.

Running the trunk line between a finished floor and ceiling usually entails removing part of the finished ceiling and perhaps cutting holes through joists above. Alternatively, you can suspend the trunk line below the finished ceiling and then box it in with paneling or wallboard.

Vertical pipes can generally be threaded through interior partition walls; exterior walls contain insulation, which makes it virtually impossible to thread piping through them. Vertical pipes can also be run through closets or concealed with bookcases or cabinets.

Installed along with the pipes—taped

right to them, in fact—is a switch circuit of low-voltage wiring. This circuit turns the motor unit on or off at the inlets when an inlet cover is opened or when the cleaning hose is inserted.

Some hoses also are electrified. Their cleverly concealed wires transmit regular, high-voltage household current to a special cleaning head that contains motor-driven beater brushes. A motor-driven head is an expensive option with most systems, but it is worth the price if you frequently need to clean deeply embedded soil in heavily trafficked halls or doorways. The beater brushes on standard heads, driven solely by the inrushing air, are effective only against surface soil. If you plan to use a motor-driven head, locate each inlet within 6 feet of a receptacle so that the cord from the electrified hose can be conveniently plugged in.

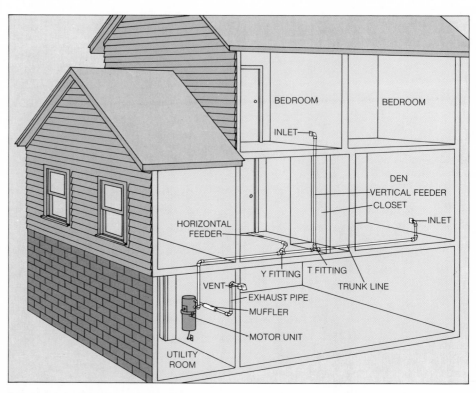

A typical piping layout. A main trunk line runs the length of this two-story house, connecting the motor unit of a central vacuum-cleaning system, located in the basement utility room, to the farthest inlet, in the first-floor den. Halfway along the trunk line, a vertical feeder line leaves the trunk line at a T fitting. Hidden in the back of a closet, the line rises through the first floor to an inlet in a second-floor bedroom. A Y fitting on the trunk line, near the T, creates a horizontal feeder line, serving an inlet in the wall between the first-floor bedroom and the living room, which in this drawing is hidden. Finally, the exhaust pipe leaves the motor unit and connects to a muffler, which quiets the outrushing air as it exits through a vent in the basement wall.

The ABCs of Plastic Piping

A catalogue of pipes and fittings. Basic to a central vacuum system is semirigid plastic pipe; flexible piping, which resembles dryer duct, can be used for tricky bends or where there is not enough room for standard fittings. Flexible pipe should be used sparingly; its accordion-folded walls cause turbulence in the line and reduce the air flow. When possible, use standard fittings—couplings, elbows, Ys and Ts—to join lengths of pipe, turn corners and create branches. Street fittings, with one end designed to fit inside another fitting, can be used with standard elbows, Ts and Ys to create compound curves in tight spaces.

In addition to these basic fittings, you will need the specialized fittings made for your system. Included in this category are flanged or adaptor elbows for connecting the pipe to the inlet, the mounting plates or retaining springs needed to fasten the elbows to the wall and the hinged covers for the inlets themselves. Although all the basic fittings are available from plumbing-supply or hardware stores, some of the special fittings must be purchased from the dealer who sells the vacuum system.

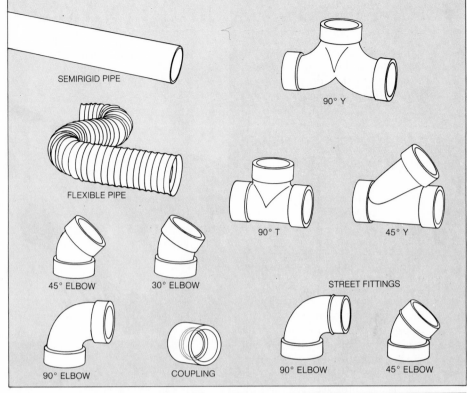

SEMIRIGID PIPE

FLEXIBLE PIPE

90° Y

90° T

45° Y

45° ELBOW

30° ELBOW

STREET FITTINGS

90° ELBOW

COUPLING

90° ELBOW

45° ELBOW

Preparing pipe ends. After cutting a length of pipe with a hacksaw, use a small knife to pare away any burrs from the inside *(right)*; these could impede air flow. Then bevel the outside of the pipe with a few strokes of a sharp file *(far right)* so that the pipe will slide easily into its fitting. Finally, rub the pipe end lightly with sandpaper to clean and degloss it.

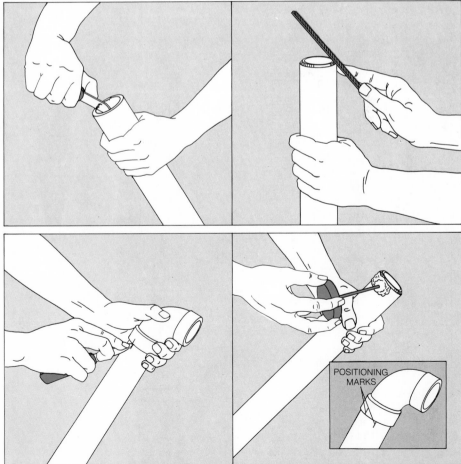

POSITIONING MARKS

Making a perfect joint. Push together the pipe and its fitting in the position in which they will be installed. Scratch a short mark on the pipe and fitting so that the two can be quickly realigned *(right)*; pull the joint apart. Using the brush attached to the cap of the pipe-cement can, dab cement liberally onto the outside of the pipe *(far right)*. Insert the pipe into the fitting, with the alignment marks an eighth to a quarter turn apart *(inset)*. Quickly turn and push the fitting to align the marks and spread the cement.

Joining flexible and semirigid pipe. Spread
pipe cement thickly over about 1½ inches of the
end of the semirigid pipe and slip the flexible
pipe over it; hold the joint motionless for about 30
seconds. Wrap the joint with a turn or two of
electrical tape or duct tape to ensure an airtight
seal. Then secure the semirigid pipe to a joist
or a stud with a pipe clamp, placing the clamp
close to the newly cemented joint.

Laying Out the System

Selecting the inlet locations. Cut a length
of heavy twine the same length as the hose that
comes with the vacuum system. Tie one end
of the twine to a heavy weight, such as a brick or
a book, and the other end to a stick the same
length as the system's cleaning wand. Using the
twine as a stand-in for the hose, plot the location for each inlet, beginning with the one farthest
from the motor location. Be sure to allow for
the necessity of looping the hose around furniture
and for reaching the ceiling point farthest from
the inlet so that you will also be able to vacuum
wall moldings as well as floors. When you have
tentatively chosen the position for the first inlet,
repeat the procedure for the others. Work
back toward the motor location, allowing for some
overlap between cleaning zones. You may
need to experiment a bit and change your inlet locations in order to reach the entire house with
the smallest number of inlets.

Next, using the inlet locations as reference points,
plan the route for the trunk line. This should
run in a straight path from the motor to the farthest inlet, taking advantage of open spaces
left by an unfinished floor or ceiling. Whenever
possible, the trunk line should also be located
so that feeder lines can be connected to it in
straight paths. Check each chosen path for
obstacles, such as heating ducts, steel beams or
masonry walls. If such obstacles do intrude,
making the route impracticable, simply reposition an inlet to avoid them.

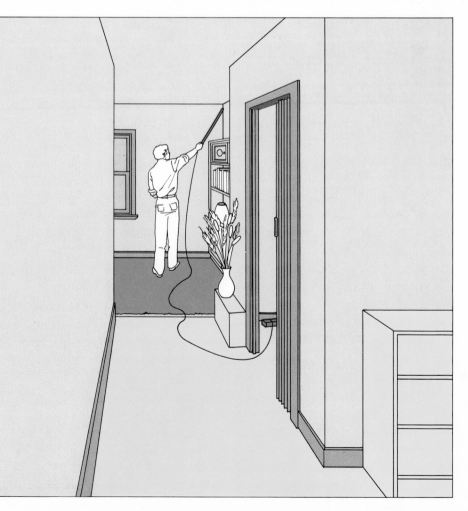

Installing a Wall Inlet

1 **Locating an access hole.** Remove the narrow shoe molding at the base of one of the inlet walls, and drill a small reference hole through the floor into the basement directly below the point chosen for the inlet. To loosen the molding safely, insert the blade of a putty knife behind it. Force a second knife between the first knife and the baseboard, then gently hammer a cold chisel between the two knives. Lever the loosened molding away from the baseboard, and drill the reference hole. Insert a scrap of wire down through the hole to make it easier to locate the hole from the basement.

If the trunk line is to run across the attic, remove any ceiling molding in the same way and drill a hole through the ceiling into the attic.

2 **Cutting into the partition wall.** Fit a drill with a 2¼-inch hole saw and cut an access hole through the subfloor into the partition above. To center the access hole in the partition, measure from the reference hole a distance equal to half the thickness of the partition, including the baseboard. This thickness is easily measured at a doorway. For an attic trunk line, cut an access hole through the ceiling into the partition below.

With the aid of a flashlight, use your fingers to make sure that the access hole is at least 2 inches from a stud. Check the partition interior for obstructions. If necessary, bore a new hole a few inches away and plug the first hole with the circular wood scrap cut earlier. Use a keyhole saw to cut the inlet hole, aligning it with the reference hole at the baseboard. The inlet hole's shape and size are shown in the instructions provided with the system.

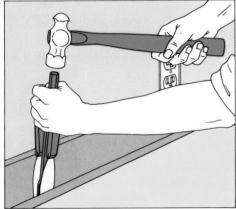

3 **Inserting the pipe.** Cut a length of pipe to reach from ½ inch below the inlet opening to the level of the trunk line—either at the center of the joists or just below them. Tape 18-gauge, two-conductor wire to the outside of the pipe, trimming the wire to extend 6 inches beyond each end of the pipe. Feed the wired pipe into the partition wall (*right*) until a helper, at the inlet opening, can reach in and pull the wire through the opening. Then, while you steady the pipe from below, have your helper cement a flanged or adapter elbow to the top of the pipe (*far right*).

Flanged elbows, such as the one shown here, have a widened face at the top, containing mounting holes for the inlet plate (*page 76, Step 4*). Some systems have an alternative fastener—an adapter elbow with a projecting circular lip that accepts a special wire retaining spring.

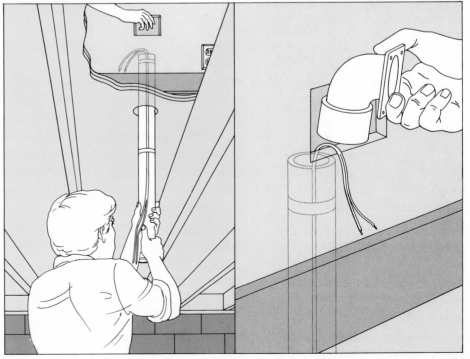

4 **Securing the elbow.** To anchor a flanged elbow to the inlet opening, first pull the ends of the low-voltage wires through one of the middle-sized holes in the mounting plate. Then angle the plate into the opening *(below, left)*, and screw the plate to the holes in the flange elbow, using the screws supplied with the plate. For a system without mounting plates, anchor an adapter elbow to the opening. First, pull the elbow and the wires through. Snap the retainer spring over the elbow; push the elbow back against the wall, locking the spring into the lip *(below, right)*.

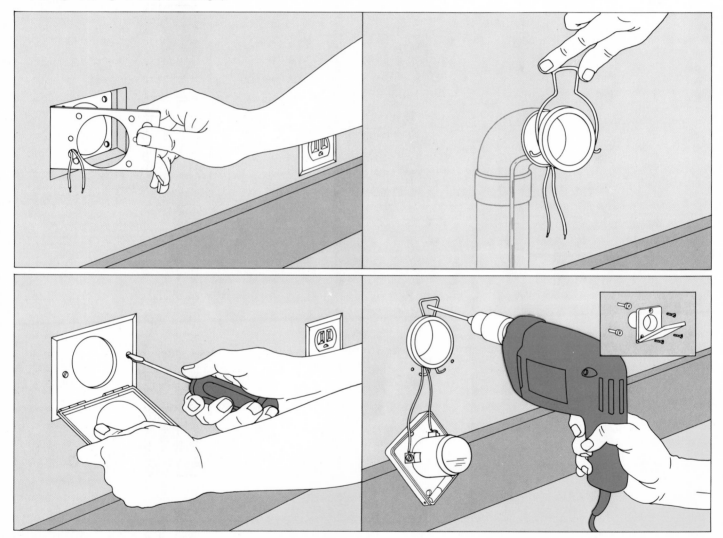

5 **Adding the inlet cover.** Connect the low-voltage wire to the terminals on the back of the inlet cover. If your system employs a mounting plate *(above, left)*, simply screw the cover onto the plate. In systems without plates, hold the cover in place against the wall and mark the position of the mounting holes. Remove the cover, then at the marks drill holes *(above, right)* large enough to accommodate plastic anchors. Add the anchors and screw the cover in place *(inset)*.

Replace the shoe molding—removed to drill reference holes—and nail it to the floor.

Installing a Floor Outlet

Adding an extension to an inlet cover. To compensate for the thickness of a floor, extend the tube at the back of the inlet cover so that it will meet the T fitting that joins it to the trunk line. If the cover is attached to a flanged fitting, as in this example, obtain a specially shaped extension collar *(lower inset)* from the vacuum dealer. Cut the collar to the correct length with a hacksaw, cement it to the inlet tube, and tape a length of low-voltage wire to the assembly. Connect the low-voltage wire to the inlet terminals. Then anchor the inlet and fittings in the usual way.

To adapt a spring-held arrangement, use an ordinary T fitting and extend it with a length of ordinary piping—but cap the piping with a special lipped adapter *(upper inset)*, to which the inlet-cover tube can be attached. The lipped adapter is available from the vacuum dealer who sells you the system. Trim, cement and wire the inlet connection as above.

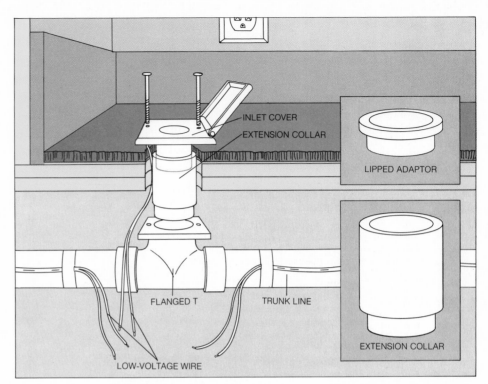

INLET COVER

EXTENSION COLLAR

LIPPED ADAPTOR

FLANGED T

TRUNK LINE

EXTENSION COLLAR

LOW-VOLTAGE WIRE

Assembling the Trunk Line

Supporting the piping. Starting at the feeder line farthest from the motor unit, assemble lengths of pipe and fittings to run the trunk line back to the motor. When the trunk line runs below joists *(right, top),* support it every 4 feet with lengths of perforated metal or cloth strapping, slung under the pipe and suspended from two nails driven into the joist. When the trunk line runs across joists in a ceiling that will later be finished *(right, bottom),* bore 2¼-inch holes through the centers of the joists and thread the pipe through the holes; use thin-walled pipe in such installations. When the trunk line runs across attic joists, lay the pipe on the joists— but connect feeder lines to the side rather than the bottom of the trunk line. For this side connection, use a T fitting and a street elbow.

After the entire system is assembled, make any necessary final adjustments; then cement the joints. Run low-voltage wire along the trunk line, taping it to the pipe at 2-foot intervals. At every feeder line, cut the trunk-line wire and connect it to the feeder-line wire with wire caps. Join the wires in threes *(inset),* each group containing one feeder wire, one incoming trunk-line wire and one outgoing trunk-line wire.

Hanging the Motor Unit

1 **Attaching the mounting plate.** Center the mounting plate over a stud, and screw it to the stud through the plate's center holes, positioning the plate so that the motor unit will clear the floor, ceiling and adjacent walls by the distances specified in the unit's instructions. If you are mounting the plate on a masonry wall or if no stud is conveniently located, use wall anchors and insert the screws through the four holes near the corners of the plate. Lift the motor unit onto the hanging pegs at the four corners of the mounting plate.

Because a central vacuum system needs a lot of current—some units require nearly 18 amps for start-up—the unit must plug into its own 20-amp circuit. Unless you are sure of your wiring skills, have a qualified electrician add the new circuit to your service panel and run it to a receptacle within 3 feet of the motor unit.

2 **Connecting the motor to the system.** Cement together the last lengths of pipe and fittings needed to bring the trunk line to the intake port on the motor unit. Make the final connection to the intake port with the hose clamps or compression fittings provided with the system—do not cement the piping to the unit. Finally, before plugging in the unit, connect the trunk line's low-voltage wire to the low-voltage terminals.

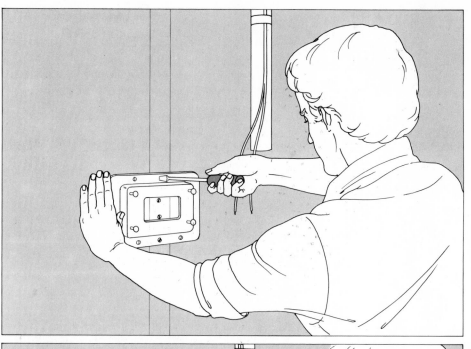

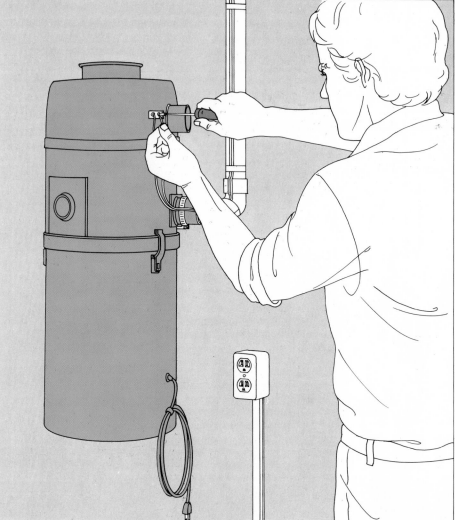

Hooking Up an Exhaust Line

Venting a central vacuum system outside calls for the same pipe-fitting techniques used in building the trunk line. You will also need to cut a hole through an exterior wall, using a hole saw for wood siding, a star drill for masonry.

The vent hole should be near the unit and should be located an inch or two lower than the motor's exhaust port, to keep condensation from running back into the unit. If the unit is hung in a basement, make sure that the vent hole is above ground; if necessary, use elbows to route the piping upward from the unit, then pitch it downward to the hole.

If the exhaust is within earshot of a neighbor's house—or your own patio—add a muffler somewhere in the exhaust line to reduce the level of noise vented outside. Mufflers are available as options from the vacuum dealer; they include fittings on each end and are simply cemented into the exhaust line in place of an equivalent length of pipe.

Finally, at the end of the exhaust line, add a vent cap similar to the kind used for a clothes dryer. The cap will keep rain water out of the pipe and deflect the unit's dusty exhaust downward as it is blasted out through the wall.

Venting the System Outdoors

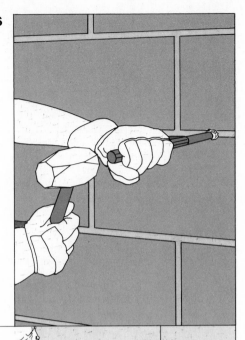

1 Making the vent hole. To cut through drywall and wood siding (*below*), fit an electric drill with a hole saw ¼ inch larger in diameter than the piping. Cut a hole through the inside wall surface between studs. Push aside any insulation, and mark the outline of the hole on the sheathing. Drive a nail through the sheathing and siding in the center of the outline. Pull out the nail and, working outside the house, center the hole saw over the nail hole to finish cutting the vent hole.

To cut through a masonry wall (*right*), hold a star drill perpendicular to the wall and strike its end with a small sledge hammer. Wear gloves and safety goggles to guard yourself from flying chips. Rotate the drill slightly and strike it again. Continue hammering and rotating the drill until it pierces the wall. Enlarge the hole with a cold chisel to fit the vent pipe.

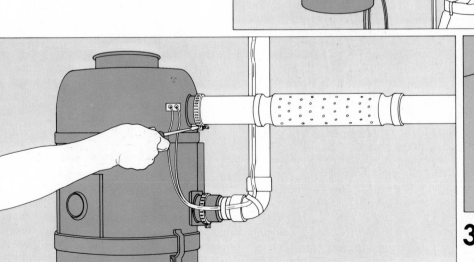

2 Assembling the exhaust pipe. Cement the muffler to a short piece of pipe and insert the pipe into the exhaust port of the motor unit. Secure the pipe to the port with a hose clamp. Cut a second length of pipe to span the distance from the muffler to the outside wall. Slide the pipe through the vent hole, then back against the muffler; cement the pipe to the muffler.

3 Adding the vent cap. Lay a generous ribbon of caulk around the outside of the exhaust pipe where it exits from the house. Push the vent cap over the pipe and seat it firmly in the caulk. Fasten the cap to a wood wall with rustproof wood screws or nails. Use concrete nails or screws and masonry anchors to fasten the cap to a brick or concrete-block wall.

Removing Dirt from Labor-saving Appliances

Virtually all major appliances, from kitchen ranges to trash compactors, demand periodic cleaning. To simplify the task, manufacturers design their machines to be partially dismantled. Control knobs pull off or unscrew; kick plates and floor-level grilles snap out; the tops of many washers and ranges lift up; oven doors are detachable. Most of the fittings inside a refrigerator or an oven, or on top of a range, come out and can be washed at the kitchen sink.

Despite their ponderous size, most major appliances can be pulled out from the wall so that you can clean under and behind them. If they have wheels or rollers, they should be pulled straight out, in one smooth motion, to prevent damage to the floor. Appliances without wheels can be walked out by lifting and shifting them from side to side. To move an electric range away from the wall, open the oven door slightly and grasp the top of the doorframe in both hands; then lift and pull the range toward you. But never move a gas appliance—even flexible gas lines can rupture.

The equipment used for the cleaning is simple. Washing is done with sponges and soft cloths. Stubborn dirt is removed with scrubbing pads—nylon pads for plastic and painted surfaces, steel wool for metal and porcelain enamel. A long-handled, soft-bristled brush—such as an old-fashioned radiator brush—is essential for reaching into crevices under and around appliances, where dust, lint and animal hair collect. And a vacuum cleaner with upholstery-brush and crevice-tool attachments is helpful for sucking up loose debris.

Similarly, although commercial preparations such as oven cleaners and spray-and-wipe solutions are handy, they are not necessarily more effective than generic stand-bys. Mild detergent, ammonia and baking soda will take care of most appliance cleaning problems. The one product to avoid is abrasive powders, which are likely to dull the finish and make the surface more dirt-prone.

A mild detergent is the best cleaner for any appliance, inside and out. Ammonia will cut through baked-on grease that detergent cannot handle, and a saucer of ammonia left in a very dirty oven overnight will loosen the soil. Be careful, however, not to use ammonia on aluminum trim; it will discolor the metal.

Baking soda kills odors as well as, and sometimes better than, many commercial deodorants. To freshen a refrigerator, especially the drain pan, wash it with a solution of baking soda; then leave an open box of soda in the refrigerator to banish future odors.

Mix cleaning agents with warm water. Use only 1 tablespoon of detergent to 1 gallon of water; otherwise, the sticky residue will be hard to rinse away. To clean a dirty oven, use ½ cup of sudsy ammonia to 1 gallon of water; to freshen a refrigerator, use 2 tablespoons of baking soda to 1 quart of water. Wash fittings—racks, shelves, crispers and broiler pans—in the kitchen sink; for other surfaces, sponge on the cleaning solution. Always rinse off the cleaning solution with clear water; left behind, the residue will trap dirt.

Apart from these standard cleaning techniques, each appliance has specific requirements, dictated by its design and function. For parts that may need special attention, check the use-and-care manual provided with the appliance. If it is missing, write the manufacturer for a copy. Dismantling and cleaning techniques common to various kinds of appliances are shown on the following pages. The maintenance tips below should help you clean your appliances more effectively and less frequently.

☐ REFRIGERATORS: Keep door gaskets scrupulously clean—stickiness strains the gasket and may tear it. Do not let the ice in the freezer compartment get more than 1 inch thick, and do not pry out loosened ice with a metal instrument—you may puncture the evaporator coils.

☐ FREEZERS: A freestanding freezer needs the same care as a refrigerator-freezer unit. If condenser coils are inside the freezer walls, allow 3 inches of air space between the freezer and the wall of the room; this will prevent the motor from overheating and possibly breaking down.

☐ RANGES: Except for their heating elements, gas and electric cooktops are similar and get the same care. Ovens, however, vary. Standard ovens have a smooth porcelain finish and can be cleaned with detergent, ammonia or oven cleaner. Continuous-clean ovens have a rough porcelain finish, designed to disperse grease during baking; they can be cleaned with detergent or ammonia, but not with a commercial oven cleaner. Self-cleaning ovens burn away dirt at a special high setting; in most, the porcelain drip pans and broiler pan can also be cleaned in the oven—but check the use-and-care manual for exceptions. In self-cleaning ovens, the area outside the fiberglass door gasket must be cleaned by hand, but do not wet or scrub the fiberglass.

☐ MICROWAVE OVENS: Wipe spatters off the plastic interior with detergent immediately. In ovens with a browning element, steam off baked-on spots by boiling a cup of water in the oven.

☐ CLOTHES WASHERS: Wipe up spilled laundry powder and additives immediately; if they are allowed to collect in corners, they will corrode the finish. If a white mineral deposit forms inside the washer, change to a detergent with a higher phosphate content or install a water softener. Clean out the lint trap after each load of laundry.

☐ CLOTHES DRYERS: For the machine to operate efficiently, air must circulate unimpeded; clean the filter after every load and the exhaust system twice a year.

☐ TRASH COMPACTORS: Food particles will cause odors; rinse out containers before depositing them in the compactor.

☐ DISHWASHERS: Empty the filter after each wash load, and check the sink air vent periodically for debris; to gain access to the air vent, unscrew its dome-shaped cover. Although the interior of a dishwasher is self-cleaning, spills on the edge of the door and the opening must be washed by hand.

☐ COFFEE MAKERS AND IRONS: Every month or two, flush thoroughly with pure vinegar or a commercial demineralizer; rinse immediately with fresh water.

Deodorizing and De-icing a Refrigerator

Melting ice with minimal mess. Remove all foodstuffs from the refrigerator, wrap them in newspapers and pack them in corrugated boxes. Turn the temperature-control knob to OFF. Then remove all shelves, dividers and drawers except for the freezer tray. Set metal pans of boiling water in the freezer compartment and, as the ice on the freezer walls begins to melt, loosen it gently with a plastic windshield scraper. Do not scrape ice from exposed cooling coils; this should be allowed to melt away on its own—scraping could damage the delicate coils. As the water in the pans cools, pour it out and replace it with more boiling water.

While the ice is melting, wash the refrigerator interior, the inside of the door, and the door gasket with detergent in warm water (*right*). Rinse all surfaces with clean water and towel dry.

When the freezer compartment is fully defrosted, you should wash, rinse and dry its interior surfaces. Carefully slide out the freezer tray and pour off accumulated water. Then wash, rinse and dry the freezer tray, along with the shelves, dividers and drawers.

Replace the removable parts, and reset the temperature control. Replace the foodstuffs and leave the refrigerator door shut for at least half an hour to allow the appliance to reach normal operating temperature again.

FREEZER TRAY

DOOR GASKET

TEMPERATURE-CONTROL KNOB

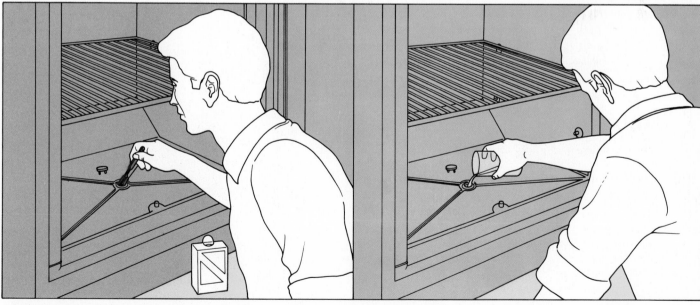

Cleaning the drain tube. If the refrigerator drains through an opening in the interior floor, scrub the drain tube with a moistened toothbrush sprinkled with baking soda (*above, left*) whenever you defrost the refrigerator. To reach the drain tube, pull out the crisper drawers and remove the plastic drain cap.

Pour clean water (*above, right*) in to rinse the drain; replace the cap and drawers.

Removing and washing a drain pan. To gain access to the drain pan, snap out the grille from the bottom front of the refrigerator by grasping both ends of the grille and lifting up as you pull out; you may need to open the refrigerator door to release the grille. Slide out the drain pan—the two most common types are shown below,

left and right. Wash the pan with detergent and warm water, rinse it with water and dry it; then slide it back into position under the refrigerator, and snap on the grille.

Wash the drain pan twice a year, or whenever you clean the drain tube *(page 81)*.

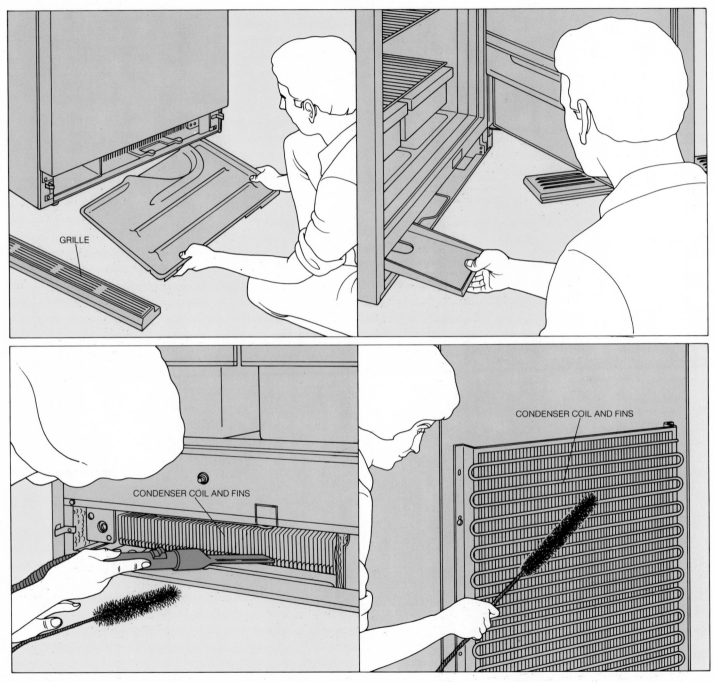

GRILLE

CONDENSER COIL AND FINS

CONDENSER COIL AND FINS

Dusting condenser coils and fins. The winding condenser coils and narrow metal fins that disperse the heat from a refrigerator are located either at the bottom front *(above, left)* or at the rear *(above, right)* of the appliance. To expose and clean coils and fins located at the bottom of a refrigerator, snap off the floor-level grille below

the door as at top. Then use a long-handled brush to loosen dirt and dust over, under and around the coils and fins. Vacuum up the debris, using the crevice-tool attachment.

To expose the coils and fins on the back of a refrigerator, roll or walk the appliance away from

the wall. Then brush off the coils and fins, or use a vacuum cleaner fitted with an upholstery-brush attachment.

Clean bottom coils and fins twice a year, more often if you have pets that shed. Yearly dusting is enough for rear-mounted coils and fins.

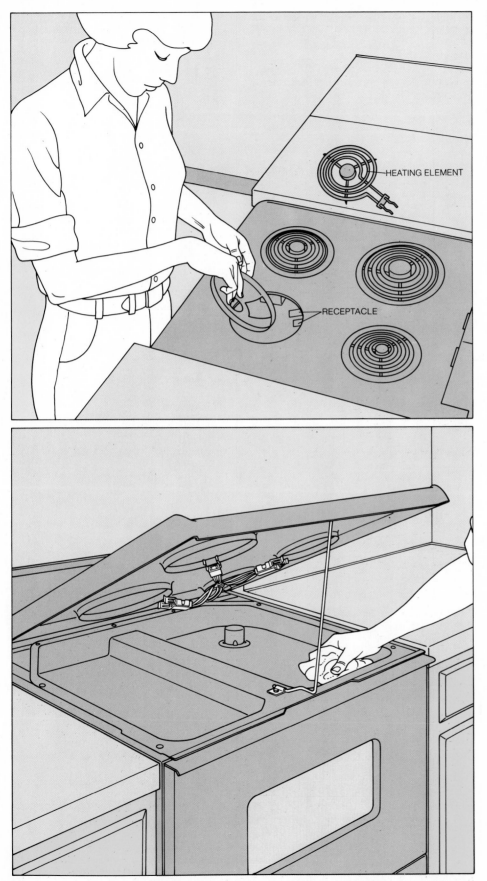

Dismantling an Electric Cooktop and Oven

Removing the cooktop accessories. To remove the spiral heating elements, lift them and pull, snapping the electrical contacts out of the receptacles under the cooktop. On some stoves, the elements are not detachable; simply lift these up at one side. Remove the drip pans, trim rings and accessories such as control knobs; wash them in a detergent solution or, if they are heavily soiled, in an ammonia solution. Do not wash the heating elements; they are designed to burn themselves clean.

HEATING ELEMENT

RECEPTACLE

Getting beneath the cooktop. Most cooktops are hinged at the rear; lift the front edge of the cooktop and prop it up with the hinged support rod that is usually attached underneath. If there is no rod, hold up the cooktop with one hand. Cooktops that are not hinged are usually removable; simply lift the entire cooktop off the range and set it aside.

To clean beneath the cooktop, use a vacuum-cleaner crevice tool to collect crumbs and dust, then sponge the interior with a detergent solution. To loosen baked-on spots, use a nylon scrub pad dampened with ammonia.

Unhinging the oven door. To make ovens more accessible for cleaning, the oven doors can be removed from their hinges. If the door is one that has an intermediate stopping position— an electric oven's door, for example, can be left partially open for broiling—open the door as far as the stopping position and, maintaining the door at that angle, pull it straight off its hinges (*below, left*).

Some oven doors have latched hinges that can be locked in an open position; this feature prevents the hinges from snapping back against the doorframe while the door is being removed. To lock these latches, open the oven door all the way and push each latch down into the locked position (*below, right*). Then just pull the door straight outward, off its hinges.

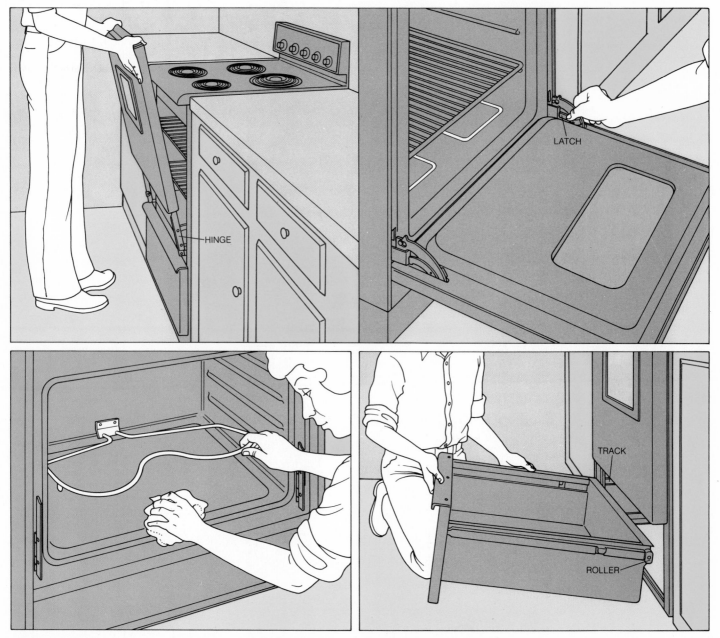

Cleaning the oven. Remove the oven racks and wash them separately, as you did the cooktop accessories (*page 83*). Then wash the oven interior and the interior surface of the oven door with the solution recommended on page 80 for your type of oven. To make the oven surface accessible for cleaning, the lower heating element pulls out or swings up on a hinge; the upper element may click down out of its brackets.

Detaching the bottom drawer. To make the floor area underneath the storage drawer of an electric range accessible so that it can be cleaned, you can simply remove the drawer from its tracks. To release the storage drawer, first slide it toward you as far as it will go, then lift the front of the drawer to disengage the rollers, and pull the drawer free. Sponge out the interior of the drawer with a solution of detergent and warm water, and vacuum or wash the floor underneath the range.

GAS PORTHOLES

BURNER

Getting At the Innards of a Gas Range

Removing and cleaning gas burners. With the drip pans and burner grids removed and the cooktop propped open *(page 83)*, carefully lift out the gas burners. Most burners simply rest in place; some may be held by a single screw beside them. Wash the burners, the drip pans and the burner grids with detergent and warm water, using a toothbrush to reach into tight spots. If the burners are especially dirty, use a solution of ammonia and warm water to cut the grime. Insert a pin or the end of a straightened paper clip into gas portholes to clear them of food or dust. Let the burners dry completely before replacing them; damp burners will not light.

Cleaning beneath the cooktop. With the cooktop propped open and gas burners removed, vacuum crumbs and dust from the interior with a crevice-tool attachment. Be careful not to joggle pipes and wires, and stay away from pilot lights—the suction will extinguish them. After you have cleared away loose debris, wash the surface, using a sponge moistened with detergent or ammonia and water; for stubborn spots, use a nylon scrubbing pad or steel wool. Rinse the surface well and dry it with an absorbent cloth. Replace the burners, and make sure the pilot lights are working before you lower the top.

Scrubbing down the oven. Remove the oven door *(page 84)* and take out the oven racks; then place your fingers through the vent holes on each side of the oven floor, lift the front end slightly to clear the doorframe, and slide the floor straight out. Wash the oven floor and the racks with detergent and warm water; for burned-on grime, use ammonia solution or steel wool. In some gas ovens, the side walls are also designed to come out for cleaning. To remove these panels, first slide out the floor of the oven, then release all of the screws along the edges of the side panels and lift the panels away from the wall. Scrub the remaining oven surfaces, including the interior surface of the oven door, as described on page 84.

Removing the broiler drawer. The broiler drawers in some gas ranges are removed in the same way as the bottom drawer of an electric range *(page 84)*; others have latches on the bottom. To remove this type of broiler, open it all the way and slip an index finger under each latch. Raise the latches and pull the broiler toward you until it is stopped by the pegs riding in slots on the bottom of the drawer. Then lift the broiler straight up and remove it. To replace it, reposition the slots on the pegs and push the broiler back about an inch, engaging the latches.

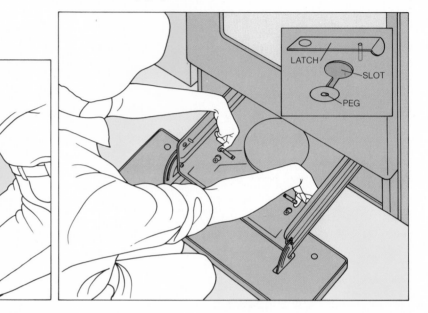

Tending To the Needs of a Clothes Washer

Removing and cleaning the lint trap. For optimum performance, a washing machine should be cleaned of collected lint at the end of each wash load. The way you clean the lint trap depends on its design; the three most common types are illustrated here *(inset)*. The card trap slides in and out of a slot in the upper rim of the washer tub; remove the trap and rap it sharply against a paper towel to dislodge the lint. The brush trap sits in a pocket on the washer rim; lift out the trap and draw a coarse-toothed comb through its bristles to remove the lint. The basket trap, which also serves as a detergent receptacle, fits over the agitator shaft; pluck out the small balls of lint with your fingers.

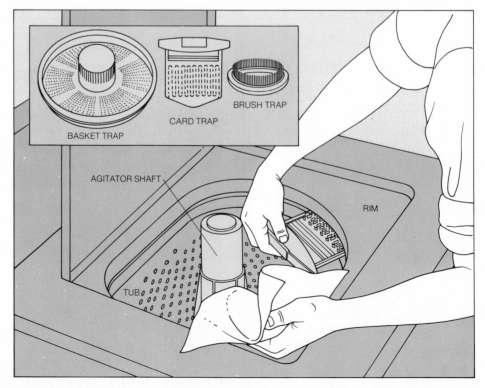

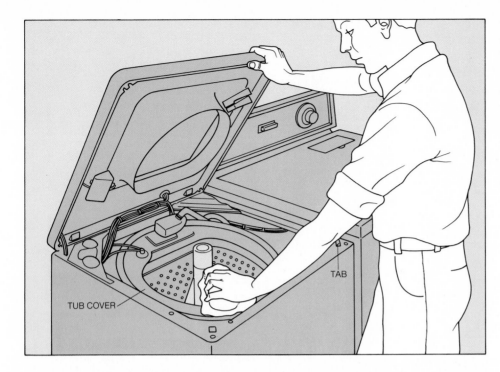

Washing off spilled detergent. To remove encrusted detergent powder that collects on the tub cover, raise the hinged washer top; if the top is held down by concealed tabs, release the tabs by inserting a putty knife under each front corner of the top and pressing in. Hold the top up with one hand while you use a water-moistened sponge to wipe away encrusted powder and sticky laundry additives from the tub cover and from the sheet-metal edges of the washer cabinet. Rinse the sponge often and continue wiping until there is no residue left on any metal surface. Dry the rinsed areas with an absorbent cloth.

TAB

TUB COVER

Keeping Air Flowing through a Clothes Dryer

Disposing of trapped lint. Remove and clean the lint trap in a clothes dryer after each load. If the trap is located beneath a flap at the top of the dryer *(top left)*, simply lift the flap, pull out the trap by its handle and peel off the feltlike layer of lint. Then reach down into the trap compartment with a long-handled brush to gather any lint that has escaped through the screen.

To clean a disk-shaped trap, which is located either on the door or on the back of the drum, pull the disk out of its circular receptacle and scrape off the lint. On a door-mounted trap, clear the air vents around the dryer opening with a long-handled brush *(bottom left)*.

To clean a floor-level lint trap, located behind a narrow trap door *(bottom right)*, lower the door and pull the trap straight out to scrape it clean. Then use a long-handled, soft-bristled brush to reach into and dislodge lint and dust from the trap receptacle; if the accumulation is especially heavy, vacuum up the debris with a crevice-tool attachment.

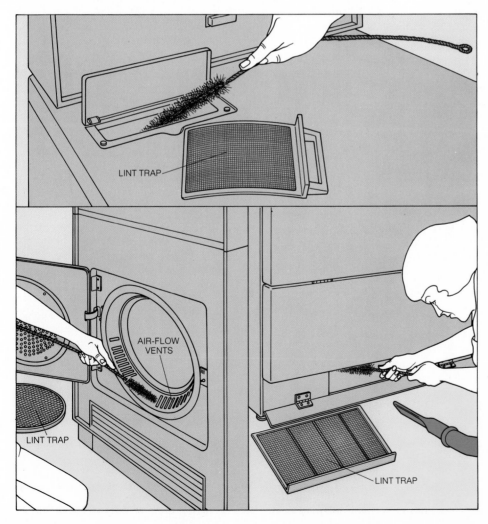

LINT TRAP

AIR-FLOW VENTS

LINT TRAP

LINT TRAP

Clearing the exhaust hose and vent. A dryer's exhaust system vents hot air from an opening in the back of the dryer, through a pipe or a flexible hose to an opening in an outside wall or a window. Clean the system once or twice a year to keep lint, dirt, leaves and even small animals from interfering with its function. First, loosen the clamp that connects the hose to the exhaust vent, and brush debris from inside the vent. Brush or vacuum lint from inside the hose; if the hose is very long, you may have to clean it in increments, telescoping sections as you work..

If the exhaust system uses a pipe rather than a hose, detach the end of the pipe from the exhaust vent and separate the pipe into sections; brush or vacuum the sections individually.

Finally, check the outdoor vent to be sure it is covered by its flap; if the flap is damaged or missing, install a new one in its place. Vent flaps are available at hardware stores.

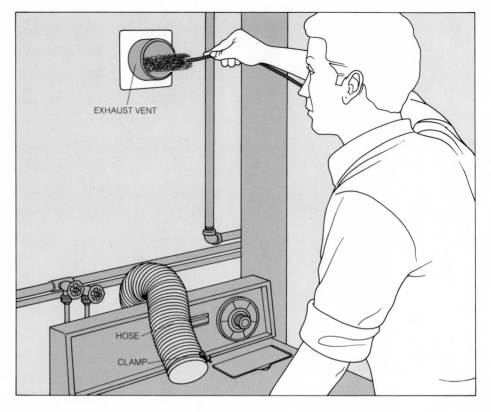

Removing Stray Debris from a Trash Compactor

Sanitizing a trash compactor. If a trash compactor's drawer is removable, disengage it by pulling the drawer out as far as it will go; then depress the roller latches on each side of the drawer and pull the drawer farther, sliding the bottom rollers off their runners. Wash the drawer interior with detergent and warm water; rinse and dry. Then vacuum and wash the inside walls of the compactor body. Watch for broken glass in both places. Then set the drawer rollers back in their runners and push the drawer shut.

If the compactor drawer is not removable, pull it out as far as you can; wash and rinse as above. Clean the inside of the body by reaching over the top of the opened drawer with a long-handled brush or a vacuum-cleaner hose.

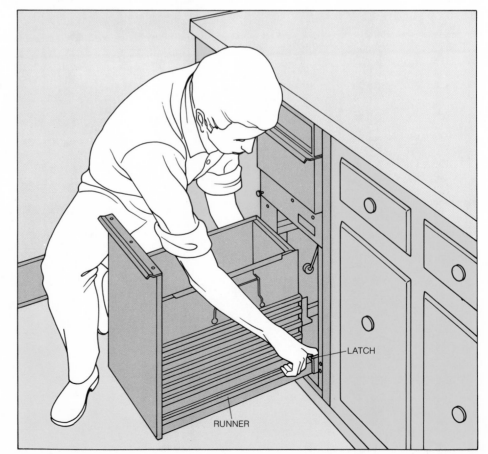

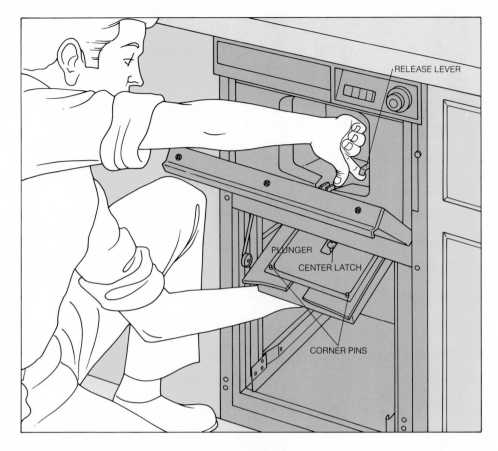

Detaching a compactor plunger. To disengage a removable trash-compactor plunger, open and, if possible, remove the compactor drawer. Then open the door at the top of the compactor to expose the plunger-release lever. Steady the bottom of the plunger with one hand while you lift the release lever with the other; be careful of glass shards, which may lodge on the bottom of the plunger. Remove the plunger from the compactor, brush glass shards from its surface, then wash the plunger with detergent and warm water and rinse it.

To replace the plunger, push it up until its center latch clicks into place. If it does not engage, the plunger latch and corner pins are not aligned with their respective fittings. Turn the plunger around and push it up again. Close the drawer and turn on the compactor, then open it and check that the plunger is still securely seated.

Detaching a Dishwasher Filter for Cleaning

Cleaning a dishwasher filter. Empty a dishwasher filter whenever it collects food particles, stray silverware or broken glass. To remove a crescent-shaped filter *(above, left),* which sits beside the spray-arm shaft, press the tab on the side and lift the filter. Rinse the filter under running water, then snap it back into place.

If the filter is a round basket seated on the spray-arm shaft *(above, right),* lift the spray arm straight up off its shaft, then lift off the filter. Hold the filter under running water and scrub it with a brush to dislodge the trapped debris. Then snap the filter back onto the shaft and put the spray arm back in its place.

Cleaning Filters That Purify Air

Among all the elements of a house that need cleaning, none is so easily overlooked as the air. Yet dust, pollen, smoke and other airborne pollutants can cause discomfort, trigger allergic reactions and cause damage to drapes, upholstery and other household goods. Airborne cooking grease, the worst offender, is actually a fire hazard if allowed to build up in vent fans and ductwork. Fortunately, most of the home's air-moving machinery screens out these impurities with filters. But filters can do their job only if they are periodically cleaned or replaced.

In addition to providing purer, more healthful air, properly maintained filters also increase the efficiency of the machinery by trapping pollutants before they can interfere with the system's fans, heating elements and cooling coils: A dirty filter in a central air-conditioning or heating system can cut air flow and increase energy consumption. For this reason, filters are easily removable for cleaning. Grease filters on kitchen exhaust fans are located on the underside of the range hood; room air-conditioner filters are always behind the air-intake grille on the front; filters on central heating and cooling systems are positioned between the return-air duct and the blower motor.

Cleaning agents and techniques for filters must be matched to the filter material. Aluminum-mesh grease filters can withstand strong detergents and scrub brushes—even the turbulence of a dishwasher. Plastic-foam filters in room air conditioners are more fragile but can be washed repeatedly in mild detergent before wearing out. The fiberglass filters of central heating and cooling systems cannot be washed, but they can be vacuumed and reused several times before being replaced.

Electronic air cleaners, which hook into a heating and cooling system, have filters that require even gentler care. These highly efficient devices scrub microscopic pollens by passing the air through a charged collector cell that consists of fragile metal fins and fine wires. The cell cannot withstand rough handling, but it is immersible and, with proper care, will last indefinitely.

Removing range-hood filters. The aluminum-mesh grease filters in range hoods detach for cleaning by methods similar to those shown here. For a three-sided box-shaped filter with a hinged bottom panel, unscrew the knob that holds the panel to the housing; the filter will drop down with the panel. For a flat filter (*left inset*), grasp the tab on the filter's edge; pull out and down to slide the filter from its channels.

For an angled filter (*right inset*), release the two latches on one side; the filter falls out.

Wash grease filters once a month in a solution of detergent and water or in the dishwasher. If the grease build-up is heavy, use ammonia instead and scrub with a brush, taking care not to disturb the weave of the mesh. Rinse the filter well and shake it dry before repositioning it.

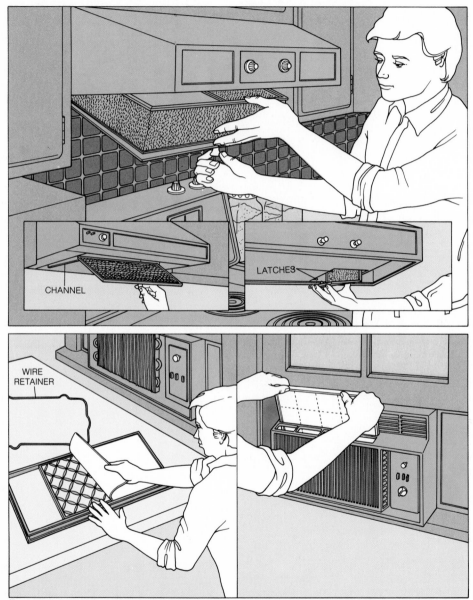

Removing room air-conditioner filters. If the air conditioner has a detachable grille (*above, left*), remove any screws that hold the grille in place, then snap it off by either pulling sharply on its bottom edge or pushing down on the top edge, depending on the model. Lay the grille face down and disengage the wire retainer or the elastic band that secures the filter to the back of the grille. Peel off the filter. Clear away hair and lint with a soft-bristled brush, then wash the filter by hand in a mild detergent-and-water solution. Rinse the filter, blot it dry and reattach it to the grille. Put the grille back in place, inserting the bottom or top edge first, then snapping the opposite corners into their respective positions with the heel of your hand.

On some units the grille is stationary and the filter slides into a slot behind it (*above, right*). To remove this kind of filter, grasp the exposed upper edge of its frame and pull the filter straight out. Wash the filter as above.

Replacing furnace filters. On older furnaces, the air filter may be located behind a removable panel, either vertical or horizontal, riding in metal channels above the blower (*below, left*). On modern furnaces, the air filter is usually located in a slot between the return-air duct and the blower (*below, right*). Inspect the filter once a month when the furnace is in use; turn off the power switch for the blower, then remove the filter. If it is heavily soiled and matted with dirt, replace it with a matching unit; otherwise, vacuum the dirty side thoroughly and reuse it.

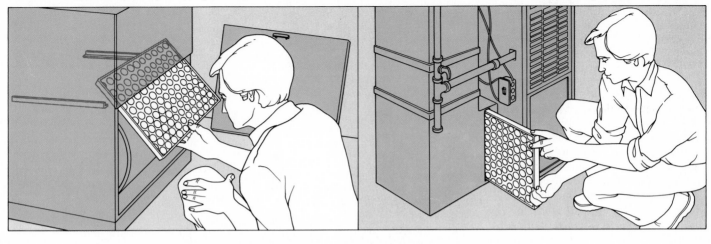

Servicing Electronic Filters

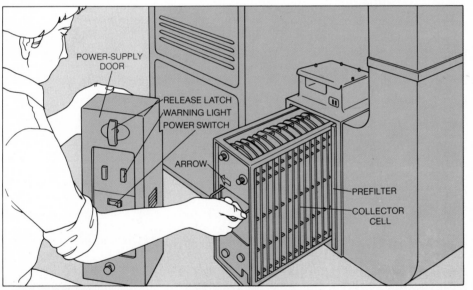

POWER-SUPPLY DOOR

RELEASE LATCH
WARNING LIGHT
POWER SWITCH

ARROW

PREFILTER

COLLECTOR CELL

1 **Removing the collector cell.** Once each month—or when the warning light or meter on the front of the cleaner indicates the need for cleaning—inspect the cleaner's finned collector cell for accumulations of dust and dirt. To reach the cell, first turn off the power switch on the cleaner's power-supply door; if there is no switch on the door, turn off the furnace blower. Disengage the power-supply door by turning its release latch; if there is no latch, simply pull the door straight out. Grasp the handle of the collector cell and slide it out. Then slide out the aluminum prefilter, which fits between the cell and the return-air duct. Check inside the collector-cell opening: Some air cleaners have a second cell placed end-to-end with the first, which also should be removed.

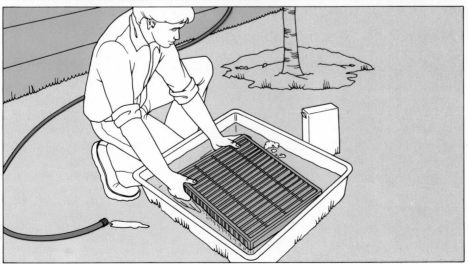

2 **Washing the collector cell.** Place the collector cell in a plastic washtub or in a bathtub. Fill the receptacle with water to cover the cell, and add ½ cup of automatic-dishwasher detergent for every 5 gallons of water. Soak the collector cell for 20 minutes, agitating it occasionally to loosen the dirt. Then remove the cell, and swish the prefilter clean in the same water. Rinse the cell and prefilter well in a tub of clear water or with a hose spray.

When the cell and prefilter stop dripping, replace them in the air-cleaner cabinet. Make sure the cell handle faces out and the air-flow direction arrow points toward the furnace. Then replace the door and turn on the power switch. Snapping noises are normal until the cell dries completely, but if they are bothersome, switch off the air cleaner and let it dry further.

Keeping a Swimming Pool Clear and Clean

Clear, sparkling water in a swimming pool is not only a delight to the senses, it is also essential to the safety and health of the swimmers. In water that is cloudy or discolored, a swimmer in trouble may be hidden from view. And neglected water is a fertile environment for bacteria, which can cause ear and eye infections.

A well-tended pool is free of the obvious dirt and debris blown in or brought in by swimmers. But chemical purity plays an important role in its pristine condition. The pool water should contain just enough chlorine disinfectant to kill bacteria and destroy the microscopic organisms that algae feed on. In addition, its pH level—a measure of acidity and alkalinity—should ensure that pool walls and hardware will not corrode or scale and that minerals will not precipitate out, causing the water to turn cloudy.

This chemical balance is usually established by a water analysis when the pool is first filled. Many pool-supply stores perform the service free. If you take them a water sample, they will test for hardness, metal content, and acidity and alkalinity. To balance these properties, they will prescribe the necessary treatment—usually including the addition of a chlorine stabilizer called cyanuric acid, which helps chlorine last longer.

Once the proper chemical balance is established, only two simple tests are routinely needed to keep it that way. One measures the pH level, and the other gauges the chlorine content in parts per million (ppm); both can be done with a test kit, available at pool-supply stores. The water should be tested daily whenever the pool is in use, every other day when it is unused. Then add whatever corrective chemicals are called for.

Chlorine is the chemical most commonly added to pool water, but it is often used in conjunction with either muriatic acid or sodium bisulfate to lower the water's pH to between 7.4 and 7.6, the level at which chlorine works best. Alternatively, sodium carbonate, also called soda ash, is added to raise the water's pH level. The amounts needed for each percentage of pH change will be listed on the container label.

Sodium bisulfate and sodium carbonate are powders and can simply be sprinkled over the deep end of the pool. Muriatic acid, a liquid, must be carefully diluted; add one part acid to three parts of water, always pouring the acid into the water and not the reverse. Then pour the mixture into the pool. In all cases, retest the pH after 6 hours and correct any imbalance. But in adding chemicals, be conservative—it is a lot easier to add more than to correct an overdose.

Chlorine can be added to pool water in several different ways. The traditional forms are sodium hypochlorite, a liquid, and granular calcium hypochlorite. Both will raise the pH level. Calcium hypochlorite also adds calcium to the water and should not be used in hard-water areas. Slightly more expensive, but designed to increase the pH less abruptly, are compressed sticks or tablets containing chlorinated isocyanurates. These are placed in the skimmer baskets of the pool's filter system *(opposite)*, in floating dispensers or in automatic chlorinators, where they dissolve slowly.

Chlorine remains effective for varying lengths of time, depending on the pH level of the water, the presence of a chlorine stabilizer, the water temperature and the amount of sunlight hitting the pool. Its effectiveness also depends on the number of people using the pool; nitrogen compounds in urine and perspiration, introduced into the water by swimmers, combine with the chlorine to produce chloramines, which greatly reduce chlorine's disinfecting properties. It is chloramines, in fact, that produce the distinctive chlorine odor of pools and the stinging, reddened eyes that go with it.

To rid the pool of chloramines, dose it every two weeks with 1 pound of calcium hypochlorite per 10,000 gallons of pool water. This treatment, called superchlorination, should be done in the evening or at a time when the pool will not be used for at least 6 hours—until the chlorine level drops below 3.0 parts per million (ppm).

Other routine cleaning chores involve ridding the pool of foreign matter, from leaves to dust, and scrubbing down the walls and floor of the pool itself. Much of this cleaning is done automatically by the pool's filter system, but the strainers and filtering devices must themselves be cleaned about once a week, depending on pool use. To determine when the filter needs cleaning, note the reading on the pressure gauge on top of the filter tank when the filter is newly cleaned; clean the filter again when this reading has increased by 10 pounds per square inch (psi). Filters are cleaned either by backwashing them or hosing them down, depending on the filtering medium—which may be sand, diatomaceous earth (commonly called DE) or clustered cartridges *(pages 96-97)*.

Even with efficient filters, some dirt will inevitably settle on the sides and bottom of the pool. For a quick cleaning, sweep the dirt toward the main drain with a long-handled pool brush. For a thorough cleaning, a more effective tool is the pool vacuum *(page 95)*, which should be used about once a week.

Debris too large to pass through the drain into the filter system can be scooped out with a long-handled net called a leaf rake or collected with a curious object called a jet vacuum, or leaf gobbler. Attached to a garden hose, the jet vacuum uses water pressure to force debris into a net bag that floats above it.

Two other cleaning chores are much less routine. Occasionally, you will have to sponge off the grime along the water line with a nonabrasive tile or vinyl cleaner designed especially for pools and available from pool-supply dealers. And in the spring, when you ready the pool for seasonal use, you will have to scrub, vacuum and run the filter system continuously for up to five days, to put the water and the pool back in usable condition. Check the pressure reading hourly if the water is very dirty, and clean the filter if it shows signs of clogging.

If the standing water in a plaster pool is so dirty that you cannot see the bottom at the deep end, the quickest way to clean it is to drain the pool and scrub it down with a strong solution of muriatic acid *(page 97)*. You must never, however, drain a vinyl pool to clean it, since the weight of the water is needed to keep the vinyl in place. The most efficient way to drain a pool is to rent a submersible pump that delivers between 50 and 100 gallons per minute; it can empty a 20,000-gallon pool in about seven hours.

Locating the Traps in a Filter System

Anatomy of a filter system. To clean the water in this typical swimming pool, the water is pumped through the filter tank. Water at the bottom of the pool is drawn through a main drain; surface water is sucked through a skimmer opening at the rim. The water goes through the pump and into the filter tank, where a filter medium traps suspended dirt; then the water returns to the pool through inlets in the wall.

Relatively large bits of debris—leaves and sticks, for example—are trapped in a basket at the base of the skimmer opening (inset top). Finer pieces, such as hair and lint, are filtered out by a strainer basket at the pump (bottom inset). Both baskets must be removed and emptied about once a week. The filter must also be cleaned on a weekly basis (pages 96-97).

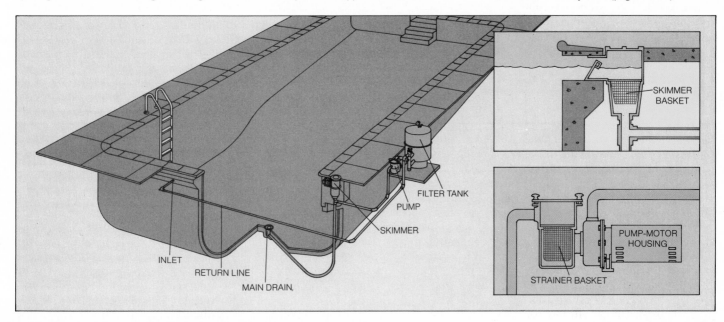

INLET
RETURN LINE
MAIN DRAIN
FILTER TANK
PUMP
SKIMMER
SKIMMER BASKET
PUMP-MOTOR HOUSING
STRAINER BASKET

Checking the Water's Chemical Balance

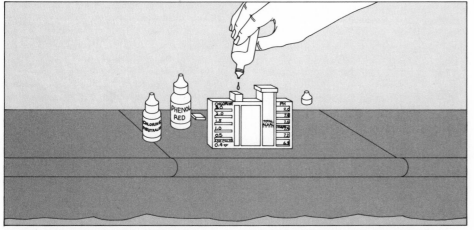

Testing pool water with a kit. A test kit has two vials, one for measuring chlorine content and the other for measuring pH, and three test chemicals: chlorine reagent, chlorine neutralizer and phenol red. To use the kit, fill the chlorine test vial with pool water taken from 18 inches below the water surface, away from inlets. Add the chlorine reagent—the instructions included with your test kit will tell you how many drops you should use. Put the cap on the vial, shake it for a few seconds and compare the resulting color with the color chart that is imprinted on the vial. Make a note of the chlorine level, measured in parts per million (ppm).

Next, fill the pH vial in the same way. Add chlorine neutralizer and phenol red. Cap the vial, shake it, then compare the resulting shade of red to the tonal chart imprinted on the vial. Note the corresponding pH reading.

Add chlorine to the pool (opposite) if the chlorine test shows less than 0.6 ppm. Correct the pH level if the test does not produce a reading between 7.4 and 7.6.

Do not use test chemicals more than 6 months old—they will give inaccurate results. Rinse the vials well with pool water after testing.

Pool-Chemical Safety

Like all highly concentrated chemicals, pool chemicals must be treated with care. For safety, observe the following simple guidelines:

☐ Never mix pool chemicals. When using more than one, allow an hour between treatments. Keep a separate measuring device for each chemical, and never allow the device to get wet. Do not reuse an empty container. Rinse it well, then discard it.

☐ Store chemicals in a cool, dry place in their original containers, off the ground and out of reach of children. Always keep chemicals covered.

☐ Never smoke while handling pool chemicals. Never leave combustible materials, such as a paper cup, in or near chemical containers.

☐ Avoid touching or inhaling any of the chemicals. Wash your hands after using them. Hose down any areas where chemicals have spilled.

☐ Read label instructions and precautions and follow them carefully.

Tracking Down the Cause of the Trouble

Getting to the root of the problem. Many of the cleaning problems that beset swimming pools spring from causes that can be corrected by adjusting either the filtration system or the water's chemical balance. The chart below and opposite is designed to help you plot a course of action by working from symptom to possible cause to recommended treatment.

For diagnosing two of the problems—water hardness and total alkalinity—you will need special test chemicals, available in kit form at pool-supply stores. The water-hardness test indicates when excessive calcium is present in the water. The test for total alkalinity indicates when the total alkaline content of all the substances in the water adds up to a figure likely to throw the

desirable pH level out of balance. Total alkalinity should range from 80 to 150 parts per million.

Other chemical correctives listed in the treatment column—such as algae inhibitor, coagulant, degreaser and antiscale solution—are sold in packaged form in pool-supply stores; recommended dosages are given on the labels.

Problem	Possible causes	Treatment
Cloudy water	Too-frequent backwashing of sand filter	Do not backwash until pressure gauge reads 10 psi above normal.
	Clogged or torn filter elements	Check the filter elements in a cartridge filter; replace any that are damaged. Add degreaser to the filter elements. Monitor pressure gauge; backwash promptly when it reaches 10 psi above normal.
	Dirt particles too fine to be trapped in filter	Add coagulant to the pool to clump dirt particles. Monitor pressure gauge closely to prevent dirt from clogging filter. Backwash promptly when pressure reads 10 psi above normal.
	High pH	Check and correct pH level. Test pH daily until it is stabilized.
	Chalking paint	Repaint the pool every 3 years.
Water turns blue, brown or black when first treated with chemicals.	Chlorine combining with metals—iron, copper, manganese—to form minute particles	Check and correct pH level. Then run filter continuously to remove metallic sediment, checking pressure frequently and backwashing as needed. Vacuum out any sediment remaining in pool.
Standing water turns green, black or reddish brown. Dark blotches and slippery spots form on walls.	Green algae	Superchlorinate, concentrating treatment in areas of visible algae growth. Run filter constantly for 6 to 8 hours, checking pressure frequently and backwashing as needed. Vacuum any remaining algae from pool surfaces. Check and correct pH level. Add an algae inhibitor.
	Black algae	Scrub algae spots with a wire brush to expose growth buds. Turn off filter. When water is still, superchlorinate, concentrating chlorine near areas of growth. Restart filter after 6 hours. Brush and vacuum dead algae from pool surfaces. Check filter pressure frequently; backwash as needed. Check and correct pH level. Add an algae inhibitor.
	Mustard algae	Put all pool tools into water, to be treated with the water. Superchlorinate; adjust the pH level to a reading between 7.4 and 7.6. Brush algae from pool walls, and add a special algaecide—designed for mustard algae—to pool. Run the filter continuously until water is clear, backwashing as needed. Vacuum any remaining algae from pool surfaces.
Foamy water	Excess algaecide	Add fresh water to dilute the concentration. Test chlorine and pH levels frequently until their readings are normal.
Chlorine odor	Nitrogen compounds in pool water reduce chlorine efficiency	Superchlorinate; check and correct pH level. Thereafter, check and correct chlorine and pH levels more frequently.
Stained walls	Low pH and low total alkalinity	Check and correct pH level with pH booster. Test total alkalinity; increase it to acceptable levels by adding sodium bicarbonate to pool.
Corroded pipes and fittings	Low pH and low total alkalinity	Treat as above.

Problem	Possible causes	Treatment
Etched pool surfaces	Low total alkalinity and insufficient dissolved calcium	Test total alkalinity; increase it to acceptable levels by adding sodium bicarbonate to pool. Use calcium carbonate to increase calcium hardness.
Scaling on pool surfaces, filter, water-heating hardware	High total alkalinity and high calcium hardness	Test total alkalinity; reduce it to acceptable levels by adding muriatic acid or sodium bisulfate to pool. Check and correct pH level as necessary. Add anti-scale solution to filter tank.
Erratic and rapidly changing pH levels	Low total alkalinity	Test total alkalinity; increase it to acceptable levels by adding sodium bicarbonate to pool. To further stabilize water chemistry, add cyanuric acid. Use stabilized chlorine for regular chlorine treatments.

Ridding a Pool of Dirt and Debris

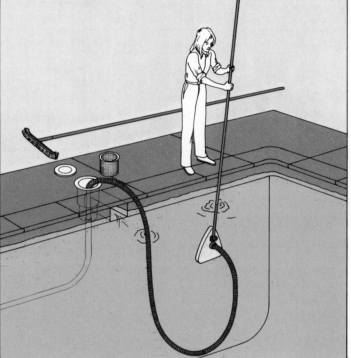

Two ways to remove leaves. To scoop water-logged leaves and debris from a pool bottom, rest the metal frame of a leaf rake—actually a long-handled net—on the pool bottom; pull the rake toward you, trapping the leaves in the net. To scoop up floating objects, dip the rake beneath the objects, catching them from below.

To use a jet vacuum, or leaf gobbler (inset), attach a mesh collector bag to its plastic base, using a fine mesh for small debris, a larger mesh for leaves. Attach a garden hose to the coupling on the vacuum plate, and a long pole to the bracket provided. Turn on the water full force, and lower the vacuum to the bottom of the pool. Push it slowly along the bottom in parallel strokes, filling the collector bag.

The jet vacuum shown here, with a brush on the bottom, is designed for vinyl pools; models for plaster pools roll over the bottom on wheels.

Using a pool vacuum. Assemble the vacuum by attaching the hose and a long pool pole to the vacuum head. Slowly submerge the vacuum head until it rests on the pool bottom, then submerge the rest of the hose so that it fills completely. Attach the hose to the suction outlet in the skimmer or to the separate vacuum outlet in the pool wall, if your pool has one. Then switch the filter system to the vacuum setting.

To operate the vacuum, guide the head over the pool walls and bottom in parallel strokes. Beginning at the center of the pool, bring the head across the bottom and up the sides to the water line. Then reverse the direction, pushing the head back to the center of the pool. Repeat this action, moving around the pool's edge until the walls and bottom have been vacuumed.

Flushing Trapped Dirt from Three Types of Filter

Backwashing a sand filter. Turn off the pump, empty the pump strainer basket and turn off the pool-water heater, if your pool has one. If the pump has a rotary valve, as shown here, turn the valve handle to the backwash position and start the pump. When water in the sight glass runs clear—usually in three to five minutes—stop the pump. If the valve has a rinse setting, turn the handle to RINSE for about 30 seconds. When the water runs clear again, stop the pump and turn the handle back to FILTER. (If the filter has no sight glass, monitor the appearance of the waste water as it drains away.) If the valve lacks a rinse setting, turn the handle back to filter and restart the pump. If the system has a cylindrical valve, as shown below, pull up the plunger handle and start the pump. When the waste water is running clear, stop the pump and push down the handle.

If your filter has four separate valves to control water flow instead of a single master valve, backwash the filter by closing the two valves that are normally open and opening the two that are normally closed. When the waste water runs clear, return the valves to their original positions.

Backwashing a DE filter. Shut off the pump and the heater, if there is one, and clean the strainer basket. If the filter has a separation tank, open its gate valve; otherwise, open its drain. Set the filter for backwashing in either of two ways: If the filter has a cylindrical valve, as shown at right, backwash it by pulling up the plunger handle. If the filter has a rotary valve, as shown above, turn the valve to the backwash setting. In either case, start the pump and monitor the appearance of the waste water—in a sight glass or at the drain. When the waste water runs clear, shut off the pump. Start and stop the pump a few times more, or until the water runs clear continuously. Return the water-flow valve to its normal position for filtering; if there is a separation tank, close the gate valve.

To replenish the diatomaceous earth, turn on the pump and clear the filter of air by opening its air-relief valve. When water trickles from the valve, close it. Mix a thin slurry of diatomaceous earth and water, and pour it into the skimmer opening at the pool. Use a 1-pound coffee can of earth for every 5 feet of filter area—or the amount listed on the system's specification plate.

Clean the separation tank by shutting off the pump, opening the air-relief valve, and removing the drain cap. Open the tank, remove the strainer bag and dispose of its contents. Hose off the bag, return it to the tank and close the tank. Close the valve and replace the cap.

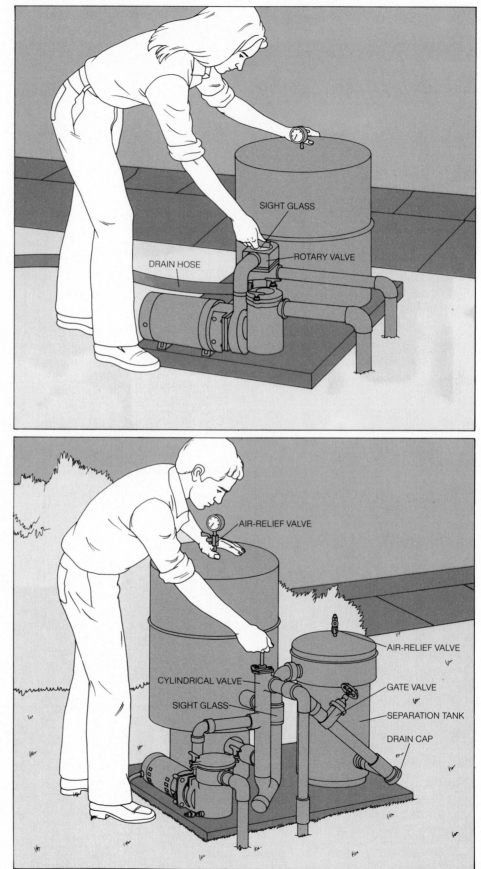

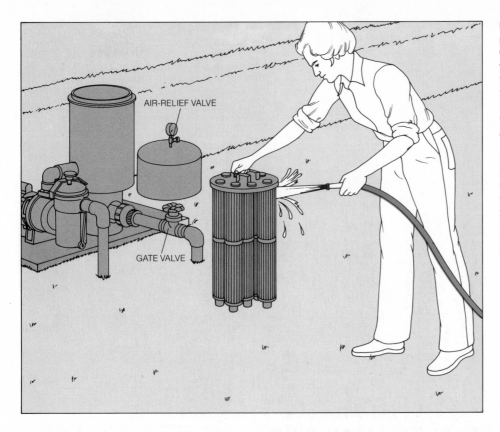

Hosing down a cartridge filter. Turn off the pump and the pool-water heater, if there is one. Clean the strainer basket, and close any gate valves leading to or from the filter tank. Open the tank air-relief valve, if there is one. Unlock the tank lid and lift out the cluster of cartridge filters. Using a garden hose, rinse off the cluster while inspecting the individual cartridges for holes and tears. Replace any that are defective.

If water alone fails to remove dirt from the cartridges, douse each one with filter-cleaning solution, available from pool-supply stores. If this treatment fails, install new cartridges. Return the filter cluster to the tank, replace the lid and lock it securely. Open any gate valves and turn on the pump. When water begins to trickle from the air-relief valve, close it.

Spring-cleaning the Pool

Scrubbing down an empty pool. Drain the pool with a submersible pump; then hose off loose dirt from the pool walls, driving it toward the main drain, and pump out this water. Using a cup and a sponge, remove any water remaining in the skimmer. Unscrew the covers of underwater lighting fixtures, remove the fixtures from their niches, then flush out the niches with the hose.

Wearing goggles, rubber gloves and rubber boots, and using a long-handled nylon brush, scrub down the walls and floor with a one-to-four solution of muriatic acid. Have a helper, similarly attired, pour the solution down the walls from a large plastic watering can. Clean the pool in sections, hosing off each section after scrubbing it; push the waste water toward the main drain. When the entire pool has been scrubbed, run the pump a final time to remove the puddle of waste water around the main drain.

To mix the acid solution, fill a 40-gallon plastic trash can four fifths full with water, then fill it the rest of the way with acid. Wear goggles and rubber gloves and do not splash. After scrubbing the pool, flush the trash can and the watering can with fresh water. To clean the main drain and the submersible pump of acid, remove the drain cover, set the pump in the drain, flood the area with fresh water and pump the water out.

Dealing With the Aftermath of a Disaster

The worst thing you can do after a fire or a flood is to sit around waiting for the insurance claims adjuster to arrive. Although the adjuster and other experts must necessarily assess and repair the damage, immediate action on your part can reduce the damage and the cleanup costs by half. In the aftermath of a flood—whether caused by a storm, a severe plumbing leak, or a fire fighter's hose—a house and its contents should be dried out as quickly as possible to prevent mildew growth, fungus attack and pervasive, lingering odors.

The first order of business in this cleaning emergency is to turn off the electricity, either by flipping the main circuit breaker or by pulling the main fuse. If you have advance warning of a flood, you can do this before you leave. If not, your first steps on returning must take you directly to the service panel *(box, below)*. Once the power is off, it is safe to begin bailing and mopping.

A little standing water in a house can be removed with mops and sponges or with a wet-and-dry utility vacuum cleaner. If you have more than an inch or two of water to deal with, rent a submersible pump from a tool-rental agency. These pumps will run for up to 3½ hours on a fully charged automobile battery; if you need to run the pump longer than that, disconnect the battery after 3½ hours, replace it in the car and recharge it by running the engine at fast idle for about half an hour.

At full speed, a submersible pump powered by a battery will expel up to 26 gallons of water per minute, emptying 2 feet of standing water from a 20-foot-square basement in four hours. If a flood has dumped more than 3 feet of water into your basement, pump it out in stages, removing no more than 3 feet in a day to prevent walls from buckling.

After most of the water is gone, you will be left with a sloppy, wet mixture of mud and debris too thick for the pump to handle. Push this muck to a door or window with a long-handled squeegee, and shovel it out. Muck left in a basement may have to be removed by forming a bucket brigade to carry it to ground level. Then rinse down the walls and the floor with fresh water, and mop up the moisture that remains.

Next, the house and its contents must be dried. Although most of the objects in the house should be dried rapidly, there are some exceptions. Leather goods and books, for example, must be dried slowly to prevent brittleness. Suggestions for ways to minimize damage in drying artwork, furniture, upholstery and bedding appear in the guide on page 103.

Drying the house itself calls for demolition and carpentry skills, because every part of the structure that has been flooded must be exposed to the air. Wall cavities must be breached so that any water trapped within can drain and so that air can circulate around structural lumber, preventing mildew and decay. Wet insulation must be removed completely and replaced with new material after the wall cavities are dry. Water pooled above a ceiling must be drained into a bucket or a trash can and the globes of any ceiling lights emptied.

After electrical power can be safely restored, you can speed up the drying process with electric fans or dehumidifiers. If weather permits, open all the doors and windows and set up fans to aid air circulation. If doors and windows must be kept closed, use a dehumidifier to take excess moisture out of the air. In cold, damp weather, use a portable space heater. Propane heaters are preferable because they are clean-burning; kerosene heaters, though effective, can leave a greasy film on walls and ceilings. Propane heaters can be rented from rental agencies; they come with canisters of fuel and a hose to connect the canister to the heater. Before using the heater, be sure to read the accompanying safety precautions and instructions.

Water and Wiring: A Chancy Combination

Any time house wiring and water come together, there is a danger of electrical shock. A cautious approach to entering a flooded house and turning off the electrical power is absolutely crucial to your safety *(opposite, top)*.

Because circuit-breaker and fuse panels are commonly built into dark basements or closets, you will need a flashlight to reach them; do not plug in a work light or try to turn on an overhead light. If there is moisture on or near the panel or if there is standing water in the room, wear tall, leak-free rubber boots and stand on a dry wooden ladder or stool while disarming the panel. Never touch any other object with your free hand while touching the panel: Electricians advise working with one hand in a pocket to avoid the possibility. Better still, use a dry wooden or plastic stick to operate the main cutoff switch or to pull the main fuse block.

If your panel is in a room with submerged electrical receptacles, you must call an electrician to turn off the power. The electrician will wear special, heavily insulated boots and gloves to approach the panel or may opt instead to dismantle the electric meter, which governs all power to the house from outside. In any case, before restoring any power to the house, you will need an electrician to check any receptacles or switches that have been exposed to water, to test all of the circuit breakers or fuses, to make necessary repairs, and to tell you how long a damaged circuit must dry before it can be used safely. Further, the electrician may be able to reconnect an undamaged circuit or two to provide temporary power for drying the house.

Turning Off the Power

Shutting down a circuit-breaker panel. Following all of the safety precautions in the box opposite, and wearing thick, dry rubber or leather gloves, use your knuckle to flip off the main breaker switch located at the top of the panel. Using the back of your hand is a safety precaution: In the unlikely event that the dampness transmits a small current to your body, any contraction of your arm muscles will automatically jerk your hand away from the panel.

Disarming a fuse box. Wearing thick, dry gloves, use a dry wooden or plastic rod to lift the handle of the main fuse block; insert the rod between the handle and the front of the block. With a hand at either end of the rod, pull out the fuse block, shutting off the flow of current to the whole house. When disarming a fuse box, take care to observe all of the safety precautions prescribed in the box opposite.

Instead of a main fuse, some older fuse boxes have a cutoff lever mounted at the top of one side of the box. To cut the power, simply push the lever to the off position with a dry rod.

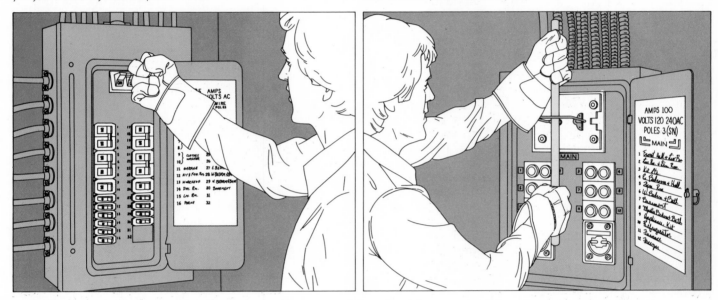

Bailing Out Standing Water

Using a submersible pump. Connect a long garden hose to the discharge fitting on the top of the pump. Wrap the power cables around the hose, and lift the pump by the hose and cables to lower it slowly into the water until it rests on the floor. Snake the hose out a window or door and extend it to the street or storm sewer. Place a 12-volt car battery in a dry spot, and start the pump by connecting the alligator clamps on the pump cables to the battery terminals.

While running the pump, periodically check the volume of water surging from the hose. If the volume drops abruptly, stop the pump by disconnecting the alligator clamps from the battery terminals; clean away any debris that is blocking the intake screen on the bottom of the housing. When you have finished pumping out the standing water, clean the pump by immersing it in a bucket of clean water and running it until the discharge water is clear.

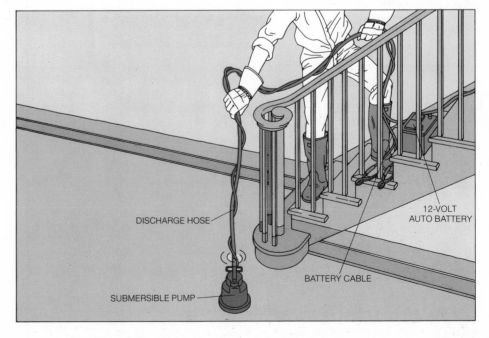

DISCHARGE HOSE

12-VOLT AUTO BATTERY

BATTERY CABLE

SUBMERSIBLE PUMP

Getting out mud and debris. After pumping out flood water, use a long-handled squeegee to push the sodden residue of mud and debris to an exterior door or window where it can be shoveled away. If you do not have a squeegee, improvise one by splitting a short length of old garden hose and jamming it over the tines of a garden rake (inset). Flush the floors and walls with clean water, and sop up any remaining moisture with a sponge or a mop.

If you shovel debris out a window, as here, protect garden beds below with a makeshift wooden trough. Construct the trough from two pieces of 1-by-12-inch lumber, nailed perpendicular to each other. If the trough must reach farther than 12 feet, use 2-inch-thick lumber.

Opening Wall Cavities for Air Circulation

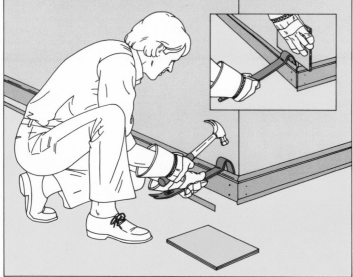

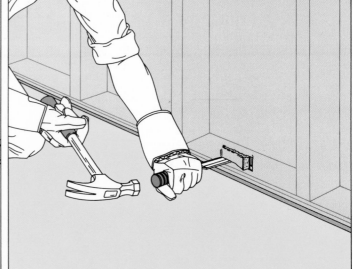

1 Prying off the baseboard. After removing the quarter-round shoe molding (page 75, Step 1), hammer the curved end of a pry bar between the top of the baseboard and the wall surface. Wedge a scrap of plywood behind the bar to protect the wall (inset), and pull the free end of the bar upward, separating the baseboard from the wall by about 1 inch. Then release the bar to allow the baseboard to spring back toward the wall, leaving the nailheads slightly exposed. Pull out the nails with the claw end of the bar. Repeat at 2-foot intervals along the wall until the entire baseboard is freed.

2 Piercing the wall for ventilation. Use a hammer and a wood chisel to open a hole about 1 inch high by 3 inches wide through the drywall or plaster, about 1 inch off the floor. Punch a similar hole directly above the first, several inches below the ceiling. Repeat between every pair of studs along the length of the wall.

To find the first pair of studs, tap along the wall with a hammer; it will sound hollow between studs. Thereafter, place holes every 16 inches.

Removing Wet Insulation from Exterior Walls

1 **Breaking away wall surfacing.** Remove the baseboard as in Step 1, opposite. Then, wearing gloves and using a heavy hammer or a pry bar, batter holes through the interior wall to a point just above the mud line left by the flood water. In drywall construction, reach into the holes and pull the sodden wallboard off the studs, removing nails as necessary to free the wallboard. In a plaster wall, insert a pry bar into the access holes and lever away the plaster and lath.

2 **Removing ruined insulation.** Push a 14-inch board between the dry insulation and the wall, just above the opening, to compress the insulation for cutting. Then, using the board as a straight-edge, slice through the insulation horizontally with a utility knife. Pull the wet insulation out of the wall and discard it.

First Aid for a Waterlogged Ceiling

Draining a water-filled ceiling. Place a bucket on the floor directly below any dripping water and, standing on a ladder, lance the ceiling with an ice pick or a nail *(below)*. If the ceiling is actually bulging under the weight of water trapped above, place a leakproof trash can beneath the center point of the bulge; then stand away from the sagging area and poke a drainage hole into it with a broom or mop handle *(right)*. Be prepared to step back quickly, because a portion of the sodden ceiling may collapse.

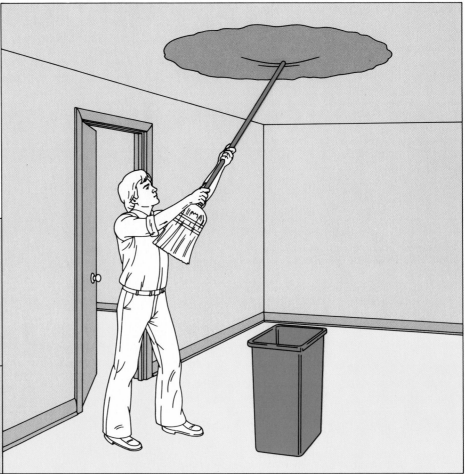

Boosting the Drying Power of Fresh Drafts of Air

Fanning the breeze along. When weather permits, open all the windows and doors of the house. Note the direction of the prevailing breeze, and speed its passage into the house by placing a fan in a window on the windward side. Set up a second fan to exhaust the air on the opposite side. If the air current is slowed by corners or if the distance between the fans is great, use intermediate fans as well.

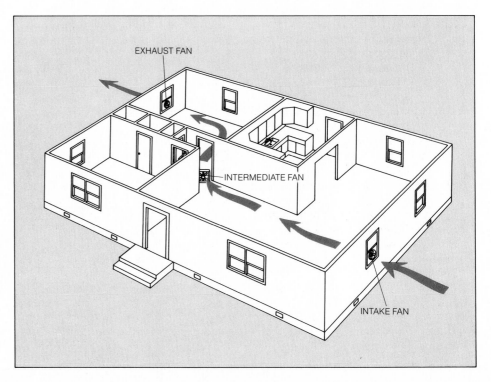

Hooking Up Emergency Heat

Lighting a propane space heater. A propane space-heating system consists of a heating unit (*far right*), connected by a heavy rubber hose to a metal propane-gas cylinder (*near right*). To set up the heater, place the two components at least 7 feet apart, with the heater resting on concrete or plywood in the center of the wet room. Open a window slightly for ventilation. Connect the regulator and hose to the gas outlet by pulling the brass mounting nut away from the metal tip of the regulator and inserting the tip into the gas outlet. Push the nut forward and tighten it, first by hand, then with a wrench. Attach the other end of the hose to the heating unit in the same way. Open the gas valve and listen for leaks. If you hear any, retighten the fittings until the hissing stops. Close the valve.

To start the heater, plug in the power cord and reopen the gas valve. Turn the thermostat knob all the way clockwise to ignite the flame. Adjust the thermostat to the desired room temperature. To turn off the heater, close the gas valve. Wait until the flame in the heating unit dies; then turn off the thermostat and unplug the heater.

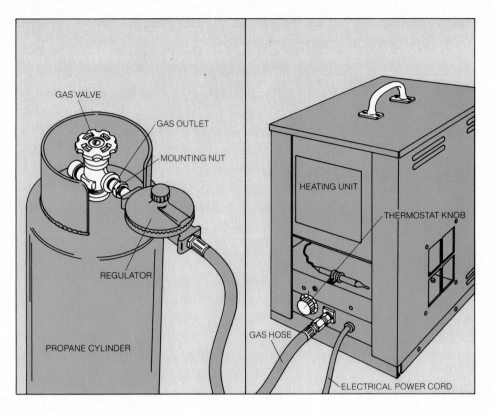

GAS VALVE
GAS OUTLET
MOUNTING NUT
HEATING UNIT
THERMOSTAT KNOB
REGULATOR
GAS HOSE
PROPANE CYLINDER
ELECTRICAL POWER CORD

Salvaging Water-damaged Furnishings

No amount of insurance can replace heirloom home furnishings or restore ruined possessions of sentimental value. Listed below are common household items that can be damaged by water and some quick actions you can take to minimize the damage.

□ AREA RUGS: Lay rugs across clotheslines so that air can reach both sides. Direct fans over them, if possible, to speed drying. Do not replace a rug on the floor until it is thoroughly dry.

□ ARTWORK: Paintings, prints and posters should be removed from their frames. If there is a paper backing, remove it at once. Store the art temporarily in a cool, dry place, away from sunlight, to await further treatment. Canvas paintings should be dried face down on a towel. Art on paper should be pressed beneath towel-covered plywood under a heavy weight; remove the plywood occasionally to let air reach the paper. If the towel is damp, replace it.

□ BOOKS: If the pages are soaked, sprinkle a few tablespoons of cornstarch or talcum powder between them; brush it off after several hours. If the pages are simply damp, stand the books on end with their pages separated for an hour; then stack them and press them for another hour to prevent the pages from crinkling. Keep drying and pressing until the pages are dry. Books that cannot be treated immediately can be refrigerated to prevent mildew.

□ CARPETS: To avoid stains, remove all furniture from the wet carpet. Open windows and doors to allow air to circulate over the carpet. If you cannot get professional help within two days, rent a steam cleaner (*page 66*) to extract most of the water.

Rubber carpet pads can withstand soaking, but natural-fiber pads, most commonly jute, will have to be replaced; take up the carpeting, and dry it as you would an area rug.

□ FURNITURE AND BEDDING: If weather permits, take wet furniture outdoors to dry, but keep it out of direct sunlight to prevent warping and fading. Remove drawers and open doors; if they are swollen shut, remove the back if possible, and push them out from behind.

Take cushions off upholstered furniture and dry them separately. Remove slip covers for cleaning. If you cannot have down-filled pillows and cushions dry cleaned immediately, tumble them in the clothes dryer with several terry-cloth towels and a pair of clean sneakers. Feather-filled bed pillows and quilts can be dried in this way or laid across clotheslines outdoors. Reposition them frequently, shaking them to distribute the feathers. Damp mattresses may be air dried or fan dried; water-logged mattresses should be discarded.

□ LEATHER GOODS: Wipe leather with a damp cloth, then with a dry cloth. Keep leather items away from direct sunlight and heat while they dry.

□ METAL FIXTURES: Wet locks should be taken apart, wiped with kerosene, and then oiled. Alternatively, squirt light household oil into the bolt opening and keyhole, and work the lock and knob to distribute the oil. Clean hinges with kerosene, then oil them.

Dry faucets and light fixtures with a towel. Coat them with petroleum jelly to keep humidity from corroding them while the house is drying.

4

Pestproofing a House

Chemical warfare. Water from a garden hose pours into a sprayer containing a concentrated pesticide. Sprayed along the house foundation and the adjoining strip of grass or soil, it will create an invisible barrier, repelling such house-invading pests as ants, crickets and box-elder bugs. When the cylindrical cap is replaced on the tank, pressure is built up by pumping the handle until there is sufficient force to release a fine mist through the trigger-controlled wand.

No home is ever completely free of pests. Termites, which destroy the very fabric of the house, may not be a problem, but fleas and ticks may find a mobile breeding ground in the fur of a dog or cat. And no sooner are mice or cockroaches banished than spiders and crickets may infiltrate the basement or bats and bees take over the attic. In their struggle to repel such guests, Americans spend billions of dollars each year for pesticides and for the services of professional pest controllers.

It is a war fought on many fronts against a host of foes. Among the most pernicious is the termite, whose appetite for wood causes millions of dollars in structural damage every year. Although the termite's range is nationwide, these insects are most destructive in the warm-climate zone that stretches across the southern part of the country. In a more limited area, the Pacific Northwest, the termite's depredations are equaled and sometimes surpassed by those of the wood-eating carpenter ant.

Rivaling the termite for notoriety is the cockroach, a remote relative of the termite that has remained virtually unchanged for 400 million years. Cockroaches can turn up anywhere, but they are especially troublesome in urban areas because of their ability to move with ease through entire apartment buildings and multifamily dwellings: An adult cockroach can pass through an opening of only $\frac{1}{16}$ inch. Although they prefer the kitchen, where they hide under stoves, refrigerators and sinks, cockroaches have made themselves at home in every room. The American habit of eating while watching television has been a boon to the cockroach, which can live for weeks on crumbs left in bedrooms, living rooms and dens. Some cockroaches have even staked out this new feeding ground by taking up residence in the warm recesses of the television cabinet.

Other pests are seasonal in their impact. The ubiquitous flea, of which there are more than 1,600 species in North America, is a summer offender that is often considered worse than the termite or the cockroach in hot, humid areas. Eggs that are dropped in the late spring from the fur of a flea-carrying dog or cat onto carpets or upholstery may hatch weeks or months later and cause a massive infestation in the house.

Americans have learned a great deal about pests and how to deal with them since the days when housewives were likely to hang the feet of a hare or a stag at the foot of the bed to get rid of bedbugs. This chapter discusses the most effective techniques for keeping pests out of the house and for evicting or destroying any of the 27 most common varieties *(pages 118-125)* that you are likely to come up against.

A Multipronged Approach to Controlling Pests

Getting rid of such unwanted intruders as ants, cockroaches, mice, spiders and wasps may not be a persistent cleaning problem, but it is often a critical one. Pests can be merely unsightly or downright hazardous. They can destroy foodstuffs, clothing, furniture, rugs or books; in extreme cases, they can even undermine the structure of the house.

A veritable arsenal of chemicals exists to combat these unwelcome guests; the weapons range from paralyzing sprays to dusts and paint-on emulsions whose effects may last many months (chart, page 113). But the first line of defense, often overlooked, is routine cleaning that reaches into the places where pests nest and feed, coupled with simple repairs that seal off their hiding places and the routes they travel.

Cleaning a house to keep it pest-free calls for thoroughness rather than specialized equipment (box, below). Used diligently, an ordinary sponge and a vacuum cleaner will remove the food particles on which pests feed, the pockets of dust in which they hide, even their eggs and larvae—and sometimes the pests themselves. The same thorough-ness, carried outdoors, will clean up many of the yard conditions that encourage large pest populations—piles of rotting leaves, puddles of stagnant water, uncut grass and unkempt shrubbery.

Minor repairs can also forestall a major pest invasion. Inspect the house for cracks that open up as a result of wear, settling or faulty construction. These are favorite hiding places for pests, and they can be passageways for pests traveling into the house from outside.

Indoors, look for these gaps between floorboards, behind baseboards, at the back of cabinets and countertops. Check the plumbing chases, especially where they pass through the backs of cabinets; when improperly sealed, these openings provide a natural route into the warm, damp, dark cavities that lie beneath—a favorite haunt of bugs.

Outdoors, inspect the foundation wall; some pests can find their way into the house through even a narrow crack. Others enter through gaps between the foundation wall and the wooden sill plate above. Carry your inspection into the attic, where a sliver of light shining through from outdoors indicates a space large enough for wasps and hornets to squeeze through. And unscreened vents in the roof or eaves are an open invitation to squirrels and bats.

Plugging, caulking and screening these cracks, gaps, holes and leaks—using the methods shown on the following pages —is often sufficient to prevent a major infestation. And sometimes such routine maintenance procedures can cure a minor infestation or, if chemical action does become necessary, they will protect your house long after the last traces of pesticide have wafted away.

However, there is one pest problem that is likely to require more complex treatment: termites. To be really effective, some preventive measures against termites must be built into a house during construction; others can be incorporated into an existing structure (page 111). Termite-proofing can be done by improving drainage around the house, increasing the ventilation in a crawl space, and creating a kind of cordon sanitaire between the soil where the termites live and the woodwork where they feed. Though major in scope, this last job requires only grading and carpentry.

Housekeeping to Keep Pests at Bay

Routine cleaning is often sufficient to prevent pest problems if you take the trouble to carry the cleaning into areas where pests shelter and feed. Remove dust and crumbs from cracks and crevices and from dark, damp places. Pay special attention to cracks between floorboards and around countertops, cabinets and baseboards; to gaps between loose flooring and tiles; to the pockets of space behind loose wallpaper; to pipe chases—the openings through which plumbing passes to reach kitchen and bathroom fixtures. Reach into the dark corners of cabinets, particularly those that are seldom used and therefore seldom opened.

In the kitchen, remove kick plates and grilles from the refrigerator and dishwasher, and vacuum the floor beneath them. Many stoves have removable broiler drawers, for access to the floor. Vacuum away the dust on refrigerator coils, and scrub the wall behind the stove to prevent grease build-up, which cockroaches and ants thrive on. Rinse out the garbage can from time to time, and keep it tightly covered.

Store unrefrigerated food in tightly sealed containers—jars, cans or plastic bags. Check shopping bags when you come in from the store, to find hitch-hiking cockroaches before they can take up residence in your kitchen. Do not allow stacks of paper bags, newspapers or magazines to accumulate; they are prime hiding places for bugs.

Elsewhere in the house, vacuum be-neath furniture and under the loose edges of carpets and rugs. Reposition the rugs and carpets periodically, or rearrange the furniture, so that no part of the rug or carpet is permanently inaccessible to cleaning. Use vacuum-cleaner attachments to remove dust from the deep crevices of upholstered furniture, the folds of drapes, and the fins of radiators and baseboard heaters. Also dust around door hinges and picture frames and under wall hangings. Occasionally, remove heating registers and vacuum or wash behind them.

Before you store seasonal clothing, clean it—especially woolen items. Then make sure the doors or drawers of the storage units close tightly. If they do not, seal them with masking tape.

Pinpointing the Outdoor Trouble Spots

FLUE LINER

GABLE VENT

DOWNSPOUT

OUTDOOR LIGHT FIXTURE

ROOF GUTTER

CRACK   CRAWL-SPACE VENT

LEAKY FAUCET

WOODPILE

STANDING WATER

Preventing a pest invasion. Many of the pests that enter a house from outdoors are encouraged by conditions that can be easily avoided. Woodpiles and compost heaps should be located far from the house foundation. So should garbage, which should be kept in cans fitted with snug lids. Uncut grass is an ideal environment for pests, and untrimmed shrubbery that brushes against the house wall provides a natural bridge through an open window.

Standing water and boggy ground especially encourage gnats and mosquitoes. Place a con-

crete splash block beneath a downspout; fix dripping faucets; fill in depressions where water tends to collect. In some cases, you may need to install drainage ditches or even underground drainage fields. Filter or frequently change the water in pools and birdbaths so that it does not become stagnant.

Fill cracks in the foundation wall *(page 109)*, and caulk gaps that open between the foundation wall and the siding and between the siding and the frames of doors and windows *(page 110)*. Install screening behind the vents that provide air

circulation through the crawl space. Repair door and window screens; at the same time, check the screens for fit, and fix them if they do not sit snugly in their frames.

Clean debris from roof gutters every fall; carpet beetles can breed in accumulated leaves or bird's nests. Screen all attic openings—gable, soffit and window vents, as well as chimney flue liners. Finally, to reduce the number of flying insects around open doors and windows in the summertime, install yellow insect bulbs in your outdoor lighting fixtures.

A kitchen that invites invasion. Everything a pest needs for survival is abundantly present in the kitchen shown at right—sufficient moisture and plenty of nooks and crannies in which to find food and shelter. Routine maintenance will dispose of most of these attractions. Repair any leaky faucet. Use caulk or simple carpentry to close any openings that lead into the cavity below the false bottom of a cabinet; these may range from hairline cracks along the floor to wedge-shaped spaces along loosened joints. Fill and seal open pipe chases *(page 110)*. Also caulk cracks around countertops, especially cracks that open behind the backsplash. Finally, resist the temptation to save paper bags; roaches, in particular, like to lay eggs in the folds.

A room ripe for takeover. The general state of disrepair of the living room at right makes it not only shabby looking, but a prime target area for pests. They will enter the house through crevices around the window frames and doorframes and take refuge in a variety of places—behind the peeling wallpaper, in cracks along the bottom of the baseboard and in dust pockets that collect in broken floorboards. All these conditions are easily correctible. The window and door cracks can be filled with spackling compound, the baseboard crack sealed with caulk, and the broken floorboards patched with splines of matching wood *(opposite)*. The loose sections of wallpaper can be reglued.

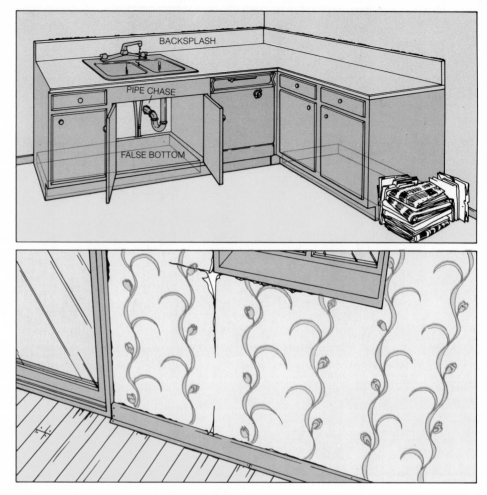

Sealing Up the Entry Points for Pests

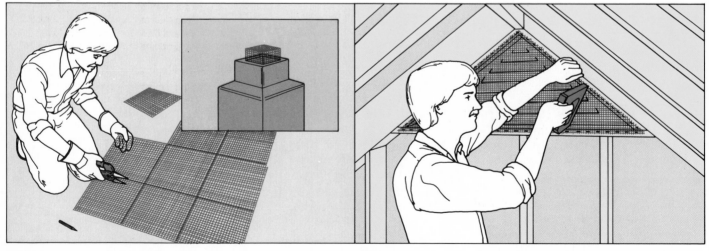

Screening chimneys and vents. To keep squirrels and birds from getting into your chimney, you can construct a box screen of hardware cloth—¼-inch galvanized-steel mesh—that will fit snugly inside the flue liner. First, hold the piece of hardware cloth over the flue and mark the flue's inside dimensions on the wire with a colored crayon, allowing for a margin of at least 12 inches on all four sides. Then cut into the hardware cloth as far as the corners of the marked rectangle, using tin snips *(above, left)*. Fold the resulting flaps along the edges of the rectangle to make an open-ended box. Fit the box into the flue liner, with the open end down, so that the mesh will protrude 6 inches above the top of the flue liner *(inset)*.

In order to screen a louvered attic vent *(above, right)* or any opening under the eaves of your house, cut a piece of window screening that is large enough to overlap the edge of the vent by at least 1 inch on each side. Then attach the screening to the inside edges of the vent, using a staple gun to fasten it at 2-inch intervals to the wooden frame all around.

Filling a crack in masonry. To prepare a crack in a poured-concrete or block foundation wall for patching mortar, widen the gap to about 1 inch, using a hammer and a cold chisel. Clean out the crack with a wire brush, then smooth a thin coat of patching mortar on the sides of the crack. After the mortar has set for about a minute, fill the crack with more patching mortar, applied with a pointing trowel. Keep the mortar moist for three or four days by sprinkling or spraying it twice daily with water.

If the mortar crumbles with changes of weather, chisel it away and clean the crack as before. Replace the mortar with mastic joint sealer, filling the crack to within ¼ inch of the surface. Soften the joint sealer with a propane torch, and press it into place with a putty knife. When the joint sealer has cooled, fill the remainder of the crack with patching mortar.

Setting in a floor spline. For a floorboard crack wider than ¼ inch, use a router with a narrow bit to make its width uniform. Cut a spline, a thin strip of matching wood, to the width, length and depth of the crack. Coat the inside of the crack and the edges of the spline with yellow glue; then tap the spline into place with a wooden mallet. Sand the patch even with the floorboards if necessary, and blend it into its surroundings with the appropriate sealer and finish (*page 16*).

If a crack is narrower than ¼ inch, it need not be filled, but it must have careful attention during cleaning to keep it from sheltering vermin.

EAU CLAIRE DISTRICT LIBRARY

Filling cracks with sealants and fillers. Out of doors and in indoor areas where moisture is present, fill narrow cracks—no wider than ¼ inch—with an all-purpose sealant applied with a caulking gun. Prepare the crack by scraping out dirt, old sealant, and flaking paint with a putty knife. Then position the tip of the caulking gun at one end of the crack, tilting the gun toward the other end. Apply even pressure to the trigger and draw the point of the gun steadily down the crack, dispensing a bead of sealant that fills the crack and slightly overlaps each edge. Smooth the bead with a wet finger or a damp cloth.

For wider cracks, such as the gap between exterior siding and the house foundation, stuff the opening with oakum or sponge-rubber weather stripping. Force it into the gap with a screwdriver, leaving about ¼ inch at the surface. Then cover the caulking with sealant, as above.

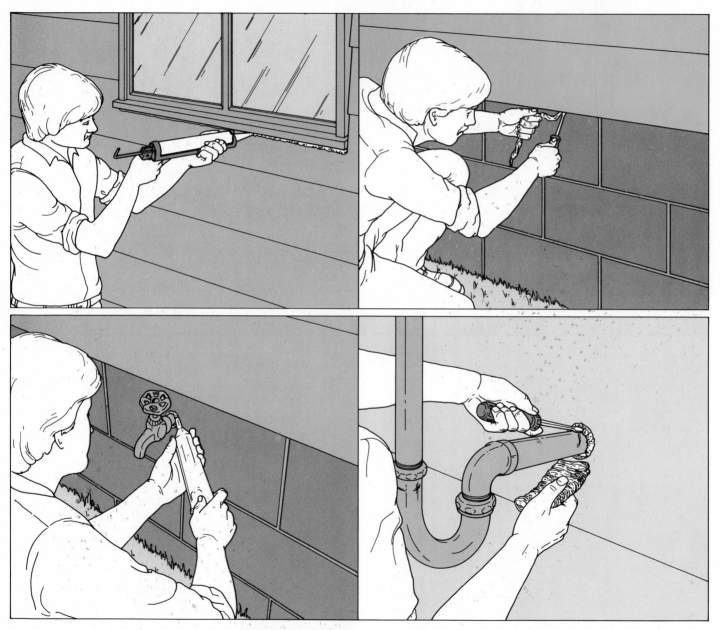

Sealing openings around pipes and conduits. To fill a narrow gap around an outdoor faucet or around a pipe or conduit passing through a foundation wall, use an all-purpose sealant packaged in a squeeze tube. Tilt the tube as you would a caulking gun (*above, left*) and squeeze the tube from the bottom. Seal gaps wider than ¼ inch with patching mortar (*page 109*).

To seal a pipe chase underneath a sink, push wads of steel wool into the gap with a broad-tipped screwdriver (*above, right*). Fill the space to within ¼ inch of the wall surface. Then fill the remaining space with all-purpose sealant; the sealant can be dispensed from a squeeze tube as above, or applied with a putty knife if the gap is a wide one.

Keeping Termites Out of a House

Although termites invade houses by tunneling into their timbers, the most common species *(page 123)* live in damp soil, entering the wood only to feed. In a termite-resistant house, all wood is kept away from the soil, and the masonry foundation has no narrow crevices in which termites can hide the mud shelter tubes that they use to travel between soil and wood. Ideally these features are put into a house when it is built—especially in termite-prone areas—but some can be added later.

To eliminate the dampness that nurtures termites, good drainage around the foundation is essential *(page 107)*. A crawl space should have one vent for every 200 square feet to keep the soil beneath the house dry, and grass and shrubs in front of the vents should be trimmed so that they do not block air flow. Clearing debris from a crawl space also helps dispel the dampness—and makes it easier to inspect the foundation for the termites' shelter tubes. If moisture persists in the crawl space despite ventilation, cover the soil with plastic sheeting or roofing felt. This will keep the dampness from permeating the floor joists above, and they will be less vulnerable to termite attack.

Wood too close to the soil is an open invitation to termites. Joists should be at least 18 inches above crawl-space soil, and at least 6 inches should separate wooden siding from the ground. Wooden steps should have a concrete base that rises at least 6 inches above the ground *(inset)*, and the base should be separated from the foundation wall by at least 2 inches. Soil used for backfill against the foundation, as well as the soil beneath a concrete-slab porch or patio, should contain no roots, tree limbs or scrap lumber; waste wood can nourish a termite colony.

Even when termites cannot travel directly from soil to wood, they can build their shelter tubes in cracks in the concrete foundation. A poured-concrete foundation, reinforced to resist cracking, is the best insurance against this possibility. On concrete-block foundations, a reinforced poured-concrete cap, 4 inches thick, forces termites to carry their tubes out into the open over exposed concrete, where they are easily detected. A top course of coreless concrete blocks with tightly filled mortar joints is a good second best.

The same termite-proof construction principles apply as well to other types of house design. On pier-type foundations, for instance, the wooden lattice that often screens openings between piers should clear the ground by at least 2 inches and should be separated from the piers by the same amount. Houses on slab foundations are subject to termite attack through expansion joints in the concrete and through the openings around pipes and conduits; these gaps must be tightly sealed with joint sealer, epoxy cement or patching mortar. On brick-veneered wood-frame houses, 8 inches of concrete foundation wall should separate the brickwork from the ground to prevent termites from traveling from soil to wood while hidden in the mortar joints of the bricks.

In basements, wood columns should not extend into or through the concrete floor; even if the wood does not touch the soil, the concrete beneath it may crack and give access to termites. And the wood frame of a basement window should be 6 inches above the bottom of a window well. It is also wise to use pressure-treated wood for all construction belowgrade; the chemicals in such wood act as a deterrent to termites.

Even with good construction details, protection against termites is not guaranteed; it is not unheard of for these creatures to build shelter tubes over long vertical expanses of exposed concrete. Careful annual inspections of foundations will detect the tubes before serious damage occurs. For extra protection, have a professional exterminator create a chemical barrier around the foundation with soil poisons.

Extermination: Taking Punitive Action

Although the cleaning and maintenance measures described on the preceding pages strike at the heart of a pest problem by depriving the pests of food, shelter and access to the house from outdoors, there will probably be times when you want to take more aggressive action. For persistent infestations of truly noxious creatures such as rats, bedbugs, ticks and fleas, call an exterminator. Professional help will also be needed in battling insects that threaten structural damage—termites, for example, or wood-boring beetles. Ridding your house of most pests, however, is a job you can do yourself. Some intruders can be chased out, screened out or trapped (opposite). For insect pests, spiders and centipedes, you will have to turn to chemicals (chart, opposite and page 114).

Your choice of a chemical should be determined by the type of pest and the area affected. Use the glossary of pests on pages 118-125 to identify your uninvited guests and to determine the most effective pesticides. Then consult the chart to learn about the specific characteristics of the recommended chemicals. Pesticides are available in many forms. They vary greatly in duration of effect and in appropriateness to the area being treated. Some smell bad, leave stains on fabrics or are unsafe to use around fish or pets.

One group of pesticides has an immediate but short-lived effect. These so-called quick-knockout agents kill pests on contact, then, within a few hours, break down into harmless by-products. Because they leave no long-lasting residues, these chemicals are often used as space sprays, misted into the air of a room from an aerosol can or a fogger—a one-shot aerosol bomb that releases its entire contents once activated.

Most other pesticides take effect more slowly: An insect coming into contact with one of these substances may not die until hours later. But they leave a deposit that may remain potent for weeks. Used as a space spray, a residual pesticide would deposit a lingering film of poison over every surface in a room. Consequently, such sprays are usually applied to limited areas, accessible to pests but not people. Outdoors, their lingering potency presents less hazard, and residuals can be sprayed on broader areas to create chemical barriers around the house.

Residuals are sold in various forms. Those packaged in aerosol cans often come with attachments that make it easier to direct the spray deep into cracks; other aerosols release their contents as foam, making it simple to place the pesticide just where you want it. Residuals are also available as paint-on emulsions and as pesticide-impregnated tapes to be applied in small strips in cabinets and around sinks. Professional exterminators mix their residual pesticides from concentrates, diluting them with water and applying them with a compressed-air sprayer. For large jobs, you too may want to mix your own solution and apply it with a household sprayer.

Many residuals also come in the form of fine dusts. These work well only in areas sheltered from moisture and household traffic, such as behind walls or in the spaces beneath the false bottoms of cabinets. However, in such secluded spots, dusts have the advantage of dispersing more widely than sprays; they are carried by the lightest air currents into the far reaches of cracks and voids. In addition, they remain potent for months or years, far longer than sprays.

Pesticides used in baits make up a third category. Generally mixed with meal or grain, these substances offer a lethal treat to rats and mice as well as to some crawling insects: cockroaches, crickets, earwigs and ants. Used against insects, baits are generally regarded only as a supplement to other treatment. Against rats and mice, however, they are highly effective alone—providing other food is not abundant. Their major drawback becomes clear when a dead rodent begins to decay in a wall void, far out of reach.

In applying a pesticide, your first concern should be safety (box, page 115). Apply the chemical to the site where the pest is likely to be found (pages 118-125), but only if the pesticide label recommends its use on that site. Remember, too, that most pests are repelled as well as killed by pesticides. To keep them from dodging the poison, leave no potential hiding places untouched. Often you will have to use dusts as well as liquids to rid yourself of crawling pests. A thorough indoor treatment may also include a quick-knockout fog, which seeps into cracks and flushes pests out into surface deposits of residual pesticide.

Be sure in advance that a pesticide is compatible with surfaces it will touch. Most aerosol sprays, as well as some liquids intended for use in home sprayers, are oil-base formulations that may stain carpets and upholstery, soften asphalt tile, dissolve the adhesive under parquet floors, and discolor linoleum and plastic. If in doubt, test a small area first. In general, a water-base emulsion, mixed from a concentrate, is less likely to mar a surface, although it may water-spot wood and upholstery.

The effect of a residual will be short-lived if you apply it to a porous surface, such as unfinished wood, where it will be absorbed quickly, or to a warm or sunny area, such as a window sill, where light and heat will cause the chemical to break down. You may need to reapply it within a few days. Residuals also wash away quickly when sprayed or painted on surfaces that are continually damp; by the same token, do not wash or sponge a treated area for several days after applying the pesticide.

Although new research and government rulings continually alter pesticides' availability and methods of application, most of the substances listed in the chart opposite are used in professional pest control and are also legally available to homeowners. Many are sold in hardware stores and supermarkets in ready-to-use form—as aerosol sprays and fogs, containing a combination of several pesticides; as liquids for sprayers; and as paint-on preparations, dusts and baits. Hardware stores may also stock concentrated pesticides for home mixing.

For other concentrates and many dusts, you may need to go to an exterminators' supplier. Here you may encounter reluctance. Wholesalers are often wary of selling to nonprofessionals, and many of their pesticides are packaged in quantities too large for treating a single house. But given the range of substances and the fact that several pesticides will usually work equally well against a specific pest, you should never be at a loss for a chemical solution to your pest problem.

Controlling Pests with Fly Swatters and Traps

For a single pest in clear view, two traditional weapons still work best—the shoe and the fly swatter. Other non-chemical means can control pests in greater numbers: Flypaper and sticky traps will hold down housefly populations. Sticky traps can also be used against cockroaches, either alone or to monitor the success of chemical treatment. A cat or a dog can prove itself a valuable ally against mice, and you may be able to feel more tolerant toward an occasional centipede or nonpoisonous spider when you know that it feeds on flies and crawling insects.

For snaring mice, nothing works better than standard spring traps, baited with gumdrops or peanut butter and placed at intervals of 3 or 4 feet in areas where mice forage. Rats, more wary by nature, may shy away from traps; poisoned baits are often more effective. If you do use rat traps, careful placement is important. Position them near the holes through which the rats enter the building; alternately, set the traps at 10-foot intervals along their runways, at a right angle to the runway wall and oriented to snap toward that wall. Use a piece of bacon for bait.

Trapping calls for certain precautions. Do not place a set trap where children or pets might find it. Be careful as you set a rat trap; accidentally sprung, it can break a finger. And you should always wear gloves while removing and disposing of dead rats and mice.

For other animal pests, there are more humane solutions: Chipmunks or squirrels that have moved into your attic or basement can be captured and released outdoors with drop-door traps, available in many hardware stores. If birds have built a nest in a chimney or a roof vent, push out the nest when the fledglings have departed, and then screen off the sheltered nook to discourage new inhabitants.

When a single animal—a squirrel, a bird or a bat—strays into your house through an open window or door, shoo it out the way it came in, urging it along with a broom. But put on a jacket and gloves to protect your arms and hands from bites. For a potentially dangerous animal—such as a raccoon, a porcupine or a skunk—or for any animal that appears ill or acts unafraid, call either the police or the animal-control center for assistance.

A Multiple Choice of Chemical Weapons

Deciphering pesticide chemicals. The labels on pesticides always indicate the type of insects against which the product is effective, but the chemical potency of the product, as well as the specific problems associated with its use, may vary with its ingredients. Those ingredients are listed on the pesticide label, most frequently in the form of common or proprietary names, although sometimes the multisyllabic chemical names are used. Both sets of names are given in the left-hand column of the chart below to assist you in identifying the chemicals you are dealing with.

Also on the label is a description of how the product should be used. In the case of surface sprays and paint-on preparations, the U.S. Environmental Protection Agency (EPA) specifies the areas to which the substance may safely be applied. This information *(right-hand column)* is also a clue to the product's potency. In general, the more toxic and long-lived substances are limited to use in cracks, crevices and small areas such as baseboards. A few less toxic chemicals, with shorter-lived residues, may be sprayed over larger surfaces—such as the insides of cabinets and the areas underneath furniture. Even with these clues to possible health hazards, however, pesticides should be used with the general precautions described on page 115.

Common name (Proprietary name)			
Chemical name	Forms used	Duration of effect	Comments and cautions for indoor use
Boric acid *Boric acid*	Dust	Works as long as the dust is undisturbed.	Effective only against crawling insects, and ineffective when wet. Unlike most pesticides, does not repel insects and drive them into hiding. Often placed in wall voids during construction for lasting protection. Although a common household chemical, boric acid is a poison.
Bendiocarb (Ficam) *2,2-dimethyl-1, 3-benzodioxol-4-61 methylcarbamate; 2,3-isopropylidene dioxyphenyl methylcarbamate*	Surface spray, dust	Residue from spray lasts 15-30 days; dust is effective for months.	Very effective against bees, ants, and wasps. Unlike most long-lived pesticides, can be sprayed over broad areas under furniture and inside cabinets.
Carbaryl (Sevin) *1-naphthyl methylcarbamate*	Surface spray, dust	Residue from spray lasts 1-15 days; dust is effective for months.	Very effective against bees, ants and wasps. Some formulations can be sprayed on broad areas under furniture and inside cabinets. As a dust, widely used as a flea powder for pets. Dust may mar carpets.

continued on page 114

Common name (Proprietary name) *Chemical name*	Forms used	Duration of effect	Comments and cautions for indoor use
Chlordane *1,2,4,5,6,7,8,8-octachloro-3a,4,7,7a-tetrahydro-4,7-methanoindane*	Liquid emulsion or suspension	Residue lasts months or years.	Once widely used, like its chemical cousin DDT, in gardens and house interiors, now used only against termites.
Chlorpyrifos (Dursban) *0-0-diethyl 0-(3,5,6-trichloro-2-pyridyl) phosphorothioate*	Surface spray, paint-on emulsion	Residue from spray lasts 15-30 days; paint-on form is effective for months.	An all-purpose pesticide, effective against a wide range of insects and spiders. Apply only to cracks, crevices and small areas. Strong smelling.
Diazinon (Spectracide) *0,0-diethyl 0-(2-isopropyl-4-methyl-6-pyrimidyl) phosphorothioate*	Surface spray, dust	Residue from spray lasts 15-30 days; dust is effective for months.	An all-purpose pesticide, effective against a wide range of insects and spiders. Should be applied only to cracks, crevices and small areas. Will damage ferns, hibiscus and gardenias.
Dichlorvos, DDVP (Vapona) *2,2-dichlorovinyl dimethyl phosphate*	Space spray, surface spray, fog, resinated plastic strip	Residue from sprays and fog lasts several hours; strips are effective for months.	As a space spray or fog, stuns and kills insects on contact. In surface sprays, its vapors penetrate cracks to flush out crawling insects. Both sprays and fogs smell bad on warm surfaces and are deadly to fish. Resinated plastic strips are used as flea collars for pets or suspended from ceilings to kill flying insects; strips should not be hung in kitchens or infants' rooms.
Methoxychlor *1,1,1-trichloro-2,2-bis (p-methoxyphenyl) ethane*	Space spray, surface spray	Residue lasts 1-7 days.	An all-purpose pesticide effective against a wide range of pests. Can be misted through a room or sprayed over broad areas. Very toxic to fish.
Malathion *0,0-dimethyl dithiophosphate of diethyl mercaptosuccinate*	Surface spray, dust, paint-on emulsion	Residue from liquids lasts 1-15 days; dust is effective for months.	An all-purpose pesticide effective against a wide range of insects, but many cockroaches are resistant to it. Can be sprayed over broad areas, but may stain carpets and upholstery. Smells strong and breaks down chemically when exposed to heat and sunlight; store in a cool, dark place.
Naphthalene *Naphthalene*	Balls, flakes	Gives off repellent vapors for months.	Used to mothproof woolen clothes and fabrics, and also to repel small mammals such as skunks and bats. Can destroy plastic hangers and buttons.
Paradichlorobenzene *Paradichlorobenzene*	Balls, flakes	Gives off repellent vapors for months.	Same as naphthalene.
Propoxur (Baygon) *0-isopropoxyphenyl methylcarbamate*	Surface spray; earwig, ant, roach, and cricket baits; resinated tape	Residue from spray and tape lasts 15-45 days; bait is effective indefinitely.	An all-purpose pesticide effective against a wide range of insects, but should be applied only to cracks, crevices and small areas. Gives out penetrating vapors.
Pyrethrins *Pyrethrins I and II; cinerins I and II; allethrin*	Space spray, fog, dust	Residue from spray and dust lasts minutes to hours.	The basic ingredients in most flying-insect aerosols; quickly stuns and kills flying insects. In fogs, it also irritates and flushes out crawling insects. Relatively safe because it breaks down quickly once applied, but some people become violently allergic to it. Very toxic to fish.
Resmethrin *(5-benzyl-3-furyl) methyl 2,2-dimethyl-3-(2-methyl propenyl) cyclopropane carboxylate*	Space spray, surface spray, fog	Residue lasts 1-15 days.	Similar to pyrethrins, and especially effective against yellow jackets. Very toxic to fish, but less irritating to humans than pyrethrins.
Silica gel	Dust, in surface sprays	Works as long as the dust is undisturbed.	Effective against crawling insects, but not when wet. Wear a dust mask while applying it, to prevent irritation.
Warfarin *3-alpha-acetonylbenzyl-4-hydroxy-coumarin*	In rodent baits	Effective indefinitely.	Mixed with meal or grain to poison rats and mice; sometimes several doses are needed. Poisonous to humans and pets, but only in large amounts.

Safety Precautions for Pesticides

Pesticides can be poisonous to humans and pets as well as to the vermin they are formulated to combat. To avoid accidental ingestion or contact, always read labels carefully before use and follow the directions scrupulously. Do not mist any pesticide labeled as a surface spray into the air or across broad expanses. Never expose food, dishes or food-preparation surfaces to pesticide, and in a bathroom, put away all toilet articles. Do not let children or pets occupy a room to which residual liquids or sprays have recently been applied.

Place dusts or insect baits where they will be inaccessible to children and pets—beneath appliances or under the false bottoms of cabinets. If you have small children, control rats and mice with traps rather than poison baits, and set the traps out of children's reach.

Most aerosol sprays and fogs, as well as pesticide concentrates, are flammable. Extinguish cigarettes and open flames, including pilot lights, while you spray, fog or mix a concentrate. Ventilate a treated room either during or after spraying or fogging, depending on the label directions. Foggers are designed for rooms of specific sizes; to avoid a flammable concentration of vapors, do not use a fogger in a room smaller than the specified size.

To avoid getting a liquid or spray pesticide on your skin, wear rubber gloves and long sleeves as you apply the chemical. Always wash thoroughly afterward, and wash immediately if you splash any pesticide on exposed skin.

If you have asthma, hay fever, or a history of allergic reactions, do not apply pesticides yourself. Dusts and sprays, especially those containing pyrethrins, can be particularly irritating. Have a professional treat your house, and be sure to say beforehand that you may be sensitive to the chemicals.

Just as important as the proper use of pesticides is their careful storage. Keep pesticides, along with the sprayers or dusters you use to apply them, in cabinets that are out of children's reach and locked for extra protection. Never mix different pesticides, and always store leftovers in the original containers.

Never dispose of a container that still contains pesticide; keep it until you have used all of its contents. Then, if it held a liquid, rinse it out three times; use the rinse water as you did the pesticide, in similar areas and in the same quantities. Before throwing out pesticide containers, put bottles in a bag and break them with a hammer; puncture and crush nonpressurized cans; and wrap aerosol containers in newspaper.

If you discover on your shelves a container of pesticide more than two or three years old and you do not find its active ingredients listed on the chart opposite, call the department of agriculture for your state or the nearest branch of the EPA, to find out whether the substance is still approved. If not, ask for disposal instructions.

Techniques for Applying Sprays and Dusts

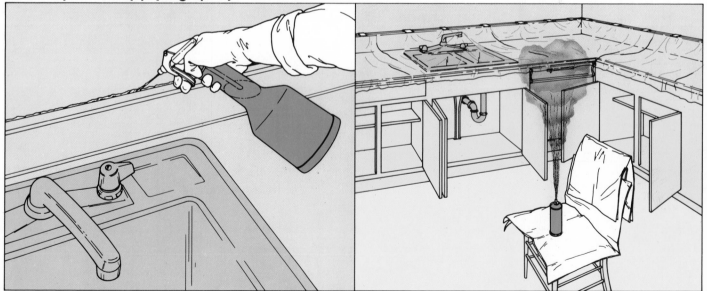

Using space and surface sprays. To treat cracks, crevices and small areas along baseboards, around countertops, and in the corners of cabinets and cupboards, use an aerosol can or a trigger-type household sprayer with its nozzle set to deliver a pin stream, for narrow cracks, or a coarse spray. Hold the sprayer close enough that the spray hits only the area to be treated *(above, left)*, and move the sprayer along the crevice at a rate that leaves a visible film of dampness but no puddles or pools.

To treat an entire room with an aerosol fogger *(above, right)*, turn off pilot lights and extinguish any open flame. Put plastic sheeting over food-preparation surfaces. Cover fish tanks with plastic; turn off fish-tank aerators. Close doors and windows, and turn off fans and air conditioners. Open cupboards you wish to treat. Place the aerosol can on a newspaper-covered chair in the middle of the room, and discharge it. Leave the room promptly for the prescribed length of time, and air it when you return.

Perform the same steps before and after using an aerosol space spray, but follow the label directions to mist the spray into room air.

Applying a dust. Using the original dispenser or a plastic squeeze bottle for mustard or catsup—preferably a new one with a fine hole—puff the dust into cracks and crevices and behind appliance kick plates. Apply sufficient dust to coat all visible surfaces with a thin film. To inject the dust beneath the false bottoms of cabinets and into wall voids, drill ¼-inch holes in these surfaces. On cabinet bottoms, drill one hole for every 4 to 6 square feet, equidistant from the sides of the cabinet. On a wall, drill one hole between each pair of studs, 2 or 3 inches from the ceiling. In an exterior wall with insulation, position each hole as close as possible to a stud, where there is likely to be a vertical air space for the dust to filter through.

Fit the nozzle of the dispenser into each hole and pump it two or three times. Then spackle the holes, sand the patches, and touch up with paint. When the dispenser is empty, dispose of it or save it for later dusting.

Laying Down a Chemical Cordon Sanitaire

Laying down a chemical barrier. To stem a large-scale pest invasion from outdoors, spray the bottom 12 inches of the foundation wall and an 18-inch strip of the adjacent soil with a water-base residual pesticide, applied with a compressed-air garden sprayer. Mix the pesticide from a concentrate, following the instructions on the label. Pump pressure into the tank with the pump handle, and apply the pesticide to the wall. Hold the wand 8 to 12 inches from the wall, wetting it visibly without allowing the pesticide to drip or form pools, and move the wand back and forth so that the entire length of the wall is evenly covered. If you have a pest problem in the basement, wet down the inside of the window wells, too, but avoid the windows themselves.

When you have completed the wall treatment, apply a 2-inch band of residual pesticide across the doorsills and first-floor window sills; carry the pesticide treatment approximately 1 foot up the inside faces of doorframes and window frames as well. To form this protective band, you can use the compressed-air sprayer, an aerosol surface spray or a paint-on emulsion.

Destroying the Nests of Outdoor Pests

Getting rid of wasp nests. To dispose of the pendulous nests of yellow jackets and hornets, found on branches and beneath eaves, use a special aerosol wasp spray, designed to shoot a narrow stream over a long distance—about 10 or 15 feet. Working at dusk, when the insects are inactive, and with the breeze behind you, direct the stream of pesticide into the nest opening for three to five seconds. Then spray the exterior of the nest until it drips. After 24 hours, if there is no sign of activity, knock down the nest and destroy it.

Use the same spray to treat the honeycomb nests of umbrella wasps and the tubular nests of mud daubers *(page 124)*, thoroughly soaking the nest. Again, work at dusk.

To destroy underground wasp nests, wait until nightfall, when the insects are inside, then blow two or three puffs of bendiocarb or carbaryl dust into the nest opening with a squeeze bottle. Immediately cover the entrance with a shovelful of moist earth. For beehives and wasp nests built within walls, see pages 118 and 124.

Caution: Do not attempt to treat bee or wasp nests if you are hypersensitive to stings or if you have asthma, hay fever or other allergies. Call in a professional exterminator.

Poisoning an anthill. Spray any water-base residual pesticide into the nest openings, using the sprayer attachment of a garden hose or a compressed-air sprayer. Thoroughly soak the ground around the openings with pesticide— up to several quarts for a large anthill. Then hose down the nest with plain water, so that the pesticide will be carried deep into the soil.

If ants have penetrated the house, spray visible nests with any residual surface spray. If the nest is inside a wall or beneath the false bottom of a cabinet or cupboard, drill holes and dust the cavities with bendiocarb or carbaryl *(opposite)*. If the ants have tunneled into wood to nest, you may need professional help *(page 118)*.

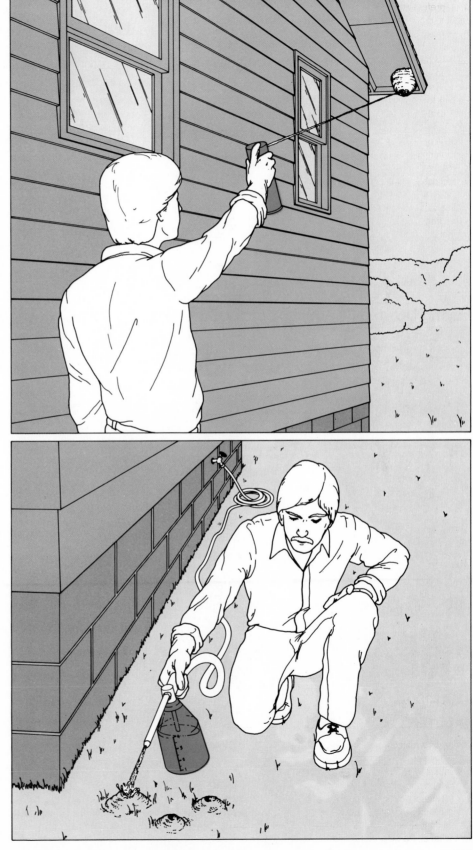

A Glossary of Common Pests

Not all pests that invade a house are harmful, but few of them are welcome. Even the friendly cricket on the hearth will chew holes in clothing if given half a chance. To control these intruders, it is essential to identify them. Some of them, such as termites and winged ants, look very much alike but are treated quite differently. It also helps to know their nesting and feeding habits and their typical invasion routes. With these facts in hand, you can decide on a course of action, which in extreme cases is likely to include chemicals. The pest profiles that follow are intended to provide this kind of guidance. They should be used in conjunction with the chemical chart and the application instructions on pages 112-117, which together explain how the pesticide should be used.

Raccoons, squirrels and other small animals that sometimes wander into the house do not appear in the glossary because they can usually be chased out or trapped humanely, using the methods described on page 113. Gnats and midges are not profiled here. They are controlled by the same methods used for mosquitoes, with the exception of screening. These tiny creatures will slip through the meshes; the only way to keep them out is to close the window against which they cluster.

If you cannot identify an insect or spider, try to capture it in a jar. In most cases, the county agricultural agent can tell you what it is and how to control it. To locate the agent, check your telephone directory's listings for the United States or local government.

Ant. Most species nest outdoors and find their way into the kitchen, attracted by sweets or grease. A few, however, nest indoors: in a wall cavity, beneath flooring, or in a pile of undisturbed litter. Carpenter ants, black and about ½ inch long, occasionally tunnel into damp wood to nest; they can do some structural damage.

Many ants—carpenter ants are a notable exception—travel from nest to food source along well-defined paths over window sills and doorsills and along baseboards and countertop edges. These paths should help you to control the infestation and also to locate the nest and destroy it (page 117). For infestation, apply any residual surface spray or paint-on preparation along the routes ants follow; baits containing propoxur may also help. In case of a heavy invasion from outdoors, create a chemical barrier along the foundation wall, using any water-base residual (page 116). If carpenter ants have nested in timber, try boring holes and puffing in bendiocarb or carbaryl dust, or call an exterminator.

Bedbug. Bedbugs, once the bane of travelers, feed on the blood they suck from the sleeping occupants of the mattresses in which they dwell. In severe infestations, the ¼-inch bugs cluster in cracks and crevices throughout the bedroom, as well as in seams and tufts of the bedding. You can import them in used furniture; inspect any purchases carefully before you bring them home.

To control the bugs, wet the inside of the frame, the springs, and the slats of the bed with 1 per cent malathion spray or paint-on emulsion. Also spray the mattress seams and tufts very lightly with .5 per cent malathion. Then spray baseboards, cracks between floorboards, and behind wall hangings and loose wallpaper with 1 per cent malathion. Complete the treatment by fogging the room with an aerosol containing pyrethrins. Do not replace the linens or occupy the room for at least two hours. Caution: Never spray a baby's crib or bedding with pesticide; instead, wash the bedding and scrub the crib.

Bee. Although bees are essential to the growth of flowers and fruit, two species, honeybees and carpenter bees, can become major nuisances. To avoid painful stings, remove a honeybee hive in a wall cavity or uncomfortably close to a house. Sometimes a local beekeeper will be willing to adopt a swarm of honeybees. If you must destroy an outdoor hive, use a wasp spray (page 117); for a hive in a wall cavity, inject bendiocarb or carbaryl dust into the wall above the hive (page 116). After two or three days, remove the hive—even if you must tear away siding or wallboard to do it. The stench of dead bees and rancid honey can be overpowering, and the honey can soak through wallboard.

If a swarm of honeybees has settled in shrubbery close to your house, screen or plug all openings under the eaves or into the roof overhang to discourage the swarm from building a hive in these cavities. In dry areas, such as the Southwest, a gentle shower of water from a garden sprinkler may encourage the swarm to move on; directly spraying the bees, however, will only make them enraged.

Although they are not aggressive, carpenter bees become pests by burrowing into exposed timber to nest. To eliminate them, blow carbaryl or bendiocarb dust into the tunnels; then plug them with caulking compound.

Carpet beetle. Sure signs of infestation are a combination of damaged carpets or upholstery and the appearance of small mottled or black beetles, ⅛ inch long, crawling near windows. But it is the hairy larvae rather than the full-grown beetles that do the damage, feeding on any fabric—even synthetics—as well as on furs, stuffed animals, and the same dried foodstuffs that form the diet of pantry pests *(page 122)*.

If you find carpet beetles or their larvae on your kitchen shelves, treat them in the same way as pantry pests. In a living room, bedroom or clothes closet, vacuum thoroughly; pay special attention to baseboards, upholstery, drapes, and carpeted areas beneath furniture and behind radiators. Then throw away the dust bag; it may contain larvae and eggs. Take small rugs and carpets outside, and brush or shake them to remove eggs and larvae. Wash or dry clean clothes and blankets. Spray a water emulsion of any residual pesticide along baseboards, around the edges of wall-to-wall carpets, into cracks between floorboards and, in a closet, at the ends of clothes rods and around shelves.

To prevent reinfestation, vacuum frequently and store fabrics properly *(page 106)*. Use moth crystals in storage closets—1 pound for every 100 cubic feet. Have the dry cleaner apply a protective treatment to carpets and fabrics.

Box-elder bug. On sunny fall days, these ½-inch-long, red-banded garden bugs may swarm indoors in great numbers, leaving spots on curtains, clothing and upholstery. Outdoors, they tend to inhabit female box-elder trees. To stem repeated invasions, spray the trees in early summer with carbaryl, diazinon or malathion, using a power sprayer; as a last-ditch measure, you can cut down the trees. During an infestation, a barrier treatment *(page 116)* with any residual pesticide can help. Indoors, fog an infested room with pyrethrins. Then vacuum up the bugs.

Centipede. Most centipedes are casual intruders from the outdoors, where they thrive in piles of damp leaves, grass cuttings and compost; they also favor the damp undersides of boxes and boards resting on the ground. Clear such hiding places from the foundation of your house. If you are plagued by a large number of centipedes, create a chemical barrier around the foundation with any residual pesticide *(page 116)*.

One species of centipede, the long-legged, fleet-footed creature illustrated, breeds in the house and can be persistent, although it does no real harm. To control it, coat baseboards and crevices in damp, dark areas—in the basement, kitchen and bathroom, and in closets—with a surface spray that contains chlorpyrifos, diazinon, malathion or propoxur.

Cockroach. Universally abhorred, cockroaches justify their reputation by contaminating food, soiling walls and counters, and possibly spreading disease. To control them, use a combination of a surface spray, a dust and an aerosol fog. Begin in the kitchen, usually the area of severest infestation. Clear off counters, empty cabinets, and spray chlorpyrifos, diazinon, or propoxur into cockroach hiding places. These include the cracks and crevices along baseboards and where cabinets and counters meet walls; the inside corners of cabinets and the ends of shelves; gaps around plumbing; drawer runners; and the floor around and behind appliances. Spray the crevices on the undersides of tables and chairs. Then puff a dust—boric acid is good—across floor areas under appliances, into the spaces beneath false bottoms and, in a severe infestation, into the walls behind appliances (*page 116*). Finally, fog with pyrethrins. Let the pesticide dry; then cover the shelves with shelf paper to protect dishes and food from the chemical's residual effects.

If you see cockroaches in a living room or a bedroom, spray water-base chlorpyrifos, diazinon or propoxur lightly into crevices on the underside of furniture, around pictures and hangings, and along baseboards, ceiling moldings and the edges of shelves. Use a fog if the infestation is heavy. In a bathroom, spray one of the same pesticides as above into cracks and gaps where it will not be quickly washed away. Inject a dust into the razor-blade slot; it will filter down into the wall behind.

A second treatment with a surface spray may be needed two to four weeks later, as a new generation of cockroaches emerges from eggs that survived the first treatment.

Clothes moth. You are unlikely to see a clothes moth—these ¼-inch-long insects shy away from light—but you will see evidence of them in the damage done by their larvae to carpets, upholstery, blankets and clothing. Like carpet beetles, clothes moths prefer fur and wool, but they will feed on synthetics if dirt or stains have added nutritional value to the fabric. Clothes moths are controlled in the same way as carpet beetles, and the tips for preventing carpet-beetle reinfestation are equally effective.

Cricket. In the late summer and early fall, crickets can swarm into houses, keeping the occupants awake with their song and chewing holes in fabrics. If large numbers are entering, you will have to create an exterior barrier of any residual pesticide (*page 116*). Indoors, spray chlorpyrifos, diazinon or propoxur along baseboards and the bottoms of walls in all rooms in which you have seen or heard crickets; be particularly thorough in basements and closets and on the floors under stairwells. Also spray the floors of unused fireplaces. If the infestation is heavy, fog with pyrethrins to chase the insects into the deposits of residual pesticide.

Earwig. Terrifying in appearance but harmless to humans and household effects, earwigs occasionally leave their usual outdoor haunts in moist, shady areas of the yard—under boards and beneath tangled shrubbery—to become indoor pests. They tend to make themselves especially unwelcome by crawling into piles of laundry and bedding. A barrier treatment with any residual pesticide (*page 116*) will stem an invasion. Indoors, spray chlorpyrifos, diazinon or propoxur along baseboards and the bottoms of walls wherever you have seen earwigs—in bedrooms, closets, laundry room or basement. You can supplement the spray with a propoxur bait.

Flea. Loathed for their irritating bite and their reputation as carriers of disease, fleas can hitch-hike into your house on a pet, then spread throughout the house. First, treat the pet, following the advice of a veterinarian, and launder pet bedding in very hot water. In infested rooms, vacuum rugs, curtains, upholstery, and all un-trafficked areas beneath and behind furniture and radiators; then throw away the dust bag. Spray a water-base solution of any residual pesticide into cracks between floorboards, along baseboards, behind loose wallpaper, in crevices on the undersides of furniture and, lightly, into the seams and tufts of upholstery. Also spray crevices in the box or basket in which the pet sleeps. Then fog the room with a flea bomb containing pyrethrins or a flea-growth regulator.

You may also need to go outdoors, spraying doghouse cracks and crevices with an indoor sprayer. Soak the pet's favorite resting places with any residual, applied with the spray attachment of a garden hose. Let the sprayed areas dry before letting your pet roam the yard.

Millipede. Millipedes have more legs than centipedes—four per body segment, not two—and move more slowly. But they favor the same kind of damp, dark habitat: piles of rotting leaves, grass clippings and compost, and areas under boards and boxes. If millipedes invade the house, remove hiding places from the foundation; if their numbers are great, apply an exterior barrier of any water-base residual (page 116). Indoors, simply sweep up these harmless creatures; if they persist, apply any residual surface spray to baseboards and the bottoms of walls in any room they have invaded—usually the laundry room or the basement.

Fly. Sound window screens and snug-fitting screen doors that swing outward are the best defense against houseflies. Sanitation in the kitchen and the yard (page 107) will also reduce their numbers. If maggots appear in a garbage can, evidence that flies have been breeding there, spray the inside bottom of the can with any residual surface spray, or tape a small plastic strip containing dichlorvos inside the lid. In a room overrun with flies, use a space spray containing pyrethrins, but do not expect more than temporary control. Flypaper can also help, giving longer-lasting but less complete protection.

Mite. Of the many species of mites, most of them barely visible to the unaided eye, two are common household pests. The clover mite (above, left) can invade the house in great numbers from a lush, well-fertilized lawn, leaving reddish smears on walls and floors whenever it is crushed. Cut back grass and shrubs from exterior walls, and spray the foundation with a pesticide barrier (page 116), using any water-base residual. Indoors, fog with pyrethrins; then vacuum all infested areas.

The house-dust mite (above, right) inhabits cotton-stuffed mattresses, pillows and upholstery, and sometimes triggers violent allergies. Vacuum carpets, mattresses, furniture and floorboard cracks, and keep the house well-ventilated to avoid the moisture build-up that favors mites.

Mosquito. In warm weather, tiny, wriggling mosquito larvae will breed in any standing water around your house—in puddles in the yard, on a flat roof, or in a clogged rain gutter. Indoors, look for larvae in fish tanks and in the saucers under houseplants. Drain any infested water. For a persistent mosquito problem in a backyard fish pond, stock larvae-eating fish such as goldfish, guppies, mosquito fish, or sticklebacks.

To bar mosquitos from indoors, tight-fitting screens in good repair are essential. You can temporarily rid a room of these vexing, dangerous insects with a space spray containing pyrethrins.

Pantry pests. Dry foodstuffs can attract many different types of beetles, as well as the larvae of several species of moth. The most common of these insects—which feed indiscriminately on cereal products, dry soup mixes, dried fruits, nuts, cocoa, pet food, and spices—is the sawtoothed grain beetle illustrated here.

Pantry pests most often arrive in groceries. If you see beetles or wormlike larvae in a new package of dry food, dispose of it immediately. If the package has been on your shelves for a while, destroy it; then empty the shelves, vacuum them, and seal uninfested food in jars, coffee cans, or plastic bags with a zip-locking top. If no infestation is visible, but you suspect it, spread the food in a baking pan and sterilize it in a 140° F. oven for 30 minutes.

For a heavy infestation, spray or paint malathion around the shelf edges; if the odor of malathion is objectionable, substitute a diazinon spray. Let the pesticide dry; then, to avoid contaminating the food with residual chemicals, apply shelf paper before replacing the food.

Scorpion. Abundant in the South and especially in the arid Southwest, scorpions can deliver a painful—and sometimes fatal—sting. Indoors, they lurk in many of the same areas favored by spiders *(opposite);* you may also spot them in a bathroom or a kitchen sink, where they search for moisture. Outdoors, they hide in piles of wood and trash, and they may burrow into a child's sandbox. To control them, follow the steps suggested for spiders.

Silverfish. Silverfish range throughout the house, doing minor damage to paper, bookbindings, wallpaper, starched fabrics, and rayon. Control them with surface sprays containing chlorpyrifos, diazinon or propoxur. Apply the spray to baseboards, along the bottoms of walls, and around pipe chases. Treat closets in rooms where you have seen silverfish. For a severe infestation, inject boric acid beneath the false bottoms of cabinets and into walls *(page 116)*. Spray again two weeks later to kill any silverfish that hatch from eggs untouched by the first treatment.

Similar in appearance to the silverfish, and sometimes confused with it, the firebrat frequents areas near sources of heat, such as radiators, hot-water pipes, ovens and furnaces. Eliminate firebrats with boric acid dust; do not use sprays, which present a fire hazard. Puff the dust beneath and behind radiators and hot-water pipes, under and around ovens and furnaces, and in all baseboard crevices in warm areas.

Sow bug. Sow bugs and a related species, pill bugs, are similar in appearance and size (¼ to ½ inch). Both are harmless and prefer the same damp habitats as millipedes. Control them as you would millipedes *(page 121)*.

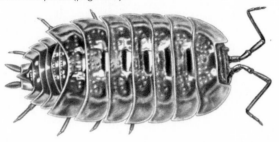

Spider. Undisturbed areas in closets and under and behind furniture can shelter spiders, including two dangerous species: the black widow *(above)*, with its characteristic red or brown spot on the underside; and, in the South, the brown recluse, distinctively marked on the top with a dark-brown spot shaped like a violin. A poisonous spider in a living room or bedroom is usually a casual intruder from an unkempt yard or a cluttered garage or basement storeroom. As a first step in controlling spiders, clear away piles of lumber, boxes and debris stored indoors or out. Wear gloves and a jacket as you work, and watch for spiders, their webs and their ½-inch-long silken egg sacs. Destroy the webs, and stamp on the egg sacs.

A barrier treatment of any residual pesticide *(page 116)* may reduce the number of spiders invading from outdoors. Indoors, use a surface spray containing chlorpyrifos, diazinon or propoxur; apply it along baseboards and in corners wherever you have seen spiders. Never stand directly below a spider to spray it; it may drop onto you, stunned but still capable of biting.

Termite. Termite control is usually a job for a professional exterminator, but homeowners should be alert for signs of these insects, which feed on wood and can cause severe structural damage. In the early spring, a swarm of winged insects emerging from the soil near the foundation, or from wood inside or outside the house, may signal an infestation. If the insects have long forewings and short hindwings, they are winged ants; on winged termites, both pairs are equally long. Termites also have thicker waists and straight, not angled, antennae. Another giveaway is the mud-walled shelter tubes through which termites travel from their underground nests to their sources of food. The tubes may lead up concrete foundation walls to the wood framing above and even ascend across an open crawl space, from the soil to the floor joists. If you see blisters or dark areas on wood floors or paneling, probe them with a screwdriver or an awl; if the wood is infested, your tool will easily sink through the thin shell of sound wood into the damaged timber beneath.

A few termite species reveal their presence with piles of small, brown fecal pellets on the floor beneath infested wood. Common along the Gulf and Pacific coasts, they nest in the house rather than underground, and build no shelter tubes. They require professional control.

For ways to protect your house against an attack of termites, see page 111.

Wasp. Many wasps anchor their nests against wood; the nests may be found in bushes, in trees or beneath eaves. Hornets and yellow jackets (*right*) build paper-like, football-shaped nests; umbrella wasps construct honeycombed, paper-like nests shaped like an umbrella canopy; and mud daubers build chambered nests of mud. Other wasps, including some yellow jackets, tunnel into the ground to nest. Destroy any wasp nest that is uncomfortably close to your house by means of the methods described on page 117.

Yellow jackets occasionally nest inside walls. Drill a hole into the wall above the nest, and puff carbaryl or bendiocarb dust into the wall cavity; then plug the hole. For a very large nest inside a wall, or one that dust does not destroy, summon professional help.

The stings of many wasps can be very painful and sometimes fatal; observe the precautions on page 117 in combating them.

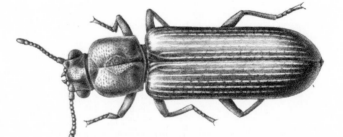

Tick. Brown dog ticks, so called because of their color, are the kind that most often invade houses. They generally arrive in the fur of dogs, then drop off and lay their eggs in carpets, upholstered furniture, cracks between floorboards and behind baseboards, and the spaces behind loose wallpaper. Brown dog ticks, unlike fleas, do not bite humans, but they are controlled in much the same way as fleas. Burn pet bedding; or spray it with any residual pesticide, wrap it in plastic, and dispose of it. In infested rooms, apply any water-base residual pesticide, as suggested for flea control. Fog the room with an aerosol flea bomb containing pyrethrins. In the yard, follow the directions for flea control. Have a veterinarian treat the dog.

Wood-boring beetle. The commonest wood-boring beetles—deathwatch beetles, furniture beetles, old-house borers, and powder-post beetles—are most likely to infest hardwood flooring, paneling and furniture. But they can attack any wood in a house—seasoned or unseasoned, hardwood or softwood, dry timber or timber weakened by moisture and fungus. Signs of their presence are the small holes that adult beetles leave as they emerge from the wood in which they have developed and, on the floor beneath the holes, small heaps of sawdust. Control is a matter for professional exterminators, but you can discourage the most common wood-boring beetles by keeping your crawl space well ventilated and dry (*page 111*). Firewood stored outdoors may harbor beetles; stamp on any you see scuttling out of the wood when you bring it into the house.

Bat. Bats may nest in attics or sheds, or in the open cavities at the top of a concrete-block wall. The odor of their urine and guano may soon become a nuisance. They can also harbor parasites—mites and bugs—that can infest the house, and they frequently carry rabies. To get rid of a stray bat or two nesting in an attic, screen off the bats' access routes while they are out for the night, using ¼-inch mesh or finer; be sure young bats have not remained inside. If a few bats are nesting in a concrete-block wall, pour moth crystals into the cavities; these will drive the bats out. Then close off the cavities or the gaps that gave them access to the wall. For large infestations, call an exterminator.

It is usually safe to chase away a single bat that blunders in an open window (page 113) or lurks around the outside of the house. But if you encounter a bat that behaves strangely—if it is lying on the floor or, outdoors, resting on a fence or shrub within easy reach—call an animal-control center. The bat may be rabid.

Mouse. Some mice live in buildings year-round, destroying foodstuffs, fabric, paper and wood; others move in from the outdoors when the weather turns cold. Sealing all gaps in exterior walls (pages 109-110), especially near the top of the foundation wall, is a first line of defense against these field mice—but remember that a small mouse can slip through a ¼-inch hole. Eliminate indoor mice with traps (page 113) or, for a large population, use bait.

Rat. Feared as disease carriers, rats are best controlled by cleanliness. Order and sanitation in the yard (page 107) will deprive rats of shelter and nesting areas. You can further discourage rats by storing lumber, pipes and boxes at least a foot above the ground, on racks or supports, to make them inaccessible for nesting.

If rats venture indoors, snap traps (page 113) and rodent baits will help you cope with them. But it is even more effective to build rats out by sealing any opening larger than ½ inch on foundation walls or siding. Use mortar, sheet metal or hardware cloth for patching, depending on the surrounding material. Roof rats, a species common in the South and along the Pacific coast, can also enter buildings under the eaves; to keep them out effectively, you must plug gaps high on the siding as well.

Picture Credits

The sources for the illustrations in this book are shown below. The drawings were created by Jack Arthur, Roger Essley, William J. Hennessy Jr., John Jones, Dick Lee, John Martinez and Joan McGurren.

Cover: Fil Hunter. 6-11: Fil Hunter. 14, 15: Frederic F. Bigio from B-C Graphics. 17-19: John Massey. 21-27: Adsai Hemintranont. 30-33: Edward L. Cooper. 35-39: Elsie J. Hennig. 41: Arezou Katoozian from A and W Graphics. 43-45: John Massey. 46: Fil Hunter. 51-55: Eduino J. Pereira from Arts and Words. 61-67: Frederic F. Bigio from B-C Graphics. 68, 69: Arezou Katoozian from A and W Graphics. 70: Fil Hunter. 72-79: Elsie J. Hennig. 81-91: Frederic F. Bigio from B-C Graphics. 93-97: John Massey. 99-103: William J. Hennessy Jr. from A and W Graphics. 104: Fil Hunter. 107-117: Walter Hilmers Jr. from HJ Commercial Art. 118-125: George A. Bell Jr.

Acknowledgments

The index/glossary for this book was prepared by Barbara L. Klein. The editors wish to thank the following: John Alderman, Century Construction Company of Northern Virginia, Falls Church, Va.; American Gas Association, Arlington, Va.; American Olean Tile Co., Lansdale, Pa.; A Plus Rental Center, Springfield, Va.; Association of Home Appliance Manufacturers, Chicago, Ill.; Bill Bader, Jones Chemical, Inc., Caledonia, N.Y.; G. W. Blanchard Co., Inc., Beltsville, Md.; Kenneth Boyer, Pro So Co, Inc., Kansas City, Kan.; Patrick Brennan, ABACUS Corp., Baltimore, Md.; Bill Butterbaugh, National LP Gas Association, Oak Brook, Ill.; Paul Campbell, Gapland, Md.; Gary Clark, Servicemaster of Greater Washington, Annandale, Va.; Mary Connell, Point Reyes Light, Point Reyes Station, Calif.; Consolidated Adhesives, Inc., Cleveland, Ohio; DAD's Discount Appliance Distributors, Beltsville, Md.; Sheryl Edge, Washington, D.C.; Federal Emergency Management Agency, Philadelphia, Pa.; Anthony D. Fiorilli, Inc., Baltimore, Md.; Ellen Fitzgerald, Washington, D.C.; Gary Fletcher, Brick Institute of America, McLean, Va.; Peggy Fulton, Washington, D.C.; Gas Appliance Manufacturers Association Inc., Arlington, Va.; Pauline Greeger, Johnson Wax, Racine, Wis.; Hobart Corporation, Kitchen Aid Division, Troy, Ohio; Robert Hund, Marble Institute of America, Farmington, Mich.; Robert Kleinhaus, Tile Council of America, Princeton, N.J.; Bill Lance, Service Manager, Culligan Water Conditioning of Greater Washington, Vienna, Va.; W. Eric Lengstrom, Washington, D.C.; Magic Chef, Cleveland, Tenn.; Marble Institute of America, Farmington, Mich.; Richard S. Mason, Wood and Stone Inc., Manassas, Va.; Ed Merchant, Merical Electrical Contractors, Inc., Forestville, Md.; Jerome B. Metelits, Aetna Rug and Upholstery Cleaners, Silver Spring, Md.; Fred Miller, Warner Parts Co., Alexandria, Va.; National Paint and Coatings Association, Washington, D.C.; Porcelain Enamel Institute, Arlington, Va.; Portland Cement Association, Skokie, Ill.; Jud Robertson, Jud Tile, Inc., Beltsville, Md.; Roper Sales Corporation, Kankakee, Ill.; Robert Rovinsky, Washington, D.C.; Mary Hall Rowland, Columbia, S.C.; Sears, Roebuck and Co., Chicago, Ill.; Scovill, Inc., NuTone Division, Cincinnati, Ohio; Simmer Pump Company, Minneapolis, Minn.; Vermont Marble, Procter, Vt.; Wallcovering Information Bureau, Springfield, N.J.; Wal-Vac, Inc., Grand Rapids, Mich.; Stanley Warshaw, Director, U.S. School of Professional Paper Hanging, Inc., Rutland, Vt. The editors also thank John Meyers, a writer, for his help with this volume.

Index/Glossary

Included in this index are definitions of some of the technical terms used in this book. Page references in italics indicate an illustration of the subject mentioned.

Acrylics, 34; scratch removal, *35*
Air cleaners, electronic, 90, *91*
Air-conditioner filters, *90*
Air filters on furnaces, *91*
Algae in pool, treatment of, *chart* 94
Ants, *118;* hills, poisoning, *117*
Appliances, 71, 80; clothes washers and dryers, 80, *86-88;* dishwashers, 80, *89;* maintenance tips, 80; moving, 80; ranges, 80, *83-86,* 90; refrigerators, 80, *81, 82;* trash compactors, 80, *88-89*
Artwork, drying, after flood, 103
Asphalt: removing from masonry, 23; surfaces, sealing, 20, *25*

Bait pesticides, 112
Baseboard, removing, *100*
Bats, *125*
Bedbugs, *118*
Bedding, drying, after flood, 103
Bees, *118*
Blacktop driveways, refinishing, 20, *25*
Blinds, venetian, *30-31*
Blood stains on masonry, 23
Blowtorch, propane, use of, *22*
Books, drying, after flood, 103
Box-elder bugs, *119*
Brass, care of, 30, *33*
Brick, 20, *21;* pressure washing, *27*
Brushes, 10
Brushing of carpets, *61;* with powder, 64
Burns in carpet, repairing, 67
Butcher-block wood surfaces, 12

Caning, *15*
Carpet beetles, *119*
Carpets and rugs: brushing of pile, *61;* burned, repairing, *67;* dry cleaning, 60, 64; drying after flood, 103; hand washing of area rug, 46, *62-63;* preservation of, 67; shampooing, 60, *65;* steam cleaning, 66; tufted, kinds of, *61*
Caulking of cracks, *110*
Caulk on masonry, removing, 23
Ceilings, 42, *43,* 44; water-filled, draining, *102*
Centipedes, *119*
Ceramic tile, 40
Chandelier cleaner, use of, *6, 39*
Chewing gum, removing: from fabric, *55;* from masonry, 23
Chimneys, screening, *108*

Circuit-breaker panel, shutting down, 99
Cleaning: air systems, *90-91;* categories of cleaning agents, 8; after flood, 98, *99-103;* precautions about chemicals, 9; specialized chemicals, *chart* 9; tool kit, *10-11;* vacuum system, central, *70, 72-79. See also* Appliances; Pest-control measures; Surfaces, kinds of; Swimming pools; Textiles
Clothes washers and dryers, 80, *86-88*
Cockroaches, 105, *120*
Coffee stains, removing, 23, 40
Condenser coils, refrigerator, *82*
Copper cleaners, 30
Countertops, scratch removal, *35*
Crawl spaces, termite-proofing, 111
Crickets, *120*

Defrosting of refrigerators, *81*
Dishwashers, 80, *89*
Drain pan, refrigerator, *82*
Drain tube, refrigerator, *81*
Drill, electric, buffing with, *24, 35*
Driveways, refinishing, 20, *25*
Dry cleaning of rugs and carpets, 60, 64
Dryers, clothes, 80, *87, 88*
Drying procedures after flood, 98, *99-103*
Dusts, pesticide, 112; application of, *116*

Earwigs, *120*
Efflorescence: *white powdery coating produced on masonry by salt rising to the surface.* Removal of, 20, *21*
Electricity, turning off, after flood, 98, *99*
Electric ranges, *83, 84*
Extermination. *See* Pest-control measures

Fabrics. *See* Textiles
Fiberglass, 34
Fiber rush, *15*
Fibers in fabrics, 48, *chart* 48-49
Filters: air systems, *90-91;* clothes dryer, *87;* clothes washer, 86; dishwasher, *89;* pool, 92, *93, 96-97;* water, installing, 40, *41*
Finishes for metal, 28, *33*
Finishes on wood, 12; blemishes, causes of, *chart* 13; floors, 16, *18;* french polish, 12, *14;* identifying, 13
Firebrats, 122
Fleas, 105, *121*
Flies, *121*
Flood, procedures after, 98, *99-103*
Floor polishers, 16, *19*
Floors: splines, setting in, *109;* vinyl, *36;* wood, 16, *17-19, chart* 17
Flushing of stains, *53, chart* 56-59

Foggers, pesticide, *115*
Foundations, pest-proofing, *109,* 111, *116*
Freezers, 80; refrigerator, defrosting, *81*
French polish, 12, *14*
Fringe of rug, hand washing, 62
Furnace filters, replacing, 91
Furniture: drying, after flood, 103; upholstered, *68-69;* wood, 12, *13;* woven, *15*
Fuse box, disarming of, after flood, 99

Garden sprayer, use of, *25, 104, 116*
Gas ranges, *85,* 86
Glass, washing, *38-39;* chandeliers, *6, 39*
Grease: on fabrics, *51;* filters for, in range hoods, 90; on masonry, *22,* 23; on porcelain and tile, 40; on wallpaper, *45*

Heaters, portable, 98, *103*

Ink stains on masonry, 23
Insect control. *See* Pest-control measures

Jet vacuum: *a device for cleaning swimming pools that utilizes water pressure to gather debris from the pool floor.* Using, *95*

Kitchens: pest control, 106, *108,* 120. *See also* Appliances

Lacquer finish: on metal, 28; on wood, 12
Laminates, 34
Leaves, removing from swimming pools, 95
Linoleum, 36
Lint traps: dryer, *87;* washer, *86*

Masonry, 20; cracks, repairing, *109;* efflorescence, 20, *21;* grease and oil, *22;* plastic, burning off, *22;* polishing, 20, *24;* poultices, 20, *23;* pressure washing, 20, *26-27;* sanding, 20, *21, 24;* sealing, 20, *25*
Metals, 28, *chart* 29, 30, *32-33;* fixtures, drying, 103; removing stains from, 23, 40; venetian blinds, *30-31*
Mice and rats, *125;* trapping, 113
Microwave ovens, 80
Mildew, removing, 40
Millipedes, *121*
Mites, *121*
Mortar, patching, use of, 109
Mosquitoes, *122*
Moths, clothes, *120*

Nap: of carpet, 61; of upholstery, 69

Oil finish, 12
Oil stains, *22*, 40
Ovens, 80, *84, 86*

Painted surfaces: metals, 28; walls and
    ceilings, 42, *43*; wood, 12, *14*
Paint stains, 23, 40
Paneling, wood, 12
Pantry pests, *122*
Pest-control measures, 105, 112;
    application of, *104, 115-117*; cleaning,
    106; ingredients, 113, *chart* 113; non-
    chemical, 113; outdoors, *104, 107-111,
    116-117*; repairs, 106, 107, 108, *109,
    110*; safety precautions, 115; termite-
    proofing, 106, *111*; types of pests, *118-
    125*; types of preparations, 112
Pile, carpet: brushing, *61*; kinds, *61*;
    reweaving, *67*
Plastic, 34; on masonry, burning off, *22*;
    repairs, *35-37*
Pools, swimming. *See* Swimming pools
Porcelain, 40
Poultices: *absorbent powders or pastes
    containing chemical solvents, used to
    dissolve and leach out a stain.* For
    masonry, 20, *23*; for wallpaper, 42, *45*
Pressure washer, 20, *26-27*
Pump, submersible, to drain swimming
    pool, 92; after flood, 98, *99*

Ranges, 80, *83-86*; hoods, filters in,
    90
Rats and mice, *125*; trapping, 113
Rattan furniture, *15*
Reed, *15*
Refrigerators, 80, *81, 82*
Residual pesticides, 112; outdoor
    application, *116, 117*
Reweaving of carpet pile, *67*
Rotary shampooing of carpets, 60, *65*
Rugs. *See* Carpets and rugs
Rust, 40; removing from glass, 38

Sandblasters, use of, 28, *32*
Sanding: acrylics, *35*; brick, 20, *21*; carpet,
    burned, *67*; french polish, *14*; stone, *24*;
    wood floors, *18*
Scorpions, *122*
Screening against pests, *108*
Sea grass, *15*
Sealing: masonry, 20, *25*; pest-control
    measures, *110*
Shampooing: carpets, 60, *65*; upholstery,
    68-69
Shellac finish, 12
Siding, wood, *14*
Silverfish, *122*
Skylights, 38
Soaking of stains, *54, chart* 56-59
Sow bugs, *123*
Spiders, *123*
Sponging of spots, *53, chart* 56-69
Spotters: *specialized cleaning solutions
    used to remove stains from fabrics.*
    Homemade, 50
Sprayer, garden, use of, *25, 104, 116*
Squeegees: for flood debris, *100*; for rugs,
    63; washing windows with, *38-39*
Stain, reapplication of, to floor, 16
Steam cleaning of carpets, 60, 66
Stone: polishing, *24*; sealing, *25*
Stoves, 80, *83-86*; hoods, filters in, *90*
Surfaces, kinds of, 7; glass, *6, 38-39*;
    masonry, 20, *21-27*; metal, 28, *chart* 29,
    30-33; plastics, 34, *35-37*; tile and
    porcelain, 40; walls and ceilings, 42, *43-
    45*; wood, 12, 13, *chart* 13, *14*, 16, *17-
    19, chart* 17
Swimming pools, 71, 92; chemical
    balance, maintaining, 92, *93*, 94; debris
    removal, 92, *95*; filter system, 92, *93,
    96-97*; spring-cleaning, *97*;
    troubleshooting, *chart* 94-95

Tarnish, removing, 28, 30, *33*
Tar stains on masonry, 23

Tea stains, 23, 40
Termites, 105, *123*; control, 106,
    111
Textiles, 47; care considerations, 48;
    cleaning kit, 50; fibers in, 48, *chart* 48-
    49; gum removal, *55*; stain removal, 47,
    50-51, *51-54, chart* 56-59; testing
    cleaners on, *52*; upholstery, *68-69. See
    also* Carpets and rugs
Ticks, *124*
Tile, ceramic, 40
Tobacco stains on masonry, 23
Tool kit for cleaning, *10-11*
Traps, rodent, 113
Trash compactors, 80, *88-89*
Tufted carpets, kinds of, *61*

Unfinished woods, 12
Upholstery, shampooing, *68-69*

Vacuum cleaners, 71; central system, *70,
    72-79*; pool, *95*
Varnish finish, 12
Venetian blinds, *30-31*
Vinyls, 34; repairing, *36-37*

Wallpaper paste, removing, 42, *45*
Walls, 42, *43*; air drying, after flood, *100-
    101*; papered, 42, 43, *44-45*
Washers, clothes, 80, *86-87*
Wasps, *124*; nests, disposing of, *117*
Water filters, installing, 40, *41*
Waxes for wood floors, 16; application,
    16, *19*; stripping, *17*
Wickerwork, *15*
Wicking out of fluid, *51*
Windows: acrylic, removing scratches
    from, *35*; washing, *38-39*
Wood-boring beetles, *124*
Wood surfaces, 12, 13, *chart* 13; floors, 16,
    17-19, chart 17, *109*; french polish, 12,
    14; siding, *14*
Woven furniture, *15*